GOD IN THE CLASSROOM

.

GOD IN THE CLASSROOM

GOD IN THE CLASSROOM

The Controversial Issue of
Religion in Canada's Schools

LOIS SWEET

M&S

Canadian Cataloguing in Publication Data
Sweet, Lois, date
    God in the classroom : the controversial issue of religion in Canada's schools

Includes bibliographical references and index.
ISBN 0-7710-8319-X

1. Religion in the public schools − Canada.   I. Title.

LC114.S94 1997   372.84'0971   C97-931493-3

The publishers acknowledge the support of the Canada Council for the Arts and the Ontario Arts Council for their publishing program.

Set in Bembo by IBEX, Toronto
Printed and bound in Canada

McClelland & Stewart Inc.
The Canadian Publishers
481 University Avenue
Toronto, Ontario
M5G 2E9

1 2 3 4 5   01 00 99 98 97

To the memory of my father, William D. Sweet,
whose gentle ways and unconditional love continue to inspire

Contents

Acknowledgments

In the spring of 1995, I applied for an Atkinson Fellowship in Public Policy. Created to further the tradition of liberal journalism in Canada, as first practised by the former *Toronto Star* publisher, Joseph E. Atkinson, this fellowship makes possible intensive research on a topical public-policy issue. I proposed to examine the interplay between religion and education in contemporary Canadian society. In particular, I was intrigued by the growth of independent religious schools. I wanted to understand what motivates hundreds of thousands of parents to reject public education in favour of schools that ghettoize their children on the basis of religion. I especially wanted to understand the wider, social implications for our increasingly multicultural country. How could public policy address these issues? I wondered.

When I submitted my proposal, I never dreamed that two years later I'd not only still be immersed in this subject, but my own views would have undergone such a transformation. It wasn't that I was hostile to religiously based schools when I began, but I did feel strongly about public education. To me, public education carries both a promise and a hope – promise of an academically sound education that's open and accessible to all. A hope of fostering in future citizens the skills and attitudes necessary for sustaining relationships of trust and solidarity and equality. I was wary of a movement that seemed to have the potential to undermine both.

Investigating this issue proved to be a challenge, as well as an eye-opener. And I owe much to those people who generously opened their homes, their schools, and their lives to me. However, initial thanks must go to members of the Atkinson Fellowship Committee, who believed this project was worth supporting. The fellowship gave me the luxury of time in which to research, travel, and write; it also proved to be the most satisfying and wonderful year of my life. My thanks to the Atkinson Fellowship Selection Committee's members, Dr. Burnett Thall, Professor Abraham Rotstein, Professor Paul Fox, Dona Harvey, and John Honderich, committee chairman. Thanks also to Adele Jushka, committee secretary, who thoughtfully and cheerfully took care of all my administrative needs.

To John Honderich in particular I owe an enormous debt. Publisher of the *Toronto Star*, John is a warm, humane person who combines high journalistic standards with a profound sense of social justice. In all of my dealings with him – both on staff at the *Toronto Star* and as an Atkinson Fellow – he was supportive, fair, and always open to a good debate.

To Charles Pascal, executive director of the Atkinson Charitable Foundation, my thanks for pushing to make this book a reality. After my five-part series for the Atkinson was published in the *Toronto Star*, Charles was adamant that it should be expanded into book form. Without his confidence in the material and in me – and his steadfast persistence that a publisher should be more than happy to have both – this book would not have been written.

Thanks also to early supporters of the project: Ursula Franklin, Gerry Hall, Ian Urquhart, Judy Steed, Bruce Barnes, and Susan Mayse. Gerald Vandezande of the Ontario Multi-faith Coalition for Equity in Education was an ongoing source of encouragement

– even when he knew we sat on opposite sides of the fence on this issue. Professors Ken Badley and J. Donald Wilson were not only important sources of research material, but both went out of their way to accommodate me when the rigours of research seemed insurmountable. Ken got up at an unearthly hour to undergo an intensive interview at 6 a.m., while Professor Wilson gave up precious holiday time to meet with me.

The help that Peter Evans provided is incalculable. Despite an immensely busy schedule, he consistently made time to talk about the project with me, suggested areas of further research, and challenged many of my presumptions about education. He also managed to come up with words of encouragement precisely when I thought I couldn't possibly go on!

People were very kind to me during the course of my travels and for that I am very grateful. In Newfoundland, my thanks especially to Professors Alice Collins and Bill McKim, Art Baggs, and Janet Henley Andrews. Professor Christopher Sharpe took on the formidable task of making sure I got everything remotely connected to the Newfoundland schools' referendum issue, and he and Mary Jane Puxley graciously introduced me to the wonderful sights of St. John's.

In Montreal, my thanks to Professors Jean-Pierre Proulx and Michel Pagé for their patience in explaining the intricacies of the Quebec system of education and for allowing me access to their academic papers. Also in Montreal, many thanks for the help I received from Glenn Smith, David Daniel, Sat Sharma, Bashir Hussain, and Manjit Singh. And I benefited greatly from the wealth of Dr. Bernard Shapiro's experience and the depth of his knowledge.

In Vancouver, my thanks to Doug Todd for his helpfulness, and to Sarjeet Singh Jagpal for an engaging interview. University of British Columbia Professor Jean Barman was very helpful academically, but she was also immensely friendly and very supportive of this project. Aileen Van Ginkel in Fort Langley, B.C., was also very supportive; I appreciate the thoughtfulness with which she approaches this issue. In Edmonton, my thanks to Sandra Anderson, Professor Bruce Wilkinson, John Bergen, Vangic Bergun, and Brault Kelpin. In Ottawa, many thanks to Judy Bernstein, Bob Harvey, Nizam and Qasem Mahmud, and Peter Senécal. And my thanks to Habiba Khalid in Oakville for the generosity of her friendship.

Gary Duthler of the Federation of Independent Schools in Canada was not only an important source of research, but he consistently challenged many of my presumptions. That he did so with patience, and in the spirit of Christian love, is a tribute to him and his faith. My thanks and appreciation also to Bernie Farber of the Canadian Jewish Congress, Rabbi Irwin Witty of the Toronto Board of Jewish Education, Elaine Hopkins of the Ontario Federation of Independent Schools, John Vanasselt of the Ontario Alliance of Christian Schools, Robert Koole, John Vanderhoek, and Lee Hollaar of the Society of Christian Schools in British Columbia, Catrin Owen of the Edmonton Public Schools, and Alan Borovoy of the Canadian Civil Liberties Association.

At the *Toronto Star*, Lesley Taylor Ciarula and Trish Crawford dug into *Star* archives on my behalf, and John Ferri made useful editorial comments. I'm deeply indebted to Toronto lawyers Peter Jervis and Peter Lauwers, who readily took time out of very busy schedules to explain legal complexities. Both care passionately about this issue and I found their insights extremely helpful. Toronto lawyers Robert Charney and Brian Kelsey also contributed to my understanding of this issue, and Roger Hutchinson, principal of Emmanuel College, provided useful comments.

Thanks to my mother, who provided me with a home away from home while I was researching the Essex County portion of this book. Edith Woodbridge, founder of Friends of Public Education, was very helpful and I appreciate the access she gave me to the archives in Harrow. Thanks also to Hugh Murray, and to Joan Flood, for her generosity and kindness.

Mieke Bos at the Royal Netherlands Embassy worked hard to ensure that I got all the interviews and visits to Dutch schools that I requested, and she did it with warmth and a friendliness that had me admiring the people of the Netherlands before I even arrived. Once there, Cypriaan Brom and Professor N. L. Dodde of the University of Utrecht helped me make my way. In France, Michel Arseneault was a fluent translator and a knowledgeable and friendly companion.

Thanks also to Tony Burman, executive producer of CBC-TV's *The National* and *The National Magazine*. He supported the making of a two-part documentary for *The National Magazine* based on my Atkinson Fellowship research. And I am indebted to producer David Cherniack for the title of this book. He worked with me on the documentary and named it "God in the Classroom," a title that seemed equally appropriate here. Needless to say, it does not exclude those people who don't worship a deity. "God" is used to encompass the idea of addressing questions about the meaning of life that go beyond the material. As a practising Buddhist, David meant no disrespect to non-theists, and neither do I.

During the course of this project, I met many wonderful people who contributed to this work, and also greatly enriched my life. Spending time with people from a variety of religious traditions, I couldn't help but be moved by the depth of their convictions and impressed by their commitment to living them out. That they took the time to explain their beliefs to me was key to my gaining insight into this issue and is something I will cherish forever.

I'm very grateful to all who agreed to be interviewed and who shared their experiences and insights. While I know many will disagree with the conclusions I came to, I appreciate the fact that it was possible to engage in such lively and thought-provoking discussions – and I hope we'll have more in the future. I wish it were possible to thank everyone by name; however, the list would be interminable. So, instead, a heartfelt "Thank you!" to all, many of whom will be introduced by name in the chapters that follow.

Wherever I went, I met with enthusiasm and interest and a kindness that sometimes overwhelmed me. I especially appreciate the time I spent in schools – the tours and the opportunities to meet and talk with students, teachers, and principals.

The experience of working with people at McClelland & Stewart was very rewarding. To Avie Bennett, chairman and president, and Doug Gibson, publisher, my sincere thanks for their confidence in this work and for making my first attempt at writing a book such a satisfying one. Pat Kennedy, my editor, was a joy to work with. She's sharp and perceptive and sensitive, and I thoroughly enjoyed both her professionalism and her love of Indian food.

Now that the book is completed, I'm amazed that I still have friends left. There were times when I was so absorbed in my work that I gave short shrift to those whose friendships mean so much to me. Being the good friends that they are, however, they were quick to forgive and offered support in a variety of forms whenever and wherever possible. Thanks to Kelly Crichton, Mel Watkins, Nancy Epstein, Molly Kane, Tracy Morey, Karen Shaver, Renate Mohr, Mike and Jean Macpherson.

Judy Maddocks deserves a special note of thanks. She provided ongoing support for my work – in fact, she believed in it long before I did – and her friendship is important to me. Thanks also to Matthew Watkins for introducing me to the music of Nick Drake.

My children – Chinta, Luke, and Kate Puxley – were used to having me immersed in my work, but they have never had to put up with one project for quite so long. However, they were infinitely patient with the demands it placed on both my time and my energy. Throughout the process, they expressed an interest in the book's progress – and in my state of mind – that, in retrospect, I find quite incredible. They are lovely, loving people and I feel privileged to share their lives.

It was my husband, Peter Puxley, who had the most to put up with, however. He lived with all of the ups and downs a project like this involves, never knowing, when he came home at day's end, whether I'd be in the depths of despondency or raring to read him the latest chapter. Through it all, he was an oasis of calm and boundless good nature. Peter buoyed me up when I was discouraged and was unwaveringly supportive. Despite all the demands in his own professional life, he was always available to discuss my work and his critiques were fundamental to this final product. Throughout our years together his love has been unselfish, constant, and expressed in myriad ways. To him I owe everything.

I

OF PROTESTANTS AND PAPISTS

We had five churches: the Anglican, poor but believed to have some mysterious social supremacy; the Presbyterian, solvent and thought – chiefly by itself – to be intellectual; the Methodist, insolvent and fervent; the Baptist, insolvent and saved; the Roman Catholic, mysterious to most of us but clearly solvent, as it was frequently and, so we thought, quite needlessly repainted.

Robertson Davies, *Fifth Business*

It was in this kind of Canadian community that I was born and raised. When I was little, it never occurred to me that people might not attend church on Sunday. Going to church was simply an integral part of everyone's way of life, I thought. Every Saturday night I had a special bath in preparation for wearing my Sunday clothes the following day. And, of course, no one I knew worked on Sunday unless the demands of sowing a crop or harvesting it required around-the-clock labour. (In which case, it was understood that God would forgive the transgression.) Nor was Sunday a time for being entertained, unless you considered paying a visit to a relative or neighbour a form of entertainment. Mind you, there wasn't a lot to do, anyway. My family didn't get a television set when those of all my school friends did because our minister repeatedly preached against its acquisition. Television promotes an immoral lifestyle, he'd intone. But once his sermons on this topic ceased – he himself having bought a television set – we, too, got one. However, there was a firm injunction against watching it on Sundays. And we never did.

As I grew older, I began to realize that not everyone in the community lived the way we did. Not everyone went to church, for starters. And many of those who did belonged to a different denomination. This was confusing, but ultimately comprehensible. What was utterly incomprehensible was the community down the road. A mere three miles away, it might as well have been halfway around the globe for all that I understood about it. Although we had a lot in common – both were southwestern Ontario farming communities – the things we didn't share were actually what defined us. My community was founded by black slaves escaping to freedom via the Underground Railroad, and the whisky producer Hiram Walker's railroad line out of Windsor. In their enthusiasm for a new life, they believed they'd stumbled upon a place "flowing with milk and honey." So they named it New Canaan. Unfortunately, the land, being clay, didn't meet their expectations. They left. My ancestors – white, English-speaking, and Protestant – arrived.

McGregor, the community down the road, was obviously named by, or for, a Scot. But you'd have been hard-pressed to find a Scot within its borders when I was growing up in the fifties. Instead, it was composed of white, French-speaking Catholics. While language created a barrier between us, it wasn't the primary obstacle to communication. That was religion. Catholics were different. Catholics were "other." I didn't know much about them, except that they had to eat fish on Fridays, and that the women had to cover their heads whenever they entered their huge, imposing church. I did know, however, that we weren't to become friends, even to interact. I knew this because of all the effort that I saw being made to keep us apart. In particular, we didn't attend the same schools. They went to their Catholic school and we went to our public (read Protestant) school. Even at a tender age, this seemed to me peculiar. After all, since birth, it seemed, I'd been told that God loves everyone. But what I experienced, as a result of separate schooling, was that some people were so different that I was to have nothing to do with them. We Protestant and Catholic children had no opportunity to talk with each other, to study together, or to play together. And when the sole opportunity did occur, I, for one, was so afraid of the stereotypic "other" that I had no idea how to handle an actual relationship with someone so seemingly different as a Catholic.

I was around eight years old when a local farmer from McGregor got into some sort of disagreement with his priest. In retaliation, he sent his two children to our school. To us, those children were aliens. They were the "other" personified. So, we tormented them with the particular cruelty of children. I often led the taunting and went out of my way to socially ostracize the girl. She, after all, was different, and I wasn't about to let her forget it. How dare she think she had the right to play with us! Little did I know that I was a bit player on a much larger social stage. The inter-religious conflict taking place in that school yard had been played out in Canadian communities since before Confederation. In fact, it's safe to say that it's been one of the defining characteristics of this country. The effect of that historical conflict has been to confuse and cloud our judgment on the subject of religion and its appropriate place in our lives and those of our children.

Today, I'm anxious to understand the implications of religious difference. Perhaps more than anything, I want to understand the "other" now that a new set of demographics has transformed the "other" into the "others." Canada is rapidly changing. We are no longer the country of my childhood, with a Christian majority, albeit of different sects. Today, we are a pluralistic, multicultural, multi-religious nation. The people we work with are just as likely to be Sikh, Muslim, Hindu, Buddhist, Jewish, or atheist, as United Church or Catholic. For many, religion and culture are totally interconnected. In fact, for many, religion *is* culture. It dictates the way they view the world, including their neighbours, how they dress, what they eat, and how they spend their time and money. As a result, it's increasingly inappropriate, and inaccurate, to assume that, just because we share a country, we share certain basic assumptions about life. Muslims, for example, maintain that Allah (God) is integral to every detail of their daily lives, a position that is anathema to people who consider belief in God an illusion.

I don't believe we can afford to stereotype others on the basis of religion, any more than we can afford to stereotype on the basis of gender, sexual orientation, or race. We share too much as fellow human beings to create such artificial barriers. Life is both too short and too precious to do so. But as history so abundantly suggests, lack of meaningful contact with those who are different from us and lack of insight into, or understanding of, their belief systems are bound to reinforce ignorance, misunderstanding, and stereotyping. A major part of the problem today is that religion is something people rarely talk about outside religious institutions – except perhaps in the most guarded and polite terms. It's considered too divisive, too explosive, too sensitive, even too embarrassing in an age of overwhelming secularism. Religious belief has been conveniently relegated to a social category stamped "private." People who hold religious beliefs and attempt to bring them into the public arena are generally considered anachronistic at best, fanatics at worst.

Yet the human quest for a spiritual dimension is not only very real but is the source of considerable meaning for many people. Somehow or other, we as a society have lost sight of that. And there are perfectly good reasons why we've done so. We all know enough history to understand that millions of people have died – and continue to die – in wars based on religious differences. Today everyone has heard about the injustices inflicted on the innocent by some members of religious institutions (native children in religiously run residential schools immediately jump to mind). And perhaps many of us have experienced firsthand the oppressive nature of religious institutions: their rigid rules about appropriate gender behaviour, their suppression of critical thinking, or their outright hypocrisy in publicly promoting one thing – tolerance, say – while practising quite another – intolerance towards members of other religions, other races, or towards those with a different sexual orientation, to cite a few. Perhaps, too, many have experienced, or heard their parents tell of experiencing, the wrath of a church that refused to acknowledge the reality of divorce, or that encouraged women to bear children the family couldn't afford, or that admonished women to stay in violent relationships. And many members of minority religions recall only too well their sense of utter isolation and alienation in a classroom full of children reciting the Lord's Prayer, or singing "Away in a Manger" at Christmas.

Without doubt, religious institutions, with their bureaucracies, their petty, competitive feuding, their rules, and their (all-too-often) misogynist, autocratic leaders can be incredibly oppressive. But it's a gross oversimplification to maintain that that's what constitutes religion or the spiritual quest. It's also far too convenient. It means we can blithely ignore the challenge that the spiritual dimension raises. It means we can write off those who seek to raise uncomfortable questions about the lack of spiritual values in public policy. It means we can target as un-Canadian members of minority religions who attempt to cling to their religious symbols. (In the course of my research, I continued to hear the old racist saw "If they don't want to be like us, why don't they go back to where they came from?") And it also means we can continue to call ourselves a country without actually making an effort to understand, at any meaningful level, who our neighbours are if they happen to be religiously different from us.

In short, we're a society that's lost sight of the importance of the spiritual. While there are many areas in which this vacuum is expressed, one of the most blatant – and I would say important – areas is in our schools. This is a point that's not been lost on the tens of thousands of parents across the country who've opted to send their children to independent, religiously based schools rather than enrol them in the public system. Nor is it lost on those who continue to send their children to public schools, while bemoaning the lack of values, religion, acknowledgement of the spiritual – call it what you will – within the public system. That this vacuum is felt, even by those who would not call themselves devout – or even particularly religious – is significant. To me, it points to the recognition that something is wrong when religion becomes a prohibited classroom subject in a democracy. It can also indicate a recognition that one of the few hopes we have for a peaceful, multicultural future is to begin to know our neighbours. And I would argue that one of the ways to do this, early on, within the classroom, is to learn about the religious/spiritual underpinnings of others.

To continue on our current path is obviously no solution. In fact, it seems as if what's happening today is a study in extremes. There are children who are getting the religion of their parents in spades, because they attend religious schools. And, because the object of these schools is to instruct the children in their own brand of religion, they get little, if any, education about anyone else's – and certainly no exposure to children who adhere to a different belief system. On the other hand, children in the public system get virtually no education in religion, because the topic is considered too hot to handle. In fact, there's often an attempt made to paper over religious differences, pretending that everyone in the classroom is somehow the same. But I'm convinced that, if we ignore the deeply held religious beliefs of others, we do so at our peril. It's impossible to understand behaviour without understanding motivation, and few things are as motivating in life as religious belief. It's even common to hear people ardently maintain that they hold no religious belief, and then cling to this conviction with a tenacity that smacks of religious fervour – and that can be equally intolerant.

Ironically, we seem, as a society, to have shifted a full 180 degrees. We've gone from times when the religious were often intolerant of the non-religious, or those of a different religion, to today, when it is those who hold religious convictions who are subjected to societal intolerance. It's often implied that anyone holding a religious belief system must be either brainwashed, intellectually challenged, or in dire need of a psychological crutch. This intolerance also takes the form of ignoring, even prohibiting, religion in our schools. What goes unsaid is the fact that secularism, or secular humanism, is also a value system and is often embraced as a kind of religion. Yet, secularists are usually blind to the religious nature of their beliefs, arguing that schools must necessarily be secular because secularism is "neutral." This is an illusion that should be challenged. Of course, these are usually the same people who argue that the State – in the form of provincial ministries of education – knows best what children should learn. Today, in most provinces, the decision has been made to opt for "neutrality" – a position anything but neutral in its impact, and one that makes no one but secularists happy.

Still, it would be foolish to ignore the perils involved in advocating a place for God in the classroom. Only Christian supremacists would petition for a return to "the good old days" when every school day in every public school began with a dutiful reading from the Bible and ended with a prayer to the Christian God, with two hours per week of Christian religious instruction thrown in for good measure.

Indoctrinating children in religious dogma isn't what I'm suggesting. Besides, the courts have reinforced the fact that, in this day and age, it's illegal for public schools to do that: the majority doesn't have the right to infringe on the religious freedom of minorities. Unfortunately, what's happened in many parts of the country is that everyone – whether a member of the majority or a minority – has lost the right to have religion in public schools. I can only understand it this way: decision-makers are terrified by the thought that they might have to cope with something as potentially contentious as religion in the classroom. Conventional wisdom seems to decree that it's much better to ride roughshod over the rights of the religious, and ignore the social benefits of religious study even to the non-religious, than to suffer some political heat.

The proper role of religion in education is an issue that doesn't lend itself to easy answers, however. Even raising the issue can be risky. For example, some people chose to attack me personally for the questions I raised in "God in the Classroom." This two-part documentary ran on CBC-TV's *The National Magazine* in September 1996, and was based on research I did for an Atkinson Fellowship in Public Policy. The majority of those callers who objected to the documentary argued that, as a result of early childhood experiences, I'd allowed my personal prejudice against religion to colour my objectivity. This reaction surprised me for two reasons. Firstly, the producer, David Cherniack, and I went to considerable lengths to treat the material in as evenhanded a way as possible. Secondly, I'm not anti-religion. While there's a lot I find objectionable in institutional religions, I in no way reject the religious impulse, the religious quest, or the religious solution. Quite the contrary. I can only interpret these reactions as rooted in the prejudices viewers themselves brought to the issue; they heard what they wanted to hear and saw what they wanted to see. While they were wrong about my prejudices, they were right about the fact that life experience affects one's perspective on issues like religion and education. How could it not? Surely it's desirable — in fact, essential — in a pluralistic society, to bring one's life experience to the public forum. Addressing one's own experience is the only way to really begin to understand how our views of each other were formed. It's also the first step in breaking down stereotypes and replacing theory with humanity.

In fact, it was the humanity of those I met during the course of this research that most affected me. As people graciously shared their beliefs and lives with me, I couldn't help but gain insight into the power and significance of religious belief. Unlike opinions, which are based on the availability of information that helps one form a judgment, religion is a leap of faith, and proofs and counter-proofs are, in many respects, irrelevant to those who believe. And that's precisely why this issue is so difficult to deal with; the tenacity with which people on both sides of this debate hold to their convictions makes it painfully clear that coming up with a solution that will satisfy everyone is an impossibility. This is because many of the devout will only accept a system that promotes their particular religion. And many secularists will only accept a system that prohibits religion. But to ignore the importance of the role of religion in education in the hope that the issue will go away is simply to postpone the eventual day of reckoning. This issue may seem to be merely simmering now, but in fact it's extremely close to the boil. And when it erupts, watch out! Coping with the fallout will be much more difficult than dealing with today's uneasy quiet.

Ironically, none of this is something that I would have dreamed of saying a mere decade ago. Instead, I would have been one of those advocating the perpetuation of the status quo: letting Catholics direct their tax dollars to their own separate schools; saying "Good riddance and good luck" to those who put their kids in independent religious schools; supporting the public system in its observance of religious "neutrality" as the only way to maintain the integrity of the system. And I would have had good grounds for doing so. I would have argued that in those provinces where Catholic schools are publicly funded, it's because they have a constitutional right to it, and that that right is sacrosanct. I would have noted that parents have the legal right to give their children any kind of education they want, including a religious education, as long as they are willing to pay for it themselves. And I would have fiercely argued against religion in public schools on the grounds that, not only would it be potentially divisive, but that children need to be protected against the profound evils of religious indoctrination.

So, what changed? Well, everything, from the country to me. In a way, both have come of age. Canada, now home to a wide variety of people from a wide variety of places, is finally moving into the twenty-first century. We have a perfect opportunity to show the world what kind of society a liberal democracy can produce when it is truly dedicated to pursuing the pluralistic ideal. We could be celebrating our incredible diversity of peoples and devising ways of giving voice and equal place at the table to this mix. We could actively seek to find ways that lead to greater understanding of, and appreciation for, each other. And one of the ways we could do this, I'm convinced, is through an education system that acknowledges religious difference and actually educates children about those differences in the classroom. I like to think of it in terms of "religious literacy." Although the religious landscape of Canada is only one of the changes that new patterns of immigration have brought about, it is an important one. And, in a very real way, this new religious reality provides an opportunity for all of us not just to learn about the beliefs and values of those who are different from ourselves, but to be challenged to question, and to grapple with, what we ourselves believe about the nature of human existence. In fact, it's only when we've actually tested our own beliefs that we're capable of truly respecting the beliefs of others.

I guess that's the way in which I have most dramatically changed. Call it maturing, the ageing process – whatever – I, like so many other baby boomers, have accepted that the spiritual dimension of life must be addressed. There is no escaping the profound questions that human beings have been attempting to answer from time immemorial. Who am I? Where did I come from? What is the meaning of life? How do I find meaning in my life? Is there life after death? While we all, ultimately, have to pursue and answer these questions for ourselves, we can benefit greatly from learning the ways in which others have answered them. Not only that, but knowing how others answer those questions provides insight into different ways of being. This is because each culture answers them in its own, unique way. And the way it answers them has resulted in a variety of actions that symbolize people's commitment, or discipline, to their religion. Some, for example, include not cutting the hair (Sikhism), or praying at prescribed times five times a day (Islam), or not eating pork (Judaism and Islam). Today, in multicultural Canada, it seems essential that we know such basics. Besides, an education system that ignores the human search for meaning through spiritual belief is, to me, inadequate and does a grave disservice to its students.

Children have the right to receive an education that presents the human experience in all its complexities and multiplicities. This includes the ways in which the quest for meaning has expressed itself through the development of religious thought. In early Canada, it was assumed that a good education demanded that children get a firm grounding in the tenets of Christianity – the concept of "original sin," for instance, being a given. But the growth of secularism changed all that. In addition, Western civilization has been awakening to the fact that children aren't simply miniature adults; they have special needs that must be addressed in order for them to develop into fully functioning, socially contributing adults. Along with the growth of psychology, the concept of "children's rights" has developed.

When I was growing up, it never occurred to me that I had any rights. Rights – either individual or collective – weren't a subject of public discourse. Children were considered the property of the adults who bore or raised them. As long as those adults conformed to the social standards of the community, they could do with those children as they pleased. My children, on the other hand, not only frequently hear the expression "children's rights" bantered about on TV or read about it in books, but they understand that the concept has meaning in relation to their own lives. The fact that the notion of children's rights has entered our collective consciousness has had an impact, I think, on this issue. We've interpreted the idea that children have the right not to be indoctrinated along religious lines to mean that public-school children should be freed from exposure to religious thought in general. To me, this amounts to throwing out the baby with the bath water. It is a form of injustice.

Obviously, those who decide what children will be taught in the public classrooms of this country don't seek to deprive them of something essential to their human growth and intellectual development. But that's how the absence of religious education feels to many parents. The problem is that someone has to draw the line and make curriculum decisions. Democracy, of course, is always hard on those who don't see the world through the same lens as the majority. In Canada today, however, all provinces understand that. They all recognize the right of parents to choose where and how their children will be educated. They accept that some may feel so strongly about the values they want their children to be exposed to that they'll insist on having them educated in their own, value-laden environment. (The hitch is that only a few provinces will contribute to the child's tuition at schools outside the public system.) What seems difficult for opponents of religion in the classroom to understand is that education is never value-less. Not only what is taught and not taught, but how it is taught, and by whom, conveys a set of values. The question is: Whose values?

Even if we as a society accept that there's a need for some kind of education about religion in the classroom, figuring out how to address that need presents an enormous challenge. First of all, the courts have made it clear that we have to differentiate between "religious education" and "education about religion." The former indoctrinates, the latter illuminates. But we're in a situation right now in which most teachers haven't themselves been educated in teaching about religion. How, then, can we expect to dump this on them? And what's to be done about those groups for whom religion is inextricably linked to their identity? They can't fathom why they should allow their children to mix with children of another religion. Should we be publicly funding their independent religious schools, thereby ghettoizing children on the basis of religion? And, even if parents and students accept the importance of being educated together about religion, is there a way of doing it that's both imaginative and non-indoctrinating? And what does religious tolerance really mean? If it simply means learning to put up with, as opposed to respecting, difference, then why bother?

Sorting out this issue is all the more complicated because education is a provincial responsibility. Provincial approaches to the funding of religious schools and the way provinces handle religion in the curriculum vary wildly. Canada runs the gamut, from a public-education system in Newfoundland that is composed entirely of Christian denominations (and will apparently retain remnants of that, despite recent constitutional change) to British

Columbia, which partially funds all religiously based schools that follow its guidelines, to Ontario, which refuses to fund any religious schools, other than the constitutionally guaranteed Catholic schools, and which forbids opt-in religious education (going to another classroom to take religious education). None of the provinces, however, seems to be talking with any other about how to deal with the new religious reality in their classrooms. If there is a debate occurring at the political level, then it must be conducted in whispers for all that anyone's heard of it.

But there is a debate going on, both between members of minority religious groups and within academic circles. In universities, there's a great deal of discussion about Canada's multicultural future and what's become known as "the politics of recognition," an expression coined by McGill University philosopher Charles Taylor. In *Multiculturalism and "The Politics of Recognition"* he writes:

> Our identity is partly shaped by recognition or its absence ... so a person or group of people can suffer real damage, real distortion, if the people or society around them mirror back to them a confining or demeaning or contemptible picture of themselves. Non-recognition or misrecognition can inflict harm, can be a form of oppression, imprisoning someone in a false, distorted, and reduced mode of being.

In other words, if people aren't legitimized by the society in which they live, if it doesn't accept them for who they are, then they suffer and could fail to attain their full human potential. In terms of the religious question, this means that, if children who are born into a household in which religion forms the basis for their identity attend a school that ignores or rejects that religious identity, then the children feel rejected as people. It's an outcome no democratic, pluralistic society can embrace.

Manohar Singh Bal, for example, a Toronto Sikh, describes the agony his six-year-old son experiences every day when he walks into his local public school. In keeping with their Sikh faith, the boy has never had his hair cut. And, if he remains true to his religion, he'll never get a haircut. But because Sikh males don't begin wearing a turban until around fourteen or fifteen years of age, his hair is simply tied into a bun and covered with a white handkerchief. For the child, being a member of a visible, minority religion in a secularist, public school, is the source of much grief. "Children laugh at him and call him names and say he is a girl," says Bal. "This happens because they don't understand our religion. And there is no system within the school to teach that." The Bals have spent hours discussing the situation. They're adamant that they won't cave in and cut his hair. They've seen too many Sikh parents do this in a final, desperate attempt to stop the harassment. While they understand the motivation, they believe that compromising on such an essential tenet of their religion is simply too high a price to pay. Besides, they maintain that another alternative exists which is both fairer and simpler. "Why can't there be a class in school to teach children about all the religions?" asks Bal. "We want respect and equality for all children, not just our own. We want the children to get firsthand knowledge of all the religions because they all have to live together."

While he doesn't use the word "identity," it's part and parcel of what this issue is all about. The religious identity that his child is receiving at home is not only being rejected by his peers at school, but he, as a developing person, is being harassed and rejected. Little wonder that many parents who are members of minority religions feel that their only hope lies in putting their children in their own, religiously based schools. While I empathize with the sentiment, I can't support it. To me, it runs against the grain of everything we should be attempting to do in this country. It reinforces the idea, and fear of, the "other." And, in the long run, it serves neither the interests of the larger society, nor those of the children being educated separately. There must be a better, more egalitarian, more socially beneficial, way. A serious search for such schooling involves putting ourselves, and some of the structures we take for granted, to the test. Among other things, this means re-examining the issue of the constitutional guarantee for public funding to Catholic schools in light of today's new multicultural, multi-religious reality. Education consultant Mark Holmes makes the point that we wouldn't dream of using a document drawn up in 1867 to determine the rights of a variety of historically oppressed groups – women being a prime example. Why, then, don't we apply that standard to this issue?

I grew up with all the assumptions and prerogatives that come with being a member of the dominant society. Even so, I experienced what it felt like to feel afraid of what I didn't understand and had no exposure to (Catholicism). But I was lucky. This was pre-1984, and Ontario had not yet brought in full funding of Catholic schools to the secondary-school level. This meant that I was able to mix with Catholics during my time at high school. While it may sound like a cliché, the fact was that my best friend during all those years was a Catholic. Twenty years later, that simply wouldn't have been an option. She would automatically have attended the local Catholic high school, while I would have gone to the local public high school – both in the same community, but worlds apart. As it was, attending the same school gave us the chance to get to know each other, and our friendship blossomed. When I visited her house on Fridays, I simply took it for granted that we'd eat fish.

Religion, however, was a taboo subject. Coming as we did from the separate-school experience, we knew, albeit unconsciously, that something so socially divisive had the potential to upset our friendship if we allowed it to interfere. And so we never discussed religion. Besides, how could we? We had no tools for such discourse, no models to point the way. Our school experiences had provided no context within which we could acknowledge that our religious inclinations were an important aspect of our humanity. As a result, we could neither share, nor respect in any meaningful way, our differences. In short, we were religiously illiterate.

In what follows, I will argue that Canada desperately needs to develop policies that foster a healthy pluralism in a much more complex society than the one in which I grew up. What this means for education is twofold. First of all, a recognition of the importance of issues of the spirit to human existence by giving them a place in the classroom. Second, an examination of the answers that different religious traditions provide to universal questions about human existence. These are essential prerequisites for achieving religious literacy, a quest that has as its object knowledge of the religious, not simply knowledge about.

Throughout this book, I make certain assumptions about the nature of education – the nature of "good" education. No doubt some will disagree, but to me a quality education is one that respects children's ability to think for themselves, to draw conclusions for themselves, and to make choices and decisions for themselves within a context and understanding of liberal democracy. That's why I think one component of "good" schools is the fostering of religious literacy, a process that, ideally, would not only give young people an awareness of the beliefs of others, but would encourage them to discover their own.

The sectarian difference and sectarian ignorance that marked my education were, unfortunately, not unusual. This was experienced through several generations all across the country. It came about because of the emphasis Canada's early education architects placed on one religion – the Christian religion. This bred excessive sectarianism, excessive piety, excessive Christian bias. I think it was that kind of experience that educators, policy-makers, and many parents reacted against – to the point of not giving religious education inside that institutional context any due at all. Unfortunately, the result has been to prevent Canadian young people from examining and exploring the nature of religious experience. It has prevented the development of a certain religious literacy so essential to successfully integrating the much wider variety of cultures and religions that typify Canada today. In the next chapter, I will take a closer look at how we got into this fix.

2

FROM DOGMA TO DEARTH

It is the duty of the teacher and a temporary teacher to inculcate by precept and example respect for religion and the principles of Judeo-Christian morality and the highest regard for truth, justice, loyalty, love of country, humility, benevolence, sobriety, industry, frugality, purity, temperance and all other virtues.

Ontario Education Act, 1850

A man who rejects the Divine authority of the Holy Scriptures is, I think, disqualified from teaching.

Egerton Ryerson, Superintendent of Education
for Ontario, 1846–1876

In 1990, the long, crude arm of the State reached out and made its presence known to Phil Friesen, a Mennonite father of three, in the northern Ontario community of Stratton. Bob Rae's New Democratic government had decreed that the Christian posters in his children's alternative religious school in northern Ontario were to be taken down and their daily Bible readings stopped. This was to be done immediately, ministry officials said, or the publicly funded school, known as the Sturgeon Creek

Alternative Program, would be closed. Friesen couldn't believe it. But under a new government memorandum, issued after an Ontario Supreme Court of Appeal decision about the role of religion in public schools, such blatantly religious acts were deemed illegal. Recounting the experience, Friesen shakes his head in dismay. "What's this country coming to?" he asks. "There's something wrong when the State orders you to take scripture verses down, and forbids you to have Bible pictures on your walls. It's a sad comment on our land."

If the founders of schools in Ontario — indeed, if the founders of Confederation — knew how education has evolved in this province, they'd be in a state of perpetual motion in their graves. Secular education was not only inconceivable to most of them, it was an oxymoron. To them, education and religion were part and parcel of the same thing — an essential good, a necessary whole. And, of course, the religion that ruled the day was Christianity. After all, it was Christians who colonized the country, and it was Christian churches and their leaders who established schools. That public schools would eventually be bereft of religion; that Catholics would be the only religious group publicly funded to retain control of their education — and even then, only in some provinces — would have been unimaginable. It's a long story, but one that's worth the telling even if it is unwieldy and complicated. Certainly, the only way to understand what happened at Phil Friesen's school is to go back to where it all began.

And if I seem to spend an inordinate amount of time describing Ontario's educational history, it's in the interests of illuminating the present. The early debates and conflicts over education were fierce, and affected the educational development of every province. When provinces joined Canada, they were required to agree to the provisions of the constitution of 1867. These spelled out their obligation to fund Catholic separate schools in the province — but only if they were in existence at the time that province joined.

The first school in Ontario was both French and Catholic. It opened at Fort Frontenac (now Kingston) in 1676. The first elementary school was also French and Catholic. It was founded in 1786 in what is now Windsor. Within a short period of time the Church of England (Anglican) started several English-language schools. Had that trend towards denominational schools continued, then today we'd probably have Presbyterian schools, Baptist schools, United Church schools, and so on. Certainly, there was no love lost among the various denominations. There were bitter fights and huge rifts between Catholics and Protestants and within the numerous Protestant sects over the role of religion in schools.

The schools had one element in common, however: they were all private. In those days, public monies weren't used to support education. In order to send their children to school, parents either had to be flush enough to afford the fees, or they had to depend on the charitable bent of the school's organizers. When the push for publicly financed schooling did come, it came from John Graves Simcoe, the first lieutenant-governor of Upper Canada after the province was officially established in 1791. It certainly wasn't publicly funded education as we know it today. Simcoe believed the State should subsidize the education of the children of the upper classes only ("The Children of the Principal People of This Country," as he so delicately put it). Presumably he thought the lower classes should fend for themselves, or had no need of education, social mobility not being a realistic expectation.

Anyway, his idea was that the State should pay for the education of upper-class children, because they would eventually become the country's leaders. Besides, he argued, why spread limited resources thinly, thereby benefiting no one? Simcoe got his way. The first piece of educational legislation enacted by the parliament of Upper Canada was the District Public (or Grammar) School Act of 1807. One hundred pounds a year was to be given to a grammar school in each of the eight administrative districts. The beneficiaries were indeed the children (read the sons) of the upper class, and the tone was decidedly Church of England. Today's élite Upper Canada College in Toronto, for example, began, in the words of the historian Robert Stamp, "as the most lavishly state-aided school in the first half-century of Ontario's history."

But the blatant classism and sectarian bent of the publicly supported private schools became points of heated contention. So in 1816, the government passed the Common School Act. While the Act was designed with the best of intentions, the small amount of money set aside for common schools did little to improve the education opportunities of lower-class children. The Act also called for regular devotional exercises and a regular period of religious instruction. This was a source of great irritation for non-Anglicans, who felt that including a religious component was a power-grab by establishment denominations and constituted a limitation on their religious freedom. The Act, however, was historically significant. As the University of British Columbia education historian, J. Donald Wilson, points out, it would "mark the beginning of state acceptance for education of the masses."

Quite a struggle lay ahead, however. Leaders of the Church of England (Anglicans) adamantly maintained that they had a God-given right to control education. They were a force to be reckoned with, after all. Under the Constitution Act of 1791 one-seventh of Crown or public lands was set aside "for the support and maintenance of a Protestant Clergy." A lot of money flowed from these lands – the proceeds of logging, rental, or sales – and for several decades leaders of the Church of England claimed that revenue as their own. Wealth and the traditional status of the Established Church enhanced their influence. As prominent advisors to the province's governors, they used that influence to try to bring education under their control. They argued that, while all education should be funded by the State, it should be administered by them – the Established Church. Needless to say, this position was greatly resented by the Methodists, Presbyterians, Baptists, Catholics, and members of other denominations. "That education should be conducted by the church was never seriously questioned in the early years of the nineteenth century," writes Wilson in *Canadian Education: A History*. "But that the control of education should rest in the hands of one denomination, the Church of England, was quite another matter, especially since most Upper Canadians were not Anglicans."

Resentment against the Anglicans raged on other fronts besides education. It even helped to spawn the Rebellion of 1837. Shocked by news of a volatile situation in the colony, the British sent John George Lambton, Lord Durham, to Upper Canada (Ontario) and Lower Canada (Quebec) to investigate. Durham was appalled at the state of education. He estimated that only 55 to 60 per cent of school-age children attended school. Durham felt that the route to progress was "the establishment of a strong popular government [which] would very soon lead to the introduction of a liberal and general system of education," which would reflect the interests of its constituents (including religion). His report of 1839 contained many recommendations, one of which proposed universal education. Let education be available to all, he suggested. Make it neutral, not sectarian, neither Anglican nor Catholic. His report led to responsible government. His recommendations about education also laid the groundwork upon which Egerton Ryerson, who would be Ontario's Superintendent of Education for thirty years, built a provincial school system in the mid-nineteenth century.

It didn't happen overnight. First came the union of Upper and Lower Canada in 1840. Upper Canada (Ontario) became Canada West and Lower Canada (Quebec) became Canada East. One of the first pieces of business the new Canadian Parliament dealt with was the Common School Act of 1841. The idea was to improve the state of education and, also, to devise a unified school jurisdiction for both provinces. There was only one problem: both provinces had evolved their own educational structures and neither wanted to give them up. The result was a compromise that has been a continuing source of contention in many Canadian provinces ever since – the introduction of separate schools. Ironically, the word "separate" was never used. Instead, Section XI of the Act provided that "any number of inhabitants of a different faith from the majority in [either] township or parish might choose their own trustees," and "might establish and maintain one or more schools" under the same conditions as other common schools.

In contrast to today, when the defenders of the principle of separate schools are often Catholics, the originators were Protestant. The Protestants – largely Church of England and Presbyterian clergymen – fervently believing religion to be an integral part of education, argued that the Bible must be used as a textbook in the schools. Wanting only the clergy to interpret the scriptures, the Catholics were as strongly opposed to having children read the Bible as the Protestants were in favour. This led the Hon. William Morris, a spokesperson for the Church of Scotland, to warn that, "if the use by Protestants of the Holy Scriptures in their schools is so objectionable to our fellow subjects of other faiths, the children of both religious persuasions must be educated apart."

Separate schooling sparked much debate between two fiery advocates of public education in Upper Canada – Egerton Ryerson and George Brown. As education superintendent, Ryerson had the power of a bureaucratic position to implement his vision. His opponent, George Brown, a spokesperson for the radical Reformers, was editor of *The Globe* newspaper and used this position to express his strongly held views. Ryerson, however, had also been an editor – of *The Christian Guardian*, a Methodist weekly newspaper. For the ten years preceding his move to government, he had used the paper to articulate his perspective on society and provincial growth and development. It was an ideal platform. To him, man was both rational and full of sinful depravity. The solution to this human conflict, Ryerson argued, was for "some central, governing power, to rule the conscience, regulate the pulsations of the heart, and restrain the passions." He believed that only religion (Christianity, of course) could perform this educational role. Legislators were God's agents for redeeming citizens. As such, it was essential that they be as concerned with the intellectual improvement of the country as with its material prosperity. "That religion, education, and freedom stand or fall together is a truth so important that it should form an article in the practical creed of every Christian and philanthropist, and should be instilled into the mind of every child among the first lessons of his elementary instruction," Ryerson wrote in 1834 in the *Christian Guardian*.

A former Methodist minister, he vehemently objected to the claims of the Church of England to be the Established Church of Canada West. Ryerson believed that religion should unify society, and, in his opinion, the Church of England was anything but a cohesive force for unity. In fact, he maintained that its effort to impose itself as the Established Church was not only the source of bitter divisions, but that these divisions were having a devastating effect on the province. To him, the solution was obvious: let no church be the "established church." Instead, let there be Christian ecumenism. "A cordial agreement in the essentials of the Gospel ought to induce all sincere and enlightened Christians to put up with minor differences," Ryerson wrote in 1838. "I do not believe that uniformity is essential to unity among the different Christian denominations. I believe there may be uniformity without unity: and that there may be unity without uniformity. I believe there has been, and there may be again, a oneness of 'heart and soul' unaffected by minuter distinctions: a oneness . . . that resembles the identity of human nature, notwithstanding all the varieties of man."

Even had everyone agreed with his ecumenical solution, there remained the problem of implementation. Was there a way for schools to avoid sectarian indoctrination except by taking the seemingly drastic route of keeping religion out of them? Ryerson was adamant that there were certain principles upon which everyone could agree: that there is a God to whom we are all responsible; that the human soul is immortal; that God revealed himself to humans through the Bible; that forgiveness for sins is available through belief in Jesus Christ. Given the nature of today's society, it may seem almost incomprehensible that he could even broach the possibility of agreement on those points. But things were very different then. Because Christianity reigned supreme, Ryerson figured that agreement could be had on upholding those principles in the schools, while sectarian differences could be safely confined to the home and church.

Needless to say, Catholic and Church of England leaders were very opposed to his plan. For them, separate schools, based on sectarian differences, were the only plausible solution. Adam Townley, presbyter of the Church of England in Toronto, spoke for many when he wrote in 1853:

Oh, Dr. Ryerson! . . . Right well do you know that it is this very privilege of parents and pastors to educate their children as they choose for which we who advocate Denominational Schools are contending: and, with equal clearness you ought to know that by denying us such schools you are, in the present divided state of the religious world, forbidding us to exercise the most common and yet dearest right of Christian freemen – the power of educating our own children in the way and manner that we ourselves, their parents and pastors, consider most conducive to their present and eternal well-being. O most execrable oppression!

The Catholic position was best expressed by the author of an article in the *Canadian Freeman* in 1862, which read: "We object to the Common School system because the government constitutes a Protestant superintendent a better judge as to the best education to be given Catholic children than the Catholic Bishops, Priests, and parents of these Catholic children."

So where did George Brown and the radical Reformers stand? Well, they believed in "the democratic principle," which hinged on the equality of men (women, of course, did not enter the picture), unhampered by prejudice, or sectarian beliefs. In an 1861 editorial in *The Globe*, Brown argued that, if people define themselves primarily in terms of their social status or religious affiliation, then a homogeneous, democratic Canadian nation is impossible. He thought the only logical way to go was with a national system of education "by which the children of all will be brought into communion with each other, and, aided by the innate feeling of the human heart which makes every man a lover of his native land, come to look upon themselves as Canadians."

Brown's vision, while controversial in his day, is conventional wisdom to much of today's educational establishment and, indeed, to many Canadians. Gary Duthler, however, doesn't accept it. In fact, he's made challenging that presumption his life's work. A committed Christian and former teacher in the Christian independent-school system, Duthler is now the executive director of the Federation of Independent Schools in Canada. Approximately 260,000 students attend the 1,700 independent schools that belong to his federation. Of those 1,700 schools, 1,200 are religiously based. When he was working on his master's degree at the University of Waterloo, Duthler researched the origins of the common school in Upper Canada. Brown's "avowal of the religion of democratic humanism was as confessionally doctrinaire as any 'sectarianism' it purported to abhor. And, it was as totalitarian in its determination to succeed," he maintains. "Brown was thoroughly a democrat, committed to the rights of the individual and the duty of government not to interfere in those rights. But the need for universal education overrode those principles." In other words, Brown understood that universal education requires the participation of all to make it viable. So the right of parents to educate their children in their own belief systems (separately) was something he couldn't support.

And so Brown used the power of the pen to defend common schools against denominational encroachments. While he disliked the Church of England for trying to breed a privileged class, it was the Catholic Church that received his greatest indictments. Brown was convinced that the "Popish" hierarchy was trying to use separate schools as a stepping stone to gain control over many aspects of national life. He railed against the power of the Catholic clergy, which, he felt, was the greatest obstacle to Canadian progress. In 1862, he wrote, "So long as the Roman Catholics of Upper Canada believe with the *Freeman* that the clergy are the unerring guides to the views of an infallible church, there can be no cordial union between them and the great body of their fellow-citizens. Until they learn to use their private judgment in matters political, they will always be the creatures of a power which will use their votes for the benefit of the church as distinguished from that of the people."

Once again, it's important to bear in mind what times were like when this debate was raging. Feuds begun in other countries were imported here (Irish Protestants versus Irish Catholics); the French-versus-English division was as much embodied in religious differences (Catholicism versus Protestantism) as language. And education itself was the focus of much attention. This was because society was in a state of flux, and education was regarded as key to the strong development of a prosperous colony. Only through education, it was believed, could advances be made both in agriculture and in the newly burgeoning industrialism. And, of course, like today, it was hoped that education could combat illiteracy, crime, and family breakdown, while inculcating "proper" attitudes and values.

The irony, of course, is that while Ryerson and Brown were not only philosophically opposed, and disliked each other intensely, they managed to form an alliance. This alliance merged Ryerson's vision of a united society, founded on a slightly amended British constitution, and Brown's democratic humanism. Many historians maintain that this alliance was crucial to both the creation and survival of common schools in Ontario.

The framework set in place in Upper Canada wasn't followed in all of the other provinces, however. Nova Scotia and New Brunswick, for example, viewed separate denominational schools as socially divisive, while Saskatchewan and Alberta followed the example set in Ontario and Quebec. In "Religion and Education: The Other Side of Pluralism," J. Donald Wilson writes that separate schools were seen as

> a way to maintain some publicly controlled uniformity while also recognizing the validity of certain minority rights . . . with the result that the Canadian practice, generally speaking, became one of subsidizing the education of some religious minorities in confessional, separate, and dissentient schools. The accommodation of these minorities was made for educational, not religious reasons, conceding thereby that the parent is an important agent of education and that schools should be responsive to parental demands in matters relating to moral and religious education.

In 1867, when the British North America Act was signed, legal protection for denominationally based schooling was guaranteed. The BNA Act applied initially to the original signatories of

Confederation – Ontario, Quebec, Nova Scotia, and New Brunswick. But it also established a formula for other provinces who might choose to join Confederation. It guaranteed that whatever education system was in place when a province joined was constitutionally protected. Section 93 made all laws relating to education the exclusive responsibility of the provinces. And Section 93, subsection 1, stated that any denominational school "which any Class of Persons have by law in the Province at Union" couldn't be threatened.

The result is today's patchwork treatment of separate schools across the country. Catholics, for example, are fully – and publicly – funded in Alberta, Saskatchewan, Ontario, Quebec, and Newfoundland, and the Northwest Territories, but not in Nova Scotia, Prince Edward Island, New Brunswick, Manitoba, or British Columbia. Catholic schools in the Yukon are in a unique situation. All schools are owned and operated by the Yukon government, but the Roman Catholic Church has the legal right to choose Catholic teachers and to have a religious component in the school day. Newfoundland, when it joined Canada in 1949, had a school system that was completely denominational. By 1969, its schools were either Catholic, Pentecostal, Seventh Day Adventist, or Integrated (Anglican, United, Presbyterian, Salvation Army, and Moravian). In 1996, Newfoundland's Liberal government pushed for, and got, constitutional change. While the denominational bureaucracy of the system has been removed, its denominational bias hasn't. (More on that in Chapter 3.) Critics saw this as a dangerous precedent for others, but it underlined an important point: the Constitution, while an important guarantor of rights, isn't immutable. If rights given to some in a different era appear unjust and inequitable in today's context, they should be open to challenge and debate.

Manitoba, while constitutionally obliged to fund Catholic schools (since they were in existence when the province joined

Confederation), extricated itself from this arrangement in the 1890s (more in the next chapter). Today it treats them as independent schools, outside the system, but eligible for partial public funding. British Columbia also considers Catholic schools independent, outside the public system. Nevertheless, it's provided some partial funding to them since 1977. And because each province is responsible for education, there's also no uniformity on the role of religious education. It's all very complicated and makes the ideal of Canadian unity – when it comes to education, at least – look like an impossible dream.

So how did Ontario move 180 degrees, from its original emphasis on Christianity in the schools, to ordering Friesen's alternative Christian school in northern Ontario to take down its Christian paraphernalia and toe the secular line?

Well, it happened very gradually. There was no question of the centrality of religion in Ryerson's curriculum. Ryerson saw to it that religion was written into Ontario's School Act of 1850, even specifying that a teacher should be "a person of Christian sentiment." The 1855 Act stated that each school day should begin and end with prayer and Bible reading, the Lord's Prayer was to be part of the daily opening exercises, and the Ten Commandments were to be taught to all students and repeated once a week. In 1859, clergy were allowed to come into the school to teach students belonging to their denominations. This was to be done, however, outside regular school hours. Students could be exempted from religious instruction at their parents' request.

Both World Wars bolstered the impetus for religious education. People were appalled at the devastation wreaked by them. In fact, during the Second World War, there was a sense that instilling a moral purpose in the young was the only way to ensure a future. So, in 1944, a regulation was changed to make religious instruction part of the regular curriculum. Classroom teachers were given the responsibility of teaching a Bible-based course for two half-hour periods a week. Local clergy could also come in and teach the children, at the board's discretion.

Over the next decade and a half, however, increasing numbers of people voiced their objection to this religious requirement. In particular, they objected to what they regarded as the denominational bias of the teaching. By 1966, it was clear that these complaints had to be addressed, and a commission was appointed to clarify the appropriate place of religion in schools. In its final report, it recommended removing the two half-hours a week of religious education in elementary schools, and offering optional teaching of religion by clergy in secondary schools for up to one period a week.

While the recommendations weren't officially adopted by the government, the education ministry and boards of education took them seriously. They increasingly shifted curriculum teaching from religious education to a more secular emphasis on morals and values (character building). It took a couple of court cases, however, to push Ontario's public schools down a completely secular path. And it was the Canadian Charter of Rights and Freedoms (part of the Constitution Act, 1982) that made this possible. The Charter's preamble guarantees "freedom of conscience and religion." And, under Section 15(1), under Equality Rights, the Charter states: "Every individual is equal before and under the law and has the right to the equal protection and equal benefit of the law without discrimination and, in particular, without discrimination based on race, national or ethnic origin, colour, religion, sex, age or mental or physical disability."

In 1986, several parents in Sudbury, using the Charter as their basis for legal action, claimed that the section of the Education Act authorizing religious prayers – specifically the Lord's Prayer – discriminated against non-Christians. The Sudbury board defended the Act. It argued that Canada had a Christian heritage, that religious exercises were educational, not religious, and that exemption was available to any child. While the Divisional Court upheld the Regulation, the Ontario Court of Appeal disagreed. In 1988, it ruled that the Education Act infringed upon freedom of religion and conscience as guaranteed by the Charter, and was thus unconstitutional.

In its judgment, the court recognized that Ontario was changing from a homogenous society to a multicultural one. As well, the court chose to define the meaning of "religion" and "conscience." It said they comprised the right to hold such religious beliefs as a person chooses; the right to declare religious beliefs openly and without fear of hindrance or reprisal; the right to manifest religious belief by worship and practice or by teaching and dissemination; the absence of coercion or restraint (for example, direct commands or limitation of choices); and freedom from conformity (being under the tyranny of the majority), which involved having the right to refuse to participate in religious observances. The ruling had no effect on either Catholic or independent schools. But public educators were warned; the rights and freedoms enshrined in the Charter had relevance and meaning in the classroom.

In another part of Ontario, another court challenge was being heard at virtually the same time. Several parents, supported by the Canadian Jewish Congress and the Canadian Civil Liberties Association, took the Elgin County Board of Education to court. They objected to a religious-education course being taught by "born-againers" – members of a local Bible club. And they won. In 1988, the Ontario Court of Appeal ruled that offering religious indoctrination in the general school curricula of public schools – even when parents had the right to have their children exempted from the classrooms during such lessons – was unconstitutional. The court maintained that such a curriculum constitutes religious coercion and violates the rights of religious minorities. These minorities welcomed the decision. But subsequently they were upset with the Rae government's response to it – an edict, now known as Memorandum 112. That edict went much further than the court ruling. It prohibited religious instruction in schools, even when the course was optional and even where religious coercion wasn't a factor. Memorandum 112 spelled the end of Friesen's alternative Christian program.

Friesen's children's school had been operating under the Fort Frances–Rainy River public-school system for thirteen years. It had been set up to meet the needs of local Christians who wanted their children's education to include fundamentals of Christianity. While the student population was largely Mennonite, the school was open to all. The irony, to Toronto lawyer Peter Jervis, was that Memorandum 112 accomplished the very opposite of what the court intended. Instead of protecting minority rights, he contends, Memorandum 112 ensured that they were trampled. "This little school with 60, and later 115, kids, out of a total student population of 3,000 to 4,000 in that board was a minority population," he argues. Jervis also argues that the right of the Sturgeon Creek parents to practise their Christian beliefs has been denied by the secular majority. He is outraged at what happened and maintains that Memorandum 112 contradicts Canada's constitutional history.

"Where does the Constitution require that there be secularism in the publicly funded schools?" he asks. "In fact, if you read the Constitution and see what the Supreme Court has said, it says that freedom of religion means freedom from religious coercion, freedom to practise your religious beliefs, freedom from religious majoritarianism. It doesn't talk about the separation of church and state."

Indeed, the question of whether or not the Charter requires a secular school system is crucial to the future of educational policy in this country. A Toronto lawyer, Peter Lauwers, thinks it doesn't. Quite the contrary. When he researched this topic, he found the perspective of Canadian philosopher Charles Taylor very instructive. The McGill University professor argues that "a society can be organized around [a] definition of a good life, without this being seen as a depreciation of those who do not personally share this definition. Where the nature of the good requires that it be sought in common, this is the reason for its being an object of public policy. According to this conception, a liberal society singles itself out as such by the way in which it treats minorities, including those who do not share public definitions of the good: and above all by the rights it accords to all its members."

To Lauwers, who often acts on behalf of Catholic school boards, this means that government could support the preservation of French language and culture, aboriginal communities, denominational schools – and religious groups such as Friesen's. "Pluralism and multiculturalism can't survive unless they are sustained by practical measures," Lauwers told a 1996 meeting of the Ontario branch of the Canadian Bar Association. "Mere freedom to associate is not enough. This coexistence ought to be preserved and expanded, not only because it is part of our tradition, but also because it reflects basic human needs that must be satisfied if we are to experience not only life, but the good life." Mark Holmes, a former professor at the Ontario Institute for Studies in Education, notes that "it's perhaps the supreme irony of the late twentieth century that secular hegemony is being imposed in such a heavy-handed way. George Orwell was strangely unprophetic," he says. "He foresaw a totalitarian, egalitarian world enforcing conformity and terrorizing the intellectuals on behalf of Big Brother. Instead, we have an intellectual élite benevolently imposing a liberal, educational tyranny."

Certainly, Canadians who feel strongly about an interrelationship between religion and education are left with a vacuum: a public-school system that imposes upon their children so-called neutral values that are, in fact, anathema to them. This is done despite the multicultural nature of today's society – even, in fact, in the name of today's multicultural society. And while a secular school system may suit the majority of people, it's extremely offensive to members of many belief systems. Has the reaction against the Christian supremacy of Ryerson's legacy swung too far? Genuine diversity – especially if it relates to religious diversity – has been suppressed within much of public education. This outcome smacks of a dangerous, and blind, overreaction.

It could well be that this overreaction has resulted from reducing religious content in education to an issue of secularist-versus-sectarian rivalry. If public schools had had a more open attitude to religion, viewed it as a subject worthy of serious study, perhaps the response to sectarian manifestations wouldn't have been quite so absolutist. What do children who have developed a certain "religious literacy," an ability to think for themselves in matters of the spirit, a sense of their own freedom of conscience, have to fear from evidence of sectarianism? If a school system taught religion as an essential part of human experience, then the children would be equipped to handle the more flagrant expressions of sectarianism. In a way, these issues have unfolded in this manner because of an absence of broader context in which to study religion in schools. The consequence has been to bury an important area of endeavour.

Beyond that, a more tolerant system will involve some sacrifice – on all sides – because no one will get exactly what he or she wants. Lauwers makes this point when he says that genuine pluralism may require compromise on the part of some people. This is because, he maintains, pluralism is only meaningful if it's exercised in matters of importance. "This may lead to a requirement to seek an exemption from religious education," says Lauwers, "or a requirement that a commercial sign be entirely in only one official language. Liberal democracy doesn't require a complete bleaching out of all differences and distinction."

Maybe not, but that point hasn't been easy to establish in the legal arena. Courts haven't been terribly helpful in this area because they, necessarily, rely on legal precedents and legal interpretations, not moral imperatives. As a result, they often lag behind social change. Religious minorities in Ontario have attempted the lengthy, costly, and ultimately useless, legal route. Now they're at an impasse. The only option open to them, it seems, is to wage a battle on the political front. While this is the most natural place for such a move, it remains to be seen whether debate can get beyond an antagonistic, knee-jerk reaction to anything related to religious inquiry. But recognizing the importance of religion in human experience, in light of today's religious diversity, is essential if we are to redefine who we are. The possibilities and the limits of political action are suggested by examining past and present battles for Catholic education. They underline the fact that the current system of funding some religiously based schools is a political creation, and to that extent not immutable but subject to change in response to new political conditions.

3

DIVISION AND REVISION

*Until I went to college, I had no genuine contact with anyone
who wasn't Catholic. . . . Real life, the friendships, the feuds, the
passions of proximate existence, took place in the sectarian
compound, a compound, like any other, with its secrets — a secret
language, secret customs, rites, which I now understand must
have been very menacing at worst or at the best puzzling to the
outside world.*

Mary Gordon, *Getting Here from There:
A Writer's Reflections on a Religious Past*

*This is what Yahweh asks of you, to act justly, to love tenderly,
and to walk humbly with your God.*

Biblical quote framed and hung in Kevin Mulvey's office

Joan Flood marches confidently into Kevin Mulvey's office,
drops her leather coat, and settles in for an interesting hour or
so reminiscing about the past. This is no small feat, since Flood
and Mulvey were on opposite sides of the fence on an issue that
marked one of the most divisive chapters in Ontario's recent
educational history. Flood is chair of the Essex County Board of
Education; Mulvey is principal of St. Thomas of Villanova, a

state-of-the-art Catholic high school built in 1994 in La Salle, a bedroom community outside Windsor. Flood and Mulvey went through all the turmoil and upheaval wreaked in the late eighties and early nineties after Conservative Premier Bill Davis's 1984 decision to extend public funding to Catholic high schools to the end of Grade 13. Many Ontario communities had a tough time coping with the aftermath of that decision, but Essex County's experience was one of the worst.

In January 1997, I journeyed back to this part of southwestern Ontario where I grew up, in the hope that learning about the social effects of the religious-schools issue would illuminate the path we should take in the future. When I arrived, my knowledge of the divisions that had occurred in the community was mostly derived from what I'd picked up in the media. I recalled a story about an anti-Catholic slogan spray-painted on a Catholic church, public high-school students protesting the takeover of their school by Catholics, and police called in to control crowds at public high-school board meetings. While I was born and raised in Essex County, a region that's about evenly split between Catholics and Protestants, I'd been gone a long time. I figured that, like most every other part of the country, it too had changed with the times. Still, I could well imagine the religious tensions of my childhood being rekindled as a result of extending government-sanctioned segregation along religious lines.

Probably few people in that area have experienced the pain of religious tensions more than Joan Flood. She grew up on a farm several miles down the road from where I grew up, although we never knew each other. How could we? True, she was older than I was, so our high-school paths wouldn't have crossed anyway. But the salient point was that she was Catholic. So, even though the public elementary school was right next door to her family's home, she was bused nine miles away to Essex, to Holy Name School. Between the Catholic hospital, Catholic social services,

Catholic school, and, of course, the Catholic Church, she had little need for much outside contact. Her entire life revolved around being Catholic. But, within Gesto, the community in which she grew up, there were only three Catholic families. There, she experienced what it felt like to grow up a member of a minority. Every year, she watched the United Church kids play games in the school yard next door at their annual summer picnic. Every year, she longed to join them in their fun. "Then one year I got bold," she says. "I remember I was ten and I was peeking through the fence and saw my age group gathering for their race. I wanted so badly to be part of it. So I ran over and lined up with them. Then someone pointed at me and said, 'She can't be in this race. She's Catholic.' I was so embarrassed, so hurt. I ran away in tears."

Flood is the fifth of eleven children. Her father was a strict Catholic. Rosary was said every night. Fridays were meatless. A St. Christopher's medal hung from the car's rearview mirror above the dashboard, and before every ride a prayer was said to St. Christopher for safety. "Later the Church declared he wasn't a saint," says Flood. "I was flabbergasted. How could I believe in something that didn't exist? I was taught the fear of God, not the love of God."

But Flood incurred the combined anger of both the Church and her father when she fell in love with a Protestant. Things would have been fine if he'd converted and they'd married in the Catholic Church. But he didn't, and they weren't. Flood's father disowned her, refusing to see her, talk to her, or allow anyone in the family to have any contact with her. "I really didn't know my younger brothers and sisters," she says, "because no one was allowed to see me." When her second child was born, a daughter, it died in its first days. It was a difficult loss, but she was heartened when a nurse came to tell her that her father and mother were in the hospital lobby. "I wanted so much to see my mother," says Flood, "so I asked the nurse to let them come in.

But my father came in alone; he made my mother stay outside. The only thing he said to me before leaving was: 'Did you get the baby baptized?'"

Two things are immediately impressive about Joan Flood: her obvious strength and her innate kindness. They're an interesting mix, given the trials she's faced in her lifetime. And both were required during the turmoil following the extension of public funding to Catholic high schools. "I'd lived through segregation along religious lines," she says, "and I didn't want it to happen again. I truly believe in public education. Regardless of our religion, I think we should go to the same school and learn tolerance. We shouldn't be showing favouritism to one particular religion, but that's what the government did. I'm a Conservative – I even ran for them – but what Bill Davis did was wrong. He tore the community apart."

The trip to St. Thomas of Villanova – known in these quarters as simply "Villanova" – takes Flood and me through the flat fields of farm country I know so well. I'm amazed, though, at the many large luxury homes dotting the countryside. Either the local farmers are becoming very prosperous, or city commuters are enjoying a taste of country living. There's a sprinkling of snow on the ground, and everything looks fresh and virginal. I'm struck by both its sparseness and its beauty. We pass some of the community high schools – Essex, Harrow, Amherstburg. They're modest, unassuming buildings that pale by comparison when Villanova comes into view. It's a sprawling brick building with a beautiful stained-glass front where the chapel is. There are tennis courts, basketball sites, a football field complete with field house, and thirteen portables lined up next to the parking lot. I'm beginning to understand why locals refer to this school as "The Palace."

The inside is beautiful. There are a 524-seat theatre, music labs, a computer lab, an art studio, three gyms, a library chockablock with computers and lit by a skylight from which hangs a piece of native Indian mobile art. Kevin Mulvey, the principal, is warm and welcoming. He says that, in the beginning, a building of this sort was inconceivable. Initially, the idea was simply that the public and Catholic kids would share a school. And so, in 1987, they joined forces inside General Amherst High. It's within sight of the Detroit River, only a stone's throw from Fort Malden, an important fortress during the War of 1812. The deal was supposed to be short-term. Then, depending on how many students the separate school attracted, a decision would be made about whether the Catholics would get a new school or take over an existing public school.

The Amherstburg school could accommodate well over 1,000 students, says Mulvey, but enrolment was down, so there were about 350 empty spaces. Turning seven classrooms on the second floor over to the Catholic school (six for classes and one for a chapel) didn't seem like a major concession. "Things started out well," he says. "I was the principal of Villanova and we only had 87 students for Grade 9 – the idea was to add a school year each year. But as time went on, pressure on the building increased. By the time we added Grade 11, we had 450 students and that created tension. It was sort of like the case of in-laws who come to visit and then stay too long."

Students were forced to attend school in shifts, the public-school kids from 8 a.m. to 1 p.m., the Catholic kids from 1 p.m. to 6 p.m. But everyone seemed to be coping well with the inconveniences, says Mulvey, since they knew the arrangement would eventually end. The real trouble began when the site that had been picked for the new Catholic school was rejected by the municipality. The NDP government then announced that one of the public schools would be transferred to the Catholic board. That's when things got really hot. "The years 1991–92 were difficult," says Mulvey, "because the political issue of transferring a school was a problem. Students would go home and hear the anger of their parents. And when it was announced that General Amherst was one of three community high schools being considered for closure, there was a walkout of public-high students. Our students had to walk through a picket line in order to get to class. A Roman Catholic church was spray-painted with an anti-religious slogan, and a Catholic church in Kingsville was broken into. The actual issue was the accommodation of students. The emotional issue became community high schools and their closure. But some people interpreted it as a religious issue – which was precisely what we were trying to avoid."

Mulvey put his finger on what makes raising this issue so diffi-cult: challenging the public funding of Catholic schools is all too often interpreted as a masked form of bigotry, of being anti-Catholic. Catholics are sensitive on this ground for good reason: anti-Catholicism is woven into the fabric of our Canadian past. In Essex County, for example, opposition to the separate-school system dates back to 1891, when Council No. 1 of the ultra-conservative Protestant Protective Association was formed in Windsor. Stridently anti-Catholic, its members swore an oath to "denounce the Pope . . . his priests and emissaries and the diabol-ical work of the Roman Catholic Church." A prominent member of that organization was both a lawyer and city mayor. So, when Mulvey refers to an anti-Catholic slogan being painted on a Catholic church, I ask him what it said. He and Flood look at each other, then both say they can't remember. Later, I look the inci-dent up in the archives. The misspelt graffiti read, "Buy a gun. Kill a Cathlic."

This is scary stuff. Little wonder it's something everyone wants to gloss over. Crazies must have done it, say those who'll actually talk about it. It's over and done with. Best forgotten. Some claim, however, that the upheaval had a positive effect. It woke people up to the gravity of the situation. When even the Irish press took an interest in the conflict, it raised the question: Did they really want another northern Ireland in their own back yard? The answer was clearly No. And perhaps, at an intuitive level, that's what some young people were trying to say right from the very beginning.

In 1987, when an information meeting was held for graduating Grade 8 students at a Catholic elementary school, a number of them came forward. The January 14, 1987, issue of the *Amherstburg Echo* reported three students rising to say: "We don't care about money, or new equipment, or about having the honour of being 'the pioneers' [the description given to the first Grade 9 separate class to attend Amherst]. We just care about our educations, about getting jobs in the future, and about keeping the friends we've got [Catholic and non-Catholic]. All the new equipment and everything sounds great, but the rest of the idea shows that we could be split up from our friends [from non-Catholic friends, and those Catholic ones who decide not to enrol in the separate wing] . . . we've looked forward all our lives" to going to Amherst.

But public funding of Catholic high schools was the new law of the land. How could the wishes of these students be considered in light of the larger political struggle for tax-dollars, school space, and constitutional rights? Mulvey says, in retrospect, that the struggles his students encountered during their years at General Amherst strengthened them all. "We had to look at our own school and ask, 'What is it about us, and how do we show excellence?' The sharing crisis made for a solid ideology for the school. Students knew they had to be known for the quality of their school, so they had to make it a good one." He's obviously proud of the outcome. Today, he oversees 1,422 students (and growing) in a huge, beautiful school. While he acknowledges the past was difficult, he quickly breezes through it. The subject doesn't come up again.

When I meet later with parents who were involved with the PTA at General Amherst during this struggle, I find quite another perspective. Vic Bennett and Diane Pouget fought hard to keep the public high school from being taken over by the Catholic system. They're proud of the fact that the community was able to retain its school. And it's a chapter in history they don't want people to forget. In fact, at a recent reunion of General Amherst High, they were shocked to discover that the fight to save their school has been erased from the school's history. "A couple of pamphlets were produced for the bicentenary and a plaque was put on a rock," says Bennett. "The wording on the plaque was changed several times, because the Ministry of Education didn't want any mention made of what they called 'the accommodation crisis.' So our history was edited out. There's no mention in the bicentennial books. They don't want anyone to talk about it. They're very embarrassed by it. But it's our history. It happened."

And Bennett and Pouget adamantly maintain that the struggle was not rooted in bigotry. Pouget says this very forcefully, being a practising Catholic herself. To her mind, supporting public education doesn't make her any less a faithful Catholic. In fact, she and her husband never dreamed they'd send their three daughters to public schools. Both of them had attended Catholic schools and they had simply assumed their children would do the same. And they did for a while. But after going through two strikes by separate-school teachers and experiencing a variety of other bureaucratic problems with the separate-school board, they decided – long before this issue ever arose – to send their children to the local public elementary school. "When I talked to my priest about all the problems at the [Catholic] school, he was quite sympathetic at first," says Pouget. "But when I told him we'd decided to send our children to the public school, he was aghast. He said, 'Heaven forbid! Now they're never going to hear the name of Jesus again.' I said, 'Yes they are, Father. They're going to hear it in our home and at church.' We didn't lose our faith just because we decided to send our children to a public school."

Pouget describes how difficult it was to make that decision. "It was one of the hardest things I've ever done, because religion is very important to me," she says. "But that separate-school board had nothing to do with religion and everything to do with power and money. I wanted to protect my children." And that's what she thought she'd done until Villanova moved into General Amherst. Then she discovered that many of the experiences she wanted her daughters to have during their teenage years were being thwarted as a result of the sharing arrangement. Going on shifts, for example, meant that the public-school kids didn't get gym time until after 8 p.m., too late for most to trudge over to the school to begin extracurricular activities. The 8 a.m. class start made the co-op education program very difficult to administer; nobody wanted students to start working at that hour. Nor did their lunch hour of 10:32 fit easily with community placements. Home rooms became nonexistent. Student-council elections and Remembrance Day assemblies were held over the PA system and opportunities for socialization became limited. The Catholic students were supposed to use their own entrance, but, as their numbers increased, so did their use of the school. Pouget says it wasn't long before the public-school kids had no space they could call their own.

To add insult to injury, she says the separate-school board poured a lot of money into its section of the school – painting walls, replacing windows, installing carpets, air-conditioning, and drapes. They purchased new furniture, cupboards, and a school van. That part of the school that was designated public didn't get a face-lift. There wasn't the money, so it stayed shabby. "To this day, our children have never been rewarded or thanked for the sacrifices they endured," says Pouget. "During all the years of sharing, our students were portrayed as the villains, the Villanova students as the poor little orphans. . . . Our students were continually short-changed, even though our boards and the Ministry of Education assured us this wouldn't happen. We were often accused of being un-Christian, prejudiced, or anti-Catholic when we voiced our concerns. These accusations were very unfair and painful."

Things escalated to the point that parents opposed to the transfer of their school to the Catholic board dragged school chairs into the middle of Highway 18, the main thoroughfare, and sat on them, refusing to budge. Traffic came to a standstill. By the end of the day, several thousand people had come out in support of retaining their community school. Gord Freeman says he was at home that day when his wife phoned to say, "The school's been given away. Get down there and help Dee-Dee [Diane Pouget]." As he describes this, his eyes well with tears, as if the event happened yesterday. The highway sit-in lasted several days. Three to four weeks of community protest later, the NDP government announced that it had found the money for a new Catholic school.

Unfortunately, the building of the new Catholic high schools in Essex County (Villanova in La Salle and Cardinal Carter in Leamington) hasn't resolved the community dissension and division. It's understandable that, if you're going to invest in new buildings you should build well. But many argue that the Catholic board wasn't content with Chevrolets – they opted for Cadillacs – which is why both schools are locally referred to as "palaces." Unfortunately, their opulence serves to separate children into the haves (Catholic students) and the have-nots (public students). Is it bigotry to feel jealous and resentful about perceived inequality? Is trying to save your community school anti-Catholic? It's likely the same conflict would have arisen had it been Anglicans or humanists or People with Blue Eyes who appeared to be getting superior treatment to everyone else. But the fact the favoured group is one that experienced religious persecution in the past gives it additional meaning.

Today, the "accommodation crisis" is over. But there continues to be a struggle for the hearts and minds – and especially the bodies – of high-school students. Both boards compete aggressively for students. (More bodies mean more government money, and building Villanova and Cardinal Carter put the separate-school board into debt.) "They [the Catholic board] try to recruit our kids, offering a kid out of Grade 8 the chance to play football and go to Michigan," says Bryan Meyer, a chartered accountant in Harrow. "We don't even have a football team because we can't afford the uniforms." Meyer finds the situation unfair and says Protestants are discriminated against. This is ironic, given that the motivation behind full funding was to create a situation of equality for Catholics. Now Meyer wonders why Catholics have constitutional protection of their school system, while Protestants, who were also supposed to get their schools under the compromise agreement, have ended up with no protection for their religious rights. He argues that devout Protestants lost their rights when their schools became the catchall for everyone who wasn't Catholic. Public schools are required by law to be religiously "neutral," so Christianity can't receive special attention. "So Protestants lost their protection," he argues, "while Catholics kept theirs. It isn't fair."

He also bemoans the social effects of this division. "Protestant/Catholic issues died here some time ago," says Meyer. "There was intermarriage and people were getting along well. But this really brought everything back to the fore and people were forced to take sides. Functionally, I guess that things are tolerable today. But we continue to bear the scars. And it hurts to see the waste – of resources, time, energy – because of a duplication of services."

Aside from the building of Villanova and Cardinal Carter, the financial cost of perpetuating separate religious schools isn't something that people here dwell on – even though government figures I obtained reveal that eleven years of funding Catholic high schools has cost Ontario taxpayers $2.23 billion, a significant portion of which represents new spending. Instead, what they repeatedly raise are the social costs of religious segregation. "Protestant and Catholic students got along just fine when they went to one public high school," people repeatedly tell me. "Separating them set the clock back." This may be true from where they sit, but every time I hear it I can't help thinking how irritating it must sound to die-hard supporters of separate Catholic schools. This is because many supporters of separate Catholic schools convey the sense that "intermarriage" is an altogether undesirable outcome. As for "getting along together," while it might be seen as a desirable objective, it's not nearly as important to them as perpetuation of the faith. Besides, interacting can lead to intermarriage and recent history seems to suggest that this results not in more converts but in greater losses of their own numbers. Supporting separate Catholic schools, then, is seen as an act of religious survival.

But Joan Flood adamantly maintains that the purpose of education isn't to make people "distinct." She argues that public education – education that's open to everyone – is what will build a tolerant society. Students should be taught religious values, she says, "but I want them taught in such a way they can make their own choice when they grow up. Until that's done, we won't be tolerant of one another." She can't understand how her views could be called anti-Catholic when she's proposing a system in which Catholics and non-Catholics would be educated together: "We aren't rejecting Catholics. We want to be together with Catholics." She thinks Ontario should eliminate publicly funded Catholic schools in favour of one public system. This isn't a discussion in which the Catholic Church wants to become embroiled. Nor do officials see why they should have to. They need only point to the Supreme Court's ruling in the Adler case, in 1996, that Ontario is not discriminating against other religions when it refuses to fund independent religious schools. The highest court in the land has confirmed the constitutional right of Catholics to public funding of their schools.

★

But change is in the air, and it inevitably affects Ontario. Both Newfoundland and Quebec are moving away from denominational schools. And they're doing so despite constitutional guarantees. I flew into Newfoundland a month after its referendum on denominational schools in the fall of 1995. The Liberal government, under Premier Clyde Wells, wanted parliamentary approval for constitutional change. Under Term 17 of the province's agreement to join Canada in 1949, denominational schools were guaranteed. The effect was to perpetuate public funding of a huge array of schools – Roman Catholic, Anglican, United, Presbyterian, Salvation Army, Pentecostal, Seventh Day Adventist, and Moravian. Later, the United, Anglican, Salvation Army, Presbyterian, and Moravian churches joined forces to create "Integrated" schools. That left a system composed of Pentecostal, Catholic, Integrated, and Seventh Day Adventist schools. Each was governed by its own mini-bureaucracy, called an education council. The government paid the bill, established curricula, and set standards. But the churches, through their education councils, directed school boards to hire and fire teachers of their own denominations, operate religious programs, and open and close schools. In the hard economic times of the nineties, all these separate denominational schools appeared to be a luxury that many believed the tiny province could no longer afford. An estimated $25 to $30 million a year could be saved by eliminating separate denominational bureaucracies.

Besides, Newfoundland was changing. Not everyone is a Christian adherent. About 94 per cent of the population belongs to the eight different denominations. This means that children of the 6 per cent – whose parents are secular, or from other faiths, such as Judaism or Islam – have no choice but a Christian, church-run school. In addition, there seems to be appalling ignorance about other faiths. This was brought home in an anecdote someone in

St. John's told me. She said a Jewish colleague of hers was concerned about all the Christian trappings of Christmas that his Grade 1 child was being exposed to. So he went to the teacher and asked if some sensitivity could be shown to the children who weren't Christian. The teacher was very receptive and said she'd be only too happy to oblige. A couple of days later, the child came home, very excited, and said, "Daddy, Daddy, guess what we're going to do at school? How Jews celebrate Christmas!" The best of intentions obviously don't equal knowledge.

Bill McKim, a psychology professor at Memorial University, has long been concerned about the role of religion in education. In 1988, he edited a book entitled *The Vexed Question: Denominational Education in a Secular Age.* An ardent advocate of public (that is, non-denominational) education, he gives me a short history course over the time it takes to eat lunch.

He says that there's one quick answer to the question "Why denominational schools?" The religious groups couldn't get along with each other. Like every other part of the country, the first schools in Newfoundland were run by the churches. But in the late 1830s, the government decided to legislate a public-school system. There were too many nasty clashes between Irish Catholics and English Protestants; things were turning ugly and public schools seemed a good antidote. The Anglicans, however, ignored the intent of the law.

"They were in the majority and were in charge of the school board – in Conception Bay, I think it was," says McKim. "They made everybody read the Bible and the Catholics got up in arms. They said, 'There are more of them than us, and they're trying to impose their religion on us.' They yelled and screamed, so finally the government, to make the Catholics happy, said, 'Okay, you can have your own system.' The law was changed, but by this time the Anglicans and Methodists were going at it hammer and tongs about who was going to run the remaining school system. Since the government had already set the precedent of letting the Catholics have their own system, it finally broke down – this is about 1870 – and said, 'All right, you guys can have your own system too.' So, when the Salvation Army came along and wanted their own schools, then, of course, they got them, too, as did all the others who came along. That's what got preserved in the Constitution."

McKim, a born-and-bred Newfoundlander, says religious segregation was made official while an informal system of sharing power was developed between Anglicans and Catholics. For example, McKim excelled at university. In any other province he might automatically have applied for a Rhodes Scholarship. But he didn't, since he knew it wasn't the year for a Protestant to win, it was a Catholic's turn. (It went to CBC journalist Rex Murphy.) McKim says the message, the symbolism of religious segregation, was implicit: "'These [people from other religious denominations] are different people. They aren't like us. You don't marry them. You don't play with them. You don't have anything to do with them.' I can remember when I went to school in an older section of town, the school would occasionally be broken into by vandals. I remember going into assembly one morning after the school had been broken into on the weekend and things were smashed and disreputable things were written on the blackboard. And the principal told us they were 'the St. Pat's toughs.' Same thing as saying they were the Catholics. You could get yourself beaten up if you were in the wrong type of territory."

It's easy to see, when driving through St. John's, how insulated a sub-group could be from the larger community. I visit St. Pius X Junior High School, for example, and from a second-floor window see a world that is totally Catholic – church, schools, home for the aged – birth to death, all in a small enclave. The boys from Mount Cashel went to this school, and I try to imagine what their small world must have felt like. Later, when I ask a cab driver to take me to Mount Cashel, the home run by the Christian Brothers, he stops beside an empty field. The building has been bulldozed, all signs of the place in which so much suffering took place now destroyed. Pat Hogan, principal of St. Pius X, implies that the revelations of child sexual abuse that took place at Mount Cashel made people more willing to vote for removing power from the churches. "We went through a holocaust of sorts," he says in reference to it. "A really bad time. It's hard, really hard, to say what changed. . . . You know, religious rivalries were very, very strong in the late fifties and sixties. But society changed, the church changed, people's world-view changed. Religion itself didn't seem to have the same importance as it used to have."

Alice Collins, an education professor at Memorial University, doesn't think the Mount Cashel revelations were the actual catalyst for change. "Throughout the whole crisis, there were many people who would say, 'But we all had a sense that that was going on.' They just never spoke out. I think the problem was deeper. It was a problem of not being able to challenge hierarchical structures, like the church-school-state relationship that we have . . . a hierarchical structure doesn't allow you to have input and to challenge and to criticize. That's the underlying thing of what Mount Cashel represented." She maintains that the social segregation caused by denominational schooling made it very difficult for people even to be aware of other points of view. "When you institutionalize people on the basis of religion throughout a whole province," she says, "it has to have social effects – not because people are consciously intolerant of another person's point of view, but because they don't have exposure to it."

A wake-up call, of sorts, came during the denominational-schools referendum campaign. Collins says many Newfoundlanders, as a result of improved communications, of meeting new people coming into the province, or because of their own travels outside Newfoundland, were getting "rather smug in our idea that we were becoming more sophisticated. But it took only a couple of weeks of debate on the referendum to realize that just beneath the surface are all the old biases and, I have to say, in some cases, bigotry existed. So, you know, it doesn't take much to bring that out." She cites the trap the media fell into − of talking about "the Catholic vote" as if Catholics were one monolithic whole who don't think for themselves.

Still, as I sift through newspaper clippings of that period, it's clear that the Catholic and Pentecostal leadership did lead the campaign against voting for constitutional change. They ran television spots, radio and print ads. They canvassed door to door and tracked potential supporters on computers. Through it all, they emphasized two things: the Godlessness of a non-denominational education system (Bibles, the Lord's Prayer, and Christmas concerts prohibited in the classroom) and governance (as in Power-Grabbing Government). One TV ad, for example, showed a hand − the long arm of government − plucking apples from a tree. A voice explained that the churches agreed to most of Premier Clyde Wells's education reforms, but that he still wanted more. So when the hand reached for the highest apple and couldn't get it, it grabbed a chain saw and violently hacked it off. "On September 5," said the voice-over, "Vote 'No' and keep the faith in education."

The Liberal government, meanwhile, refused to campaign. Instead, it settled for distributing a brochure that outlined the proposed changes. Wells was reported as saying, "If the majority of the people in this province genuinely do not want the changes government has proposed, why should we spend taxpayers' dollars to advocate something against their interests?"

The "No" campaign was both aggressive and expensive. But the forces for change won the day − albeit barely. Only 52 per cent of eligible voters turned out. The result: 54 per cent for "Yes" (constitutional change) and 46 per cent for "No." Gerald Fallon, executive director of the Catholic Education Council, is bitter about the outcome. He sits in his office, housed in the same building as the Integrated and Pentecostal education councils. He says the different denominations have a marvellous relationship: "We operate together. We socialize together. We pray together. We work together. We're colleagues, co-workers." I can't help thinking how contradictory it is that, despite his experience, Fallon campaigned for an education system that would deny his children similar encounters.

"This referendum was a means to ask all of the people of the province to pronounce on the rights of the various groups," Fallon says. "Now, the Premier will say that there is no such thing as minority rights in Newfoundland. He will say that 95 per cent of the population of this province hold the rights on education. He's right about that. But what he's wrong about is that we do not hold these rights collectively. . . . So we [Catholics] are 36 per cent of the population and we were being told by the rest of the population, the majority, that we're going to vote on your rights. The Anglicans were voting on our rights. The United Church were voting on our rights. We told the government, 'If you're going to change, you've got to ask Catholics, do they want to give up their rights?' Ask them. Because if you had the whole population of Canada voting on the rights of aboriginals, there wouldn't be any rights for aboriginals in this country. If you had all of the population voting on the rights of francophones in this country, they wouldn't stand a chance."

This isn't an extraordinary insight, but it does point to one of the reasons for a constitution: it's meant to provide safeguards for minority rights. On the other hand, there's nothing to prevent a constitution from changing, through time. Constitutional law expert Anne Bayefsky appeared before the Standing Senate Committee on Legal and Constitutional Affairs in July 1996, when it was considering the Newfoundland amendment. She said: "From the outset, one must recognize that the Constitution is not immutable, that it ought to be open to modernization, that the process of amending the Constitution has to be one which accounts for and includes flexibility. It seems to me that one has to approach the whole project of amendment with an open mind, with the concept . . . that the Constitution ought to be considered a living tree. The question of modernization, of keeping our Constitution up to date and responsive to the needs of Canadians over time means that it is not a sufficient answer to say that there are rights here which hitherto have been entrenched . . . that they must be a barrier. By definition, that would make the Constitution inflexible and prevent change."

The person behind the Newfoundland change, Premier Clyde Wells, calls the denominational system "crazy." He's thinking of it, of course, in terms very different from those of Fallon and his supporters. To Wells, government has a responsibility to do the best by all its citizens, and that means not short-changing them on the education of their children. He bemoans the sub-average levels of reading and mathematics in Newfoundland, the duplication of services, the lack of accountability, the number of decision-making bodies.

He describes himself as someone whom his province's education system failed. I look at him, leaning back in his leather chair, against the backdrop of the premier's wood-panelled office in the legislative building, and ask how he – a well-educated lawyer, Premier of Newfoundland – can make that claim. "I can't speak French," he says, raising his palms. "And there was no opportunity to have a background in science. . . . That's the price that society pays – the price we're paying in Newfoundland at the moment." He says he didn't have the opportunity to achieve in these areas because the education system was forced to subdivide its efforts. There's no money left over for such "luxuries" as French and proper science labs when scarce resources are put into busing children long distances to attend a specific religious school – or when small communities support three, even four, schools.

Wells's proposal for constitutional change was passed by Parliament, and when the Senate refused its approval the Commons overrode it. In fact, the changes aren't as drastic as opponents alleged. Religion, for example, will still be allowed in schools. Denominational schools will continue to be publicly supported, where numbers warrant. But what many people thought could never happen – the diminution of religious control over education in Newfoundland – has begun. And people who fear that the forces of secularization are taking over need only look a little further west to Quebec. The Parti Québécois government announced in January 1997 that it would seek constitutional change in order to move Quebec's education system from a denominationally based one (Catholic/Protestant) to a linguistically based one (French/English). Needless to say, this was music to the federal government's ears. It raised the question of whether Quebec would be giving implicit recognition of the Constitution Act of 1982, which incorporates the BNA Act. Quebec has never ratified it, so using the Constitution Act as an instrument contradicts Quebec's position that it's not a valid document.

Quebec later announced it would go ahead with its plans, constitutional change or not. This is exactly what Renton Patterson wanted to hear. The author of a booklet entitled *Not Carved in Stone: Public Funding of Separate Schools in Ontario*, Patterson is militant in his opposition to the public funding of Catholic schools. A former high-school teacher, he's devoting his retirement to the cause of public education. The organization through which he's doing it is Friends of Public Education, a group started in Harrow, Ontario, during the "accommodation crisis." Patterson was teaching technical courses at a high school in Pembroke, outside Ottawa, when public funding to Catholic schools was extended to the end of Grade 13. But he says the creation of two high schools in his community – one Catholic, one public – undermined the educational opportunities available to young people. "We blew it," he says. "We had a chance to be educating young people for jobs in the modern world. Instead, we ended up with a duplication of schools and a reduction in important courses. When I was teaching, nobody could care less who was Catholic, but suddenly, it was brought to everyone's attention. I was amazed and shocked and demoralized and disillusioned because of the power I saw at work [for religious control over schools], and for what purpose?"

Since then, Patterson has been trying to educate anyone, and everyone, about the need for one public education system. Despite the fact that this is a controversial area, he claims that it's possible to eliminate funding for separate schools in Ontario without constitutional change. "All that's necessary is for the province to introduce legislation to that effect," he says. And he points to Manitoba setting the precedent: "In 1890, the Manitoba legislature used its version of our Section 93(3) in the Constitution Act, 1867, . . . to abolish its system of denominational schools," he says. "Ontario could do the same." Yet when I examine that chapter of our history it makes it obvious that Manitoba is no model for the present. The Manitoba Schools question, as it was known, dominated the Canadian political agenda for more than six years at the end of the last century. In the space of five years, Canada went through four prime ministers.

When the province of Manitoba was created in 1870, it too was allowed to make laws governing education, provided the rights of denominational schools were maintained. This meant unqualified protection for the French-speaking and Catholic minorities of Manitoba. But by 1890, the Protestant majority began raising objections to separate schools, arguing they were expensive and fostered religious divisions. Anti-Catholic feelings were exploited. In the legislative session later that year, the assembly passed a law abolishing the official use of French, denied *Canadiens* the right to a French-speaking jury in provincial courts, and replaced the two systems of education with a single non-denominational one. In February 1891, the Manitoba Court of Queen's Bench declared the Manitoba legislation constitutional. The federal government appealed the case to the Supreme Court. In October of that year, the Supreme Court reversed the judgment of the Manitoba court. So Manitoba appealed to the court of last resort – the Judicial Committee of the Privy Council in Great Britain. In June 1892, it ruled the legislation constitutional. Catholics and *Canadiens* then petitioned the federal government for support. The Manitoba Schools Crisis had begun in earnest.

Besides costing a number of politicians their careers, the schools crisis fed on sectarian hatred and divided communities. Eventually, in 1895, Canada's Privy Council agreed that the constitutional rights of the minority had been denied. The Manitoba govern-ment was ordered to restore Catholic schools, provide them a share of provincial grants, and exempt Catholics from paying taxes to support another system. Should Manitoba refuse, Ottawa threatened to seize control of education. It refused.

In February 1896, the federal government introduced a reme-dial bill, proposing to set up a separate school board that would administer all Catholic schools, appoint qualified teachers and inspectors, and select textbooks. No financial provisions were laid out for maintaining these schools. The bill did state, however, that Roman Catholics could put their municipal school tax towards supporting their own schools.

At the second reading, Wilfrid Laurier, the Québécois Catholic leader of the opposition Liberals, rose in Parliament: "Not many weeks ago, I was told from high quarters in the Church to which I belong that unless I supported the school bill . . . I would incur the hostility of a great and powerful body. . . . I have only this to say: even though I have threats held over me, coming, as I am told, from high dignitaries in the Church to which I belong, no word of bitterness shall ever pass my lips as [sic] against that Church. I respect it and I love it." With officials of the Catholic Church watching from the visitors' gallery, he then declared: "So long as I have a seat in this House, so long as I occupy the position I do now, whenever it shall become my duty to take a stand upon any question whatever, that stand I will take not upon grounds of Roman Catholicism, not upon grounds of Protestantism, but upon grounds which can appeal to the conscience of all men, irrespective of their particular faith, upon grounds which can be occupied by all men who love justice, freedom, and toleration." While Laurier knew that the constitutional rights of Manitoba's minority were being unjustly denied, he was even more concerned about whipping up Protestant and Catholic bigotry, and that drove him to seek a compromise he wasn't altogether happy with, but which would dilute some of the ugliness of sectarian emotions.

He used his consummate art as a politician to best advantage. He moved that the bill not be read a second time that day, but be postponed for six months. This was a clever strategy. During that time, a federal election would be held and, if Laurier won, it would end any further remedial legislation. The bill didn't get second reading and Laurier won the federal election by a majority of thirty seats in the House of Commons. Eventually, an agreement was struck between Laurier and Premier Thomas Greenway of Manitoba. Religious instruction was to be allowed in public schools during the last half-hour of each day. And, if numbers warranted, then Catholics could petition school trustees to hire a Catholic teacher. So it was that Manitoba Catholics came to lose their constitutional right to separate schools. Today, the province partially funds independent religious schools.

While Manitoba is clearly not a desirable model for the present, since minority rights were trampled on, perhaps the example set by Laurier has more to offer. Arguing that the Constitution be overruled is simplistic, but to view it as written in stone is equally untenable. Both serve to shut out other, more socially desirable options. What we need is a political solution that might involve constitutional change. But if constitutional change is required, it doesn't follow that a minority group would necessarily see its rights eroded. In fact, constitutional change might be the only route open to a more equitable state of affairs, in which equal protection is granted to all faiths, rather than favouring some and not others. Unfortunately, it's difficult to discuss this issue without raising the spectre of bigotry. As with Laurier, however, the motivation for change has to be the desire to compromise through a process that downplays intolerance and accommodates the maximum number of interests on a just basis.

We have a choice: We can go in the direction of religious entrenchment, or we can move in new directions requiring new solutions. One of the things we have to do, however, is to ask: "What kind of a society are we building if religious segregation is the defining experience of children?" If children themselves were to have any say in the matter, what would it be? Len Williams, who eventually became deputy minister of education in Clyde Wells's government, says both the absurdity and the tragedy of Newfoundland's segregated system of religious schooling hit him when his son David was getting ready to start school. David was excited about the prospect and chattered enthusiastically about his new adventure. He stated matter-of-factly to his mother that he'd be going to school with his best friend, Annette, who lived next door. "Well, no you're not," responded his mother slowly. "You can't go with Annette because she'll be going to another school."

Williams recounts that his son was devastated. "The long and the short of it was that we had to say, 'You're Salvation Army. You can't go to her school because you're not a Catholic,'" Williams tells me. "It made me realize that children, in their innocence, are shaped by the warped perceptions or beliefs of adults. My son couldn't care less what a Salvationist or a Catholic was. He wanted to go to school with Annette. And he should have been able to go to school with her. They should have been educated together in an environment where the basic values of schooling permeate."

I share Williams's vision. But as increasing numbers of religious groups reject public education, that ideal seems more and more elusive. While I bemoan that, it seems all the more important to try to understand the educational ideal espoused by religious schools. I decided to visit a number of them across the country to see for myself whether what they are doing is so distinct as to require separating children on the basis of religion during the most formative years of their lives.

4

THE KIPPAH, KIRPAN, AND KORAN

How natural it was and how universal to slip into the language of faith. And perhaps his mother was right. . . . The outward forms were important. . . . To be seen in the synagogue was to proclaim; this is where I stand, these are my people, these are the values by which I try to live, this is what generations of my forebears have made me, this is what I am. He remembered his grandfather's words, spoken to him after his bar mitzvah; "What is a Jew without his belief? What Hitler could not do to us shall we do to ourselves?" The old resentments welled up. A Jew wasn't even allowed his atheism.

P. D. James, *Original Sin*

I remember the first time Sikhism ever held any interest to me. I was in my 20s and went to a Sikh temple. . . . But that day, there were Sikhs visiting Vancouver from California. The most startling thing about them was they were all converts. It was the first time I'd ever seen white people who were Sikhs. . . . Then I really had an identity crisis. I thought, "Here are these white people trying to act like us, and there's me, trying to act white." . . . So they saw beauty in my religion that I didn't see. That got me thinking, "Maybe there's something in it."

Interview with Sargeet Singh Jagpal, author of
Becoming Canadians: Pioneer Sikhs in Their Own Words

To check in at the Khalsa School in Surrey, British Columbia, I must take off my shoes and put a kerchief over my hair. The latter is a little awkward, the black kerchief seeming a better size for a neck than a head. But principal Harchand Singh Gill comes to the rescue. When my kerchief is tied firmly in place, he ushers me into the Gurdwara, a large, carpeted room, just off the hallway by the office. There, the classes from kindergarten to Grade 4 are having their opening religious exercises in this place of worship. There are no chairs; everyone sits cross-legged on the floor — boys on the right, girls on the left. At the front is an elaborate canopied altar, where the huge holy book, the *Guru Granth Sahib*, lies open. I sit at the back and observe the next thirty minutes of prayer, hymn-singing, and meditation. Since everything is conducted in the Indian language of Punjabi, I'm at a loss to understand what's happening. So Jasmohanjit Kaur Gill (no relation to the principal) joins me. Head of the religion department, she's completely clothed in white, from head covering to the long robe swirling at her ankles. She wears only white, she says, in order to keep her head calm and so that others will also experience a peace of mind when they look at her.

Gill, who was educated in public schools in India, has strong feelings about this daily religious ritual. She says she's very worried about young people today, about their lack of moral values, their lack of religious identity. But, at the Khalsa School, they're required to learn about their religion, what it demands of them, what it says about the purpose of life. "The purpose of life is not to eat, drink, and, you know, fool around," she says. "This life is very precious. This is our opportunity to meditate upon God, to remember him with each and every breath we take." She explains that the Sikh belief is that each of us has lived a succession of lives before acquiring human form — as dogs, cats, snails, even germs. "We've been through all that. They have a life. They feel pain. It's the same soul that is in this body now. Yes, we're vegetarians. And the soul, in every creature, is part of God. It goes through this process until it comes to the last stage, which is man. In this stage, we can understand the purpose of life. But if we don't avail ourselves of this chance, we'll go back to being a germ, or whatever. After death, there is a judge – the Ohram-Raj. We will have to give an account of our deeds, whatever we do in this life, after death."

And that, says Gill, is why Sikh parents feel so strongly about giving their children a Sikh education. They want to do right before Ohram-Raj. "Two angels sitting on our shoulders," says Gill. "They're with us all the time. They are watching our good deeds and our bad deeds. Then, after death, they will go with us to show the whole picture of our good and our bad deeds to him. Then according to what we have done here, he will give the punishment or the reward of that." This is all said in a whisper, the religious proceedings continuing as she speaks. I ask her what the children are saying. They're saying prayers, she says, the same ones every day. "They won't even be able to understand them yet," she says. "But the thing is, if I give you candy, you taste the sweetness of candy. It doesn't matter that you know what it is."

The prayers are from the holy book and are to remind Sikhs of what it is God wants from them. "Merely reading it is nothing if you don't follow it," she says. "You must actually do what God wants you to do." For her, this means rising at 5 a.m., taking a bath, and saying prayers. "In India, every Sikh has to get up early in the morning, bathe, do his prayers, and go to the Gurdwara," she says. "In these countries, it's very hard to go to the Gurdwara, but these children are lucky. They come to this school and, automatically, this is the school rule that they have to follow. We are teaching them the Sikh religion and the Sikh way of life."

I look at the children, heads covered, dressed in black skirts or pants and white tops. They're quiet. Attentive. But here, it's as if they're wrapped in a warm cocoon. This world, after all, bears little resemblance to the one outside its walls. They can come here from kindergarten to Grade 10. But after that, they'll have to attend a public school, where there'll be no Gurdwara, no reinforcement of Sikhism. Gill says she thinks about their future all the time. "If the children are awake, if they understand maturely, then they won't change," she says. "But if they don't have the maturity, the colours of the world can affect them. There are dancing parties. Dancing is not bad. But when you drink and dance, then you are out of your senses. You don't know what you are doing. The school doesn't have dances. We provide role models, enlightening them about the evils of the world. We want them to learn morality. What real moral values are. But I look at the picture of the coming generations and I feel sad, because what they are becoming is nobody. They have too much influence of outside society."

A little girl comes to us, holding something in her hands. We hold out ours and are given a lump of "Parshad." Gill calls it "the touch of the sword – sacred food." Prepared daily, it's made up of brown sugar, purified butter, flour, and water. Then the children pray, asking God to bless the food. We eat it and the children file out.

With more than seven hundred children enrolled, the Khalsa School in Surrey is the largest Sikh school in North America. (There are three Khalsa schools in the Vancouver area alone.) A group of Sikhs, organized as the Satnam Education Society of British Columbia, originally opened this Khalsa School in Vancouver, in 1986. But when land became available in Surrey, it bought a couple of acres, built the school, and opened its doors in 1992. Initial enrolment was 273, but students just kept coming. In 1996, fourteen classrooms were installed in a new wing, and a play area was added to the basement. Still, there isn't enough room; 250 families are on the waiting list. Gill, the principal, attributes the popularity of the school to several factors. "The school is very safe. There are no problems with drugs or violence. The students are not allowed off the campus during the day. They have their own play areas in the school. We have our own bus service, so they are safely driven to and from school. We don't allow anybody on campus [without permission] who isn't a parent. Plus, we keep very high academic standards. We follow the government curriculum, but in addition we give religious education. First, we start teaching them their own language, their own mother tongue – Punjabi. Then they go for religious studies, Sikh culture, Sikh history. They also have the privilege of playing music on the harmonium." Since meeting the requirements of the government curriculum constitutes a full program, additional time for Sikhism has to be found somewhere. The Khalsa School finds it by extending the school day – it starts earlier and finishes later than public schools.

The school exudes newness, but not extravagance. The essentials are all here – spacious classrooms, a gym, computer room – but there aren't any frills. There are verses, or religious sayings, posted at various places throughout the school. "Meditate only on the Lord's name. This way, you will go to your home with honour" is how one script is translated to me. Another, "Help others in the world and they will help you and you will also be helped in heaven by God." The principal, Gill, a retired teacher from India with a very long, very white beard, leads me into various classrooms – French, math, kindergarten. We watch a group of Grade 9 girls dramatize a piece of Sikh history – the martyrdom of one of the gurus. One girl drums, the others act in time to the rhythm. The story is long, complicated, and integral to Sikh identity. Their teacher is elaborately dressed; he's wearing a tunic with a strap across his chest which holds a *kirpan* (dagger). On his head, of course, is a turban. This teacher's garb is the exception, however. Most of the other male teachers are dressed casually and aren't wearing the *kirpan*. In fact, about 50 per cent of the Khalsa teachers aren't even Sikh, in which case they simply wear the black kerchief on their heads. "Our goal is to find the best teacher in the market," says Gill. "We give our ads in the paper and the people come and we select on the basis of merit, experience. So that is why our preference is to select the best."

The school has a policy of open admission, which means it will accept non-Sikh students (although in its first ten years of operation, only a couple have come). "The philosophy of the Sikh religion is that the Sikh religion isn't just for Sikhs, but is for everyone," says Gill. "We don't turn anybody away because of race, religion, or colour. The only stipulation is that they take Punjabi and religion classes. And everybody goes to prayers in the morning." The fee, at $75 a month, is astonishingly low. This is partly because the provincial government kicks in 50 per cent of each child's tuition, and partly because of the huge financial support provided by the Satnam Education Society.

Involvement of the community of parents, teachers, and religious leaders is integral to all religious schools no matter where they exist. And, while fund-raising is usually an essential part of this, the need to raise money for tuition fees depends very much on which province you happen to live in. At Talmud Torah, for example, a Hebrew school in Edmonton, there are no tuition fees. This is because the Edmonton Public School Board, concluding that diversity is an essential ingredient of good education, worked hard to bring the Jewish school under its umbrella.

Since 1912, Talmud Torah had been operating as a private school. In fact, it was the first Jewish Day School in Canada, and opened in someone's basement with a handful of families. The Russian Jews who founded it were adamant that the values, beliefs, and traditions of their religion should be transmitted to their young through their schooling. Having fled religious persecution in their homeland, they considered a Jewish school a concrete symbol of religious freedom.

So, when a public-school superintendent approached Talmud Torah in 1975 to propose that it come under the auspices of the public board, there was tremendous opposition from within. People were afraid that joining the public system would compromise Jewish education. After all, the offer of public funding came with certain qualifiers: the school would have to be open to all; it would have to continue to follow the Alberta curriculum of education; and only certified teachers could be on staff. (Non-certified teachers were offered a certain number of years in which to become qualified.)

Honey Weinlos Isaacs attended Talmud Torah as a child, only to return later as a teacher. When I visit, she's school principal. The sun is streaming into her office, which is cluttered with photos and paraphernalia secular, as well as religious. She sits back in her chair and recalls the turmoil that resulted from the offer.

"There was a lot of fear within the community that the school would lose its autonomy," she says. "There was a lot of opposition, a lot of very heated discussion. They were worried about how joining would change us and what we'd be required to do. They also questioned open admissions. I was worried, as well. I liked what we were. But my perspective is that we've become a far better school. Being part of the larger community has been quite wonderful. We have access to all the resources of Edmonton Public and it is one of the most progressive boards in the country. And we're part of all of that, so we have access to their consultants, specialists, libraries, outstanding materials everywhere, plus the collegial. There are so many outstanding educators that you can dialogue with." And the kids? "Our students participate in athletic activities that happen after school. Our students' artwork is displayed with Edmonton Public's. We're treated as one of the two-hundred-plus schools within the Edmonton public district."

Weinlos Isaacs takes me on a tour of the school. She's a warm, engaging person, with a ready smile and is obviously well liked. With 263 students enrolled from kindergarten to Grade 6, the school is bursting at its seams. Weinlos Isaacs describes plans to build a new school on land that the Edmonton public board will lease to Talmud Torah for 99 years for a mere $1 a year. "But the cost of the building will be borne by the parent body," she says. "And they've done a good job of fund-raising – $2.5 million to date. As soon as this building sells, we've got the plans, we're ready to go." A quick smile. "We're almost there." She explains that staff, supplies, and transportation costs are paid by the Edmonton board. The Jewish community contributes the hot kosher lunch, as well as supporting the religious portion of the school day.

As we stroll the halls, meeting staff, stopping to chat to students, Weinlos Isaacs goes out of her way to qualify what goes on in the school. She keeps referring to the school as a Hebrew-language program, for example, not as a religious program. This is because, when the school joined the Edmonton public board, religious alternative schools within the public system were illegal but language-based schools were not. In 1988, Alberta changed its legislation to allow religious schools under the public system, but fear of a backlash continues to exist.

"The whole program has a Hebrew component which students can't opt out of," says Weinlos Isaacs. "But they can opt out of the non-comparable component. It isn't a lot of time – an extra 140 minutes a week – which is a couple of hours spread over a week. That's when we're allowed to teach prayer or to teach something to do with religion. And we have a junior congregation on Saturday mornings in the cafeteria." The fact that Talmud Torah involves more than simply teaching the Hebrew language is clear if one looks at its school calendar. All Jewish holidays are observed, including closing the school for the whole of Passover (usually a period of eight to ten days). In order to fulfil ministry curriculum requirements, the school starts a week earlier than its public counterparts.

Talmud Torah is a concrete example of what's possible when there's a will to co-operate and accommodate on the part of government and religious groups. Concessions were required on both sides; open admissions were a major concession for the Jewish community. But in its twenty-two-year history under the public system, the fear that non-Jews would negatively alter their school has proved groundless; only a couple of non-Jews have enrolled their children, and the experience, Weinlos Isaacs says, was positive. They learned Hebrew and made every effort to conform to the rules and standards of the school. Requiring that non-certified teachers become accredited wasn't a major concession, given that a reasonable amount of time was allowed in which to do so. But the Jewish community also had to accept that choosing new staff had to be done co-operatively with officials from the public board.

For its part, the board has relinquished administrative control over holidays, and has adopted an attitude of flexibility towards what an average school day looks like. The relationship obviously works well, and I believe it points to what's possible when the objective is providing the best possible education within a public system that's responsive to community needs. In schools where religion and the culture combine with political objectives, such as the promotion of Zionism or Khalistan (the Sikh dream of achieving their own homeland in the Punjab), there should be objections. Clearly, political indoctrination, like unquestioned indoctrination in any field, shouldn't be financed with public funds, as part of a public-school system.

Later, I visit Hillel Academy in Ottawa. It's one of forty-five independent Jewish schools in Canada, twenty-two of which are in Ontario alone. Approximately twelve thousand students, from kindergarten to Grade 13, are being educated in these Ontario schools. And, because the province provides no public support, parents must bear the cost of tuition. At Hillel, that amounts to $5,000 a year. The school, composed of nursery school to Grade 8, looks like a regular public school. But the doors are locked. I have to buzz and introduce myself over an intercom before I'm allowed to enter. It's a stark reminder that Jewish schools live under the constant threat of anti-Semitism. Mark Weinberg, director of education, greets me in the main office. He says the school is about seventy-five years old and is absolutely essential to keeping the Jewish culture alive. "And because culture and religion are so intertwined," he says, "you can't have one without the other."

He sits behind his desk, wearing a *kippah* (yarmulke). "I wear it because we're a Jewish school," he says. "It's part of the fabric of our school. Some Jewish schools only require it during Jewish studies. But we require it all day, whenever you're in the building. It's our identity."

Identity is actually the thread that binds all religiously based schools, although it's seldom described in exactly those terms. The idea is that children who are educated in a secure, familiar, affirmative environment will grow up knowing who they are and where they've come from. This will then give them the strength and self-assurance to confront the dominant culture on equal terms. This rationale for separate religious schools is common, especially among those with a strong cultural basis. And it's one of the most convincing arguments for public funding, as the Dutch experience suggests (see Chapter 7). In the Netherlands, religious schools play an important role in the healthy integration, as opposed to assimilation, of groups into society, a few exceptions notwithstanding.

Weinberg says parents often struggle with the fact that their children are immersed in a separate little world, radically different from the one that exists at public schools. "I'm the father of two sons," he says, "and my wife is in education as well. So we also grappled with this. But we decided that the advantages of being at Jewish school outweighed the disadvantages. It's the knowledge you get of the history of our people. It's the knowledge you get of the laws and customs of our people. The knowledge you get of our language." But there's a price to pay for this knowledge – and it goes way beyond the $5,000 tuition. The children are expected to carry a heavy workload. They meet Ministry of Education curriculum requirements, but they have to do in half a day what public-school children are expected to accomplish in a full day. The other half of the day, then, is freed up to devote to Jewish education. Something obviously has to give, and that something is what Weinberg refers to as "MADD – music, art, drama, dance. These areas are lacking in Jewish schools in general," he says.

Some students I talk to say this isn't a major problem. Instead, they emphasize the benefits of "learning about our roots, our Jewish tradition, the Torah, the traditions of three thousand years. This [education] is the only way to pass it down," says Michael, thirteen. "Tradition is our survival. It's very important to me."

Warren, also thirteen, explains that his parents grew up in Montreal and weren't able to attend Jewish schools. "They felt they missed a lot," he says, "and they wanted me to have the chance they hadn't had. So I thought I'd go to see how I liked it, but I knew I could leave if I didn't like it. I started at Hillel when I was four, but it wasn't until Grade 6, when I took a class with the rabbi, that I developed a new understanding of Jewish religion. I became very interested and wanted to stay on. I might go to some sort of secondary education in Jewish life."

And what are the values you're being taught? I ask. Michael jumps to respond, but he speaks slowly and chooses his words carefully. "The intentions are well meant," he says, "but the medium through which they're taught isn't ideal." I press him to elaborate. "We want to support Jewish continuity in school," he explains, "but our school does it through the Holocaust and Israel. I think there's too much emphasis on the Holocaust and not enough on the beauty of Judaism, on the commentaries. There's more Zionism, more Holocaust here. I don't think this is the best way of ensuring Jewish continuity."

Warren agrees. "A lot of our learning is based on what happened in the past, to make sure the Holocaust doesn't repeat itself," he says. "But I think that rather than look at the Holocaust. . . ." He pauses. "Well, it's frightening us. Kids get worried about it happening again. This hurts how they think about religion."

But isn't the school a reflection of what your parents want you to be taught? I ask. They nod their heads in agreement. "But Jewish assimilation is much more important than anti-Semitism," says Michael. "I go around with a *kippah* and I don't find Ottawa a very anti-Semitic city. People don't swear, spit, or make racist comments at me. I think that Jewish assimilation by intermarriage and by not bringing up children Jewish is far more deadly and more serious than anti-Semitism."

Michael, of course, put his finger on one of the advantages, albeit largely unspoken, of separate religious schools: students are far less likely to adopt the attitudes of their secular peers, or peers from other religious groups, if they spend all their school time with children of the same faith. Nor are they as likely to become romantically infatuated with them; the opportunities are far too limited. Jews are particularly concerned about intermarriage. Although not as dramatic as in the United States, where the number of people born Jewish who marry non-Jews approaches 50 per cent, intermarriage in Canada has risen dramatically during the past thirty years. But other groups are equally worried about the dangers of being swallowed up by the dominant culture through assimilation. So for many members of minority religions, their own independent schools are viewed as the first, and most essential, line of defence.

The argument that independent schools are a defence against assimilation is one of the reasons some people disapprove of them. They fear the perpetuation of group separateness through religious schools, believing that it's a form of ghettoization or religious apartheid. But must integration necessarily entail assimilation, I wonder? Perhaps in an environment where the will exists, it is possible to create a relationship in which accommodation is made on the part of both the majority and the minority and isn't simply a case of the minority being swallowed up by the majority. A relationship – such as the one between Talmud Torah and the Edmonton Public School Board – is not, I think, an example of assimilation.

At the ISNA-Islamic School in Mississauga (ISNA stands for Islamic Society of North America), principal Abdalla Idris Ali says the reaction he most commonly gets from parents coming to the school for the first time is relief. "Most of the Muslim presence in this country is relatively new," he says. "People come here and they come with a fear: What are they going to face? They have problems of language, problems of communication, problems of culture. And then when they go to a public school, they are looked at as strangers. And many times, that demoralizes the children. Now, here, everyone goes, 'Wow, this is like home.' That's the best way to describe it. We feel at home."

Our conversation is constantly interrupted. The phone rings incessantly. "Yes, yes, I understand your child was born two hours ago," says Ali, to one caller. "But at the moment, she won't be able to get in. She will be on a waiting list for the year 2000." With his hand over the mouthpiece, he explains that the waiting list for the school has swollen to five thousand. Then he grabs a pencil, writes down all the details, and sighs with mixed exasperation and pride at the overwhelming success of his school. Phone call completed, he grabs a huge, elasticized pile of index cards and throws them towards me. "Each one represents a child that wants to come here," he says. "And that's only one bundle. But we have no space. Right now, we have 350 students from kindergarten to Grade 9 at this school, and parents want more. We're trying to raise money to open a high school."

Ali says the Islamic school is simply a response to a community need. "The community suffered much within the public school in many ways," he says. "Our norms, our traditions, our values. Usually, we have a high level of protection for our children. And then they go to the public school and are subjected to things that Muslim families actually see as quite shocking. Like using bad words, using drugs, obscenity. And this is why I say, 'This is an environment that is protected to allow children to learn.' The fact that the Muslim religion has a language – Arabic – is something we teach, and we teach a course in the basic concept of religion – about the culture, the history, so that children are still in touch with their culture. Apart from that, it's just a regular school. It's a very safe environment. Like, we don't even have someone who smokes in the school. It's free of all – what you consider – the problems that we have [in society]. That's why the parents . . . trust that we will look after them the way we would look after our own children. So that is the trust we have to observe."

Ali came to Canada in 1978 from the heart of Africa, the Sudan. He never dreamed he'd end up staying and running an Islamic school. Enrolled at the University of Toronto as a PhD student in International Relations, he did not lead the life of a carefree student. Ali was responsible for supporting his parents, as well as his five brothers and three sisters back in Africa. "And I made it through university. I got my scholarship," he says. "And all of my brothers and sisters went through university. My youngest brother is a district judge now. Another is a teacher." He laughs. "I had so many job offers I could have taken when I graduated. My son thinks of me as a crazy man. He says, 'Dad, all this money.' I mean, I only earn two-thirds of what I could be making. But I say, 'I am really doing something here. I enjoy it, because I really believe in it. I choose to be here because I love it. I believe any person should not do what they don't like to do. If you enjoy doing something, that's good, because that is what makes life for you.'"

Most of the people I met at independent religious schools were clearly imbued with a sense of positive mission. In what they said, and in the ways in which they interacted with the students, they expressed the belief they were called to do this work. This isn't to deny the fact that many secular-school teachers are also imbued with a sense of mission. But adding the religious ingredient to the educational mission makes a very powerful combination. At religious schools, I met people with a highly developed commitment to an ideal. The best of them weren't simply on a religious mission, but also had high educational objectives. When those energies are harnessed, they can create very good schools.

We stroll through the school. Every time we enter a classroom, Ali greets the children in Arabic, and they respond in kind. I ask him what is being said. "I say, 'Peace be with you,'" he explains. "And the answer from the children is: 'Peace be with you and his blessings and his mercy as well.' You get this every time you walk in. They are the happiest persons on earth." This isn't an easy thing to measure. The children are very curious about the stranger in their midst, but few maintain eye contact. They're uniformed, the girls wearing the *hijab* over their heads. When they walk in the halls, they're in straight, silent lines. Within the classroom, they seem equally disciplined. From Grade 5 on ("the onset of puberty," says Ali) the girls and the boys sit on separate sides of the room. When I spend some time in a Grade 9 classroom, though, I find the students are not separated side by side, but rather between front and back. This puts all the girls at the back, the boys at the front. Then I notice that all the eye contact, all the questions, are directed at the boys. None of the girls even attempts to raise her hand to answer a question.

Later, I mention this to an educator and she tells me to read the latest studies. Gender discrimination isn't unique to Islamic schools, she says. It's incredibly widespread. Studies show that teachers invariably favour male students, regardless of ethnicity or religion. (Hence the new interest in girls-only schools in main-stream society, one of which is an alternative program under Edmonton's public system.) Despite that educator's observations about the widespread nature of gender discrimination among teachers, from a civil-rights perspective it doesn't justify to me the way in which these students are divided along male-female lines. In fact, it serves only to strengthen the impression that a religious perspective all too often reinforces an inclination to inequality.

When I comment on the disciplined behaviour of the students, Ali explains that discipline is part and parcel of the Islamic faith. "You see," he says, "humans have a tendency towards their desires. There's no doubt about it. Like, the whole thing about faith is to have some kind of a way to restrain your desires or feelings. Otherwise, people accept them as they are, right? And it's easier for people to do wrong than to do right. In our convictions and faith, there is, in me, an inclination to do good and to do bad. It is easier for me to do bad than to do good. This is why, in the Muslim faith, you pray five times a day. You fast during the month of Ramadan. You do this, you do that, so that you restrain the bad part in you and strengthen the good. Right?"

This perspective corresponds with the Judeo-Christian concept of original sin, the idea that humans are born with a natural tendency towards doing wrong, doing evil. Throughout my time at the ISNA-Islamic School, I can't discover whether students have an opportunity to examine this idea and debate its validity. This is unfortunate, because the idea of original sin is, after all, a tenet of faith. Not everyone accepts it, and there are good reasons, in fact, for rejecting it. So what happens to students who have a problem with the concept? Do they have to sit on their own views of truth? Are they punished for holding contrary doctrine? I want to know if this is a truly educational environment, or whether there are some areas that are simply not open to question. If so, then the school has moved out of the realm of education and into something

quite different. Good education, after all, demands freedom of conscience, speech, and thought – the freedom to question. Religion
and education come into conflict with each other when the tenets
of the religion sponsoring the school aren't open to examination
and honest questioning. This is a standard, of course, that's every bit
as applicable to the secular faith evident in public schools as it is to
religious schools.

When it's time for prayers, all wash their hands, remove their
shoes, and file into the gym – boys at the front, girls at the back.
Beautiful Persian-type carpets are laid out on the floor. "In public
schools, Muslims run into problems," says Ali. "No prayers at schools.
They don't have a place they would squeeze themselves into. In the
school here, when prayer comes during the school hours, that's part
of our training, part of our curriculum. And Friday is our congre-
gational prayer, so some of the parents come to the school and our
Friday for prayers is actually part of our curricula."

Seeing these children all together, I can't help but be struck by
the range of ethnic groups represented. At some public schools,
this can be a source of conflict. Ali says that doesn't happen here.
"It's the religion that binds us," he says. "Actually, the main
concept of the religion is that you cannot distinguish between
humans except by their piety and their nearness to God and goodness. One of the verses in the Koran literally means as follows: All
people, we have created you from a male and a female, and we
have set you into nations and tribes so you can come together and
know one another. And the best of human beings in the eyes of
God is not best distinguished by colour or creed. It is the person
who has piety, and goodness and service to the community."

So why, I ask him, should your children be educated separately
from my children, or the children of your neighbours? "Don't
forget, we still live in neighbourhoods," says Ali. "I live across the
street and, in all my neighbourhood, there is no Muslim. When
we leave the school, we mix with those people. But the beauty of

what we actually say is: I want people to know me as I am. And I have to know you as you are. You have to deal with me as I am. I'll deal with you as you are, right? So many things we don't have a hand in. I didn't choose my parents. I didn't choose my colour, my language. I was born in a setting in a different area and I want people to accept me as is. As a matter of fact, a concept of the faith is that one of the signs of God on earth is that people come from the same source. I mean, I can give you my blood, but still we look different, we speak different languages."

Yet the emphasis on difference, religious difference, is the chief characteristic of these schools. The Sikhs, Jews, and Muslims argue, of course, that their schools contribute to a more stable society, because their students grow up connected to their communities and their religious beliefs. This permits them to confront and interact with the wider society with confidence, and on an equal footing, without having to give up who they are. Unlike their secular peers who might feel alienated and rootless, they maintain that their graduates are better able to influence than simply be influenced. They argue that this should be seen by enlightened people as a positive contribution to society. It's a position shared by advocates of Christian schools.

5

THE CROSS AND THE CLASSROOM

I saw this poster made by teenagers: "If you were arrested as a Christian would there be enough evidence against you to convict you?" That arrow really shot me right through the heart.

Madeleine L'Engle, *The Irrational Season*

When I went in search of Christian schools, I wasn't quite sure what to expect. Pious children dutifully holding hands for morning prayers? Hellfire and brimstone in every textbook? Innocent, wide-eyed teenagers, terrified of – and shielded from – the rigours and realities of the real world? Children grown arrogant as a result of being taught their truth is "the truth," the *only* truth? Young people highly versed in God talk, but academically ignorant? Children imprisoned in a religious world they long to escape? These are some of the stereotypes of all religious schools. What's the reality?

Well, it's just about impossible to generalize about Christian schools in Canada. They're both Protestant and Catholic. They're in every province. Some are large. Some struggle to make it with only a handful of students. Some get provincial support. Many don't. Some work hard to have a community presence. Others work equally hard to remain undetected. Some pride themselves on their rigorous academic standards. Others put scholastic achievement well below memorizing Bible verses.

And it's almost impossible to get an accurate sense of national enrolment. This is because Catholic schools are separately run "public" schools in Alberta, Saskatchewan, Ontario, Quebec, and Newfoundland. But in all the other provinces, they're classified as "independent" schools – along with their conservative Protestant counterparts. There are 1,700 independent schools in Canada, approximately 1,200 of which are religiously based, although not all, of course, are Christian. Trying to find out how many Canadian children attend Christian schools is, ultimately, a frustrating – and futile – exercise. Given that, in Ontario alone, 600,000 students attend Catholic schools, let's just say there are well over one million students attending Christian schools in Canada.

If there's one common thread among the evangelical Protestant schools, it's the fact that the schools are a very clear reflection of the parents who support them. And the parents know exactly what motivates them: They don't want their children denied religious education in school, just as they don't want every religion presented as "equally important." They want their children taught their particular brand of religion with conviction. The constitution of Redeemer Christian High School in Ottawa, for example, describes the "Basis" of that school as "the Word of God, the Bible, which we hold to be in its entirety the infallible revelation of God." This is what all Christian schools share – Protestant and Catholic. Oh, they may quibble about certain interpretations of the Bible, but that's not news: Christians have been bickering with each other since Jesus' crucifixion. They do share, however, a belief in the God of the Old and the New Testaments and in his son come to earth, Jesus Christ. They also share varying degrees of scepticism towards secular public schools. Education is never neutral, they argue. Why should we send our children to people we don't know, who hold values we may reject, but who are nonetheless extremely influential in shaping our children's world-views?

I visited Christian schools in British Columbia, Alberta, Ontario, and Newfoundland. They were a cross-section: publicly funded Pentecostal and Roman Catholic schools in Newfoundland; independent, evangelical Protestant, mainline Anglican, and publicly funded Roman Catholic schools in Ontario; evangelical Protestant schools in Alberta (one under the public system and the other independent, but receiving partial public funding); and an evangelical Protestant school receiving partial public funding in British Columbia. I wanted to get a feel for them – the atmosphere, students, teachers, curricula, philosophies. This was no scientific study, merely a taste of what's out there. I tried to visit the schools with an open mind, although I admit that, from time to time, my predilection for diversity was hard to shake.

Yet vice-principal Rick Canning points to his school – the Eugene Vaters Collegiate in St. John's – as an example of diversity. It's a Pentecostal school (Grades 7 to 12), but only about 50 per cent of the 407 students are from that denomination. The rest are a mix of Catholics, Anglicans, United, Hindu, and Muslim. They come, he says, for a variety of reasons. Parents want their children to attend the neighbourhood school. They like its discipline policy. Or they might appreciate its moral bent. Regardless of the religious mix, however, there's no escaping the fact that the school is unabashedly evangelical Christian. One of the stated goals of the school, for example, is that students be "provided [with] opportunities to accept Christ as their Saviour." This message confronts them at every turn. A plaque just inside the front door reads: "Wherefore take unto you the whole armour of God, that ye may be able to withstand in the evil day, and having done all, to stand. Stand therefore, having your loins girt about with truth, and having on the breastplate of righteousness."

I read the verse several times, trying to relate it to getting an education in a post-industrial society in the latter half of the twentieth century. Students swarm around me, staring at me inquisitively, although they aren't too keen to talk with a journalist. They share none of the dress described in this verse. They're wearing baseball caps, blue jeans, and T-shirts. Some boys sport a single earring. And it's impossible to detect any relationship between their small talk and this verse. Later, when I meet with school officials, I realize that, while the message of the verse may be incomprehensible to many public-school advocates, it is integral to this school's philosophy of education. The verse epitomizes their view of the world: that life is composed of daily battles against the forces of evil, and that these battles can only be fought by being armed with the Truth – the Bible. Canning, who was raised in the Salvation Army, then converted to Pentecostalism, says the emphasis of the school is evangelical Christian, not specifically Pentecostal. But what does that mean, exactly?

"Well," he says, "it means that we have prayer, that we believe in being born-again, in living a Christian life, in trying to follow closely the kind of life that Christ would have lived." And how does that express itself in the school? "Well," he says, "we emphasize not swearing, or being abusive, or any foul language, or wearing beer slogans or cult kinds of slogans on T-shirts. We don't have dances. We emphasize to the students that they respect everybody for what they are and who they are, regardless of their belief. And to make sure that they treat people from a Christian perspective, of being valuable, of being created by God, and having some purpose in life. And along with that, we have assemblies where students can . . . talk about being a Christian and living a Christian life."

He points – as do all the Christian schools I visit – to committed Christian teachers as the key to creating and maintaining the tone of the school. I meet Janice Adams, a teacher for twenty-six years. Americans by birth, she and her husband moved to Newfoundland twenty-two years ago, specifically because it was the only place that would allow them to teach in a publicly funded evangelical Protestant school. She's very warm and totally uninhibited about her religious beliefs. "We [Vaters teachers] are a community of shared belief," she says. "To us, the most important thing we can do is to have God in our lives. To us, he's the source of knowledge, he's the enricher, he's just life – a state of life. You can't share who you are and what you are in public schools. You don't share that thing that has changed your life? You want to share it and you share it here. You have the freedom. I don't impose it, but if a child is crying over something, I'll say, 'Would you like me to pray with you?' And we have the freedom to do that. And if they say, 'No,' I don't impose it. But mostly they say 'Yes.' And I've had more than one student crying on my shoulder who, because of love and prayer, has had their life changed."

I sit in her Grade 8 class during opening exercises. She's holding a Bible in one hand, gesticulating with the other about what she's reading. She talks about Satan and his desire to lead people astray. Her theme is individual choice: that students can choose good (God) or choose evil (Satan). "Life is about choices," she tells them. "The scriptures say, 'Redeem your time.' What that means is take hold of every moment and use it to the best." When she asks for prayer requests, arms shoot up: "That my finger will be better by tomorrow." "That my Dad will come home safely." "That my uncle will be cured of cancer." She takes them all in. Then, in a quiet voice filled with love, she begins to pray for all those requests. "And Lord," she adds, "I may not have knowledge of unknown requests, but the Trinity does, and you know what it would take to free the people and bring them in and answer these requests. Lord, we pray there would be such a reliance on you and your love for us. Amen." Eyes open, math begins. And I can't help but feel a new sense of calmness in the room.

★

I get the same sense at the White Rock Christian Academy, southeast of Vancouver, British Columbia. It's part of a non-denominational evangelical church, built in 1980 to serve as both church and school. This means that what's used as a gym during the week becomes the place of worship on Sunday. There are 280 students from kindergarten to Grade 12 attending the school. A prerequisite for admission is a literal belief in the Bible. For children too young to make that leap of faith, their parents must have "accepted Christ as their personal Saviour." Susan Penner, the principal, says, "It's a given. The word of God is the truth." End of discussion.

Instead of a wide variety of Bible verses posted, as in many of the Christian schools I've visited, I see only one. "For I know the plans I have for you, declared the Lord. Plans to prosper you and not to harm you. Plans to give you hope and future." I remark on it to Penner, noting that it's everywhere – in hallways, classrooms, on students' lockers. "That's because it's meant to be the focal point for the year," she says. "Every year we have a different Bible verse." She says she chose it three months before the school year began, after a day of prayer and fasting.

"We always need to try to remember that God has a plan for us," she says. "It's not our plan. Our part is to have full confidence that God's plan is good for us." She then explains the circum-stances in which she chose that verse. "Right now, our school bookkeeper is very ill with cancer. A staff member's dad has can-cer, and we have twins in Grade 4 whose mother is having a major cancer operation soon. And we have another student in Grade 9 whose mother has leukemia. It's a hard time." And so the children and staff are constantly surrounded by the comforting assurance that there's a reason, albeit unknown to them, for their troubles. That faith will see them through.

Penner gives me a tour, explaining the school's philosophy as we make the rounds. "The vision of our school is to develop godly character," she says. "We tell the students that there is only one way between 8 a.m. and 4 p.m. that you can develop. God uses that through 'Do your homework. Obey the teacher. Obey the rules. Do what you're asked to do.' That's how that character develops. So if they don't do their homework, it isn't, 'Tough luck, you won't pass.' We say, 'You need to choose another place where it doesn't make any difference. We're not here to see you pass. We're here to see you develop character. If you refuse to develop in that area, then we can't help you.' "

There are six portables outside, the school having grown well beyond the bounds of the building. We go into a Grade 1 classroom where I spy a child's drawing pinned to the wall. It shows a stick person on a cross. The printed caption reads: "I asked Jesus, 'How much do you love me?' He opened his arms and died.'" Penner looks at it appreciatively before describing how such things as relationships, honesty, music, and entertainment are dealt with. "We had a retreat with Grade 11s and 12s," she says. "And they talked about all the things they did and didn't do. Then they looked at the scriptures and held up their experiences to the scriptures. And what's important is that the overlay fits into the basic framework. When the overlay doesn't fit onto the skeleton structure, then the overlay has to change. We're trying to say to the children, 'The skeleton structure is the word of God. Your experiences have to be taken onto the word of God, and then you have to make decisions.' The question isn't 'What's wrong with such and such?' The question is 'What's right with this?' It's not what I say, or what the school rules say, but 'Is there a biblical premise that we're violating?' If so, we need to make some adjustments. Personally, I have found in being an administrator that that's a much more freeing approach than trying to rationalize every decision. It's important for all of us to identify 'What is the basic premise upon which we live?' "

Penner, who manages to combine cool professionalism with knowing every child's name, says she taught in the public system for twenty years before joining the Christian school in 1986. To her, the Christian school spelt freedom. "So many times when I dealt with kids [in the public system] I wanted to give them an additional key for successful living, particularly in the last years when I worked in a behavioural school," she says. "I knew there was another key I could give them, only I couldn't give it to them in that environment. So when I came here it was very fulfilling for me. Because after you've tried everything personally, there is still another element, and that is your faith in Jesus Christ. . . . I find that, even in Christian families, there's a lot of heartache in our society. And I watch how, when children come to school, school is a haven for them."

As we make our way back into the school from the portables, Penner points to a new, steel-reinforced fence as symbolic of what her school is all about. She says a child – not one of theirs – was recently abducted at the adjoining mall. Within a week, parents had raised $10,000 to build the fence. "And we don't owe a cent on this school," she adds with pride. Everyone is wearing a uniform – including staff. (For staff, grey or navy skirts or navy or grey pants, white blouses or shirts, and navy sweaters.) There's an air of cleanliness and piety about the school, although Penner admits she's sometimes shocked at things that happen there. "But the issue isn't whether students blow it," she says, "but whether we can encourage them to get up and go on and not repeat it."

White Rock gets government funding, which means it meets government curriculum requirements. This wasn't always so. Until 1991, it was an Accelerated Christian Education (ACE) school. ACE is an American phenomenon, created in 1970 by a Texas couple, and has its headquarters there. It publishes its own Bible-based curriculum for Christian schools from kindergarten to Grade 12, as well as a separate one for college. Children work individually, with their own workbooks, known as PACE (Packet of Accelerated Christian Education). The "teacher" (they prefer not to have certified teachers whom, they fear, might usurp the authority of the pastor and the Bible) acts merely as a supervisor. Learning is guided by five laws: performance, goals, motivation and control, measurement and reward, and discipline. A former English teacher, Penner had a hard time accepting a program that depended on rote learning. She was bothered by the lack of intellectual challenge and wanted the school to attain higher academic standards. So she pushed it to adopt the government curricula. When it did, the school got approval for government funding – to the tune of 50 per cent of each student's tuition.

Penner's reference to ACE schools isn't the first time I've heard of them, although even many evangelical Christians aren't anxious that the public be aware of them. To them, the principle of their right to establish schools based on their own faith is of overriding importance. They don't want a public outcry about ACE undermining this principle. ACE schools (also known as "The School of Tomorrow") are fundamentalist, separatist, and highly controversial. They're also spreading like wildfire. There are 7,000 ACE schools in 120 countries around the world, about 250 of which are in Canada. Most are small, operating out of church basements.

I have a hard time finding one; they don't go out of their way to advertise their presence. But Mel Velhurst, principal of the Morinville Christian Fellowship School, northwest of Edmonton, is welcoming. A former construction worker, he's now school principal. His church, which he describes as "Pentecostal-like, but not under the Pentecostal umbrella," figured he'd be good in that role. "It was a big move," he says, "and quite a cut in salary, too, and my wife is here as secretary." But, since both were totally committed to ACE, they were willing to make the necessary sacrifices.

Velhurst explains that the school actually began in his basement in 1985 with twenty-two students. The following year, the school was able to rent an empty shop in a strip mall. As the recession hit and more shops became vacant, it eventually acquired two more. Today, the school owns all three, accommodating forty-three students in Grades 1 to 12. It's clear that the school operates on a shoestring. There's one large room where morning prayers and Bible readings are held. It also contains a couple of ping-pong tables, around which students congregate during recesses and lunch breaks. Then there are two other rooms, one containing Grades 1 to 4 and the other, Grades 5 to 12. However, they're unlike any classrooms I've ever seen. The children work individually at their own "offices." They're three-sided carrels, actually, and the students sit at them according to height, not grade. When you're working individually, after all, it doesn't matter who's beside you. They aren't allowed to talk with each other anyway. Each "office" contains two flags – a Canadian flag and what Velhurst calls "a Christian flag." The children use them to alert "supervisors." Flying the Christian flag means they're ready to have their work marked. Waving the Canadian flag might mean they need to go to the bathroom.

This is by far the most rigid Christian school I visit. The children sit so uncommonly still, the only sound being the whisper of pages turning. They wear uniforms, the dress code stipulating that "blouses are to be no lower than two finger widths below the collar bone." Even the length of the boys' hair is described in full. "Short, above ears, off of collar, and out of the eyes." The school's handbook gives a Biblical reference for this rule. I look up 1 Corinthians 11:14. "Doth not even nature itself teach you, that, if a man have long hair, it is a shame unto him?" The verse before it which reads "Judge in yourselves: is it comely that a woman pray unto God uncovered?" is evidently ignored. The girls – and female supervisors – are bareheaded.

I look at what they're working on. At the top of each PACE page is written "Ask Jesus to help you." Biblical quotes are scattered throughout. Even the names of fictitious characters hold a moral:

"Mrs. Lovejoy," "Mr. Virtuesay." Parent Crystal Terhorst explains why she rejects public education. "Things are taught there that are contrary to what we believe," she says. "Humanism, for example. That's not something I want the kids to learn." Velhurst says most ACE parents share that conviction. "Parents are the ones that have to raise their children," he says. "Parents are the ones that are accountable to God. We're just here to help the homes out. We support the home. That's all we can do. We can't go any different direction than the way the home wants to go."

That may be, but I find myself feeling really sorry for the children. They're so subdued, so constricted, so complacent. Under these conditions, it's next to impossible to get their reactions to their school. Discipline can be harsh. Corporal punishment is "exercised," as the handbook puts it, under the following guidelines: The offence, as well as the scriptural implications, will be discussed with the child. "A reasonable number of firm strokes will be administered with a strap by a staff member of the same sex. . . . Following the administering of the strokes, the staff member will pray with your child, assuring him/her of their love."

ACE schools, from what I've seen, heard, and read about them, fall so far short of acceptable educational standards that it could be argued that they actually deprive children of the right to a proper education. In fact, their very presence makes a strong case for the role of the State in setting educational standards in publicly funded independent schools and enforcing them. What's particularly appalling in the case of this school is that the Alberta government is actually condoning it by giving it financial support.

One Quebec educator tells me that the Quebec government is concerned about ACE schools but doesn't feel it can actually do anything. This is because officials believe that the only route open to them would be to remove children from their homes – obviously an extreme measure. But, he adds, the government is actually far more worried about the physical conditions in which ACE children are being educated than about what the schools are doing to their minds and spiritual lives. ACE schools are generally in home or church basements, without the facilities to cope with fires or other emergencies. "The fear is very real that, at some point, some child or children are going to die in an ACE school, and then the government will be held responsible," he says. "No one wants something like that to happen, but nor is drastic action considered acceptable. So nothing is being done, largely because they're considered a fairly marginal group."

I find other Christian schools much more open to my having contact with students. True, the encounters take place in school classrooms, in front of their teachers, which no doubt inhibits discussion. But a group of Grade 11 French students – nine of them, all girls – is refreshingly candid. They attend Redeemer Christian High, a school of 100 students for Grades 9 to 12 in Ottawa. It's housed in a former public school rented out by the local board of education. Redeemer takes up the second floor; an independent Anglican school is on the first. The school is denominationally mixed, but it's safe to call it "conservative Christian," given the pivotal role that the Bible, as "the infallible revelation of God," plays in its educational philosophy. Books such as T. S. Eliot's *The Waste Land*, James Joyce's *Portrait of the Artist as a Young Man*, and Arthur Miller's *The Crucible* on the Grade 12 English literature reading list speak of the school's non-defensive approach to wide-ranging academic inquiry.

French class takes place in the library, in the middle of which are four tables grouped together to make a square. The girls are not wearing uniforms – at least not adult-enforced ones. Instead, they're wearing the uniform of teen subculture: blue jeans, Guatemalan sweaters, Gap-like tops. One girl is wearing a baseball cap backwards. When I ask them why they're going to a Christian school, most say it's what their parents wanted, but they like it.

"It's neat here," says one girl, "because you're part of the Redeemer family, and it's so small, you get to know everybody." "Right," adds a girl called Amanda. "But that has its drawbacks. I'd like to know somebody new." The girls then describe what they appreciate at the school, which mainly revolves around the quality of teaching. "And it's neat to get a Christian perspective on everything," says Shannon. "They help you grow in your spiritual life. I mean, in biology class, we looked at the crucifixion in terms of what Christ went through on the cross. How hard it was for him to lift his head up. What he experienced biologically." Emily adds that she appreciates the fact that there's no peer pressure at a Christian school. This causes an uproar.

"I have more friends outside here than inside," says Amanda. "I profess to them that I believe in God and I love him to death, but I feel pressured here because things are forced on you. There *is* peer pressure." She hasn't quite articulated what she means, so Anna, who's sitting next to her, jumps in to lend support. "There's more pressure here than at public schools," she says, "but it's about beliefs. I could handle someone offering me a joint, but when people push their beliefs on you and want you to interpret things the way they do, it's hard."

By now, there's a general level of discomfort with the direction the discussion is taking, but Anna and Amanda persist. "Many don't understand what they believe, because they're just conforming to what they think they're supposed to believe," says Amanda. "But we're not as mixed up as kids in the public system," says Emily. "I know a lot of them make fun of God." Anna refuses to accept Emily's defence. "It might be a cry for help," she says, her voice rising. "Maybe they do it because they don't have anything to believe. One-on-one, they might admit they're hurting and lonely and need somebody. The main problem I have with private schools is we're not out there, being for people, because we're in here, into ourselves. Bickering among ourselves."

These students display a level of religious literacy that is most impressive. They have a critical capacity, an ability to examine their own beliefs in a wider context. I have no problem accepting that they're quite right in their assessment that public-school students don't have a similar literacy. It strikes me as unfortunate and absurd that these kinds of discussions can't be more a part of mainstream schools. Why should they be confined to religious schools? Defensiveness on such matters seems to me a sign of weakness, of inadequacy within the public system.

The level of discomfort in the room is, by now, very high. But Anna continues. "Nobody's going to want to come to a Christian school if they're not Christian. Sure, you learn the factual stuff here – the theoretical. But what about the practical, the experiential? And which is more important?" She gets little support from her friends. Some note that it's easier to "stand your ground" and cope with life if you're at a Christian school. But Anna persists, arguing that "school shouldn't shelter you, and I feel sheltered here."

These are interesting avenues for discussion but, later, in a Grade 12 English class (five girls, seven boys), it's virtually impossible to engage anyone in conversation. The students are withdrawn, sullen. One boy does mention that he likes the low student-teacher ratio. "Teachers here don't go out of their way to fail you," he says. "They actually care. In the public system, they get paid just as much not to do anything." Another says a benefit of such a small school is, if you try out for a sports team, you're bound to make it!

The comments of some of these students might upset their parents or school officials. But it seems to me a sign of strength when students are free to challenge and critique their situation, however uncomfortable it might make the authority figures in their lives. At other religious schools I visited I often saw students deliberately breaking rules or attempting to challenge authority through body language. But discussing their situation openly? It happened rarely. It seems only the best schools have the capacity to tolerate an open examination of their practices. It's uncommon, but it does exist.

Mainline Protestant denominations tend not to run their own independent schools, with the exception of a handful of historic, élitist schools. But there are two Anglican schools in the Ottawa area. Elaine Hopkins is principal of Bishop Hamilton School, a Christian Montessori school that operates in Ottawa and nearby Orleans. The Ottawa school has 215 children from 1½ years of age to 14; the Orleans school has 34 preschoolers from 2½ to 5 years of age. Hopkins, who's also president of the Ontario Federation of Independent Schools, clearly loves her schools, her students, and her work. A woman of boundless energy, she's also earned a reputation for being outspoken. She lives up to this reputation when asked why schools such as hers are rare among mainline churches.

"First," she says flatly, "there's a serious problem with the secularization of Christians. A lot of people who go to church don't really know what it means to be a Christian. I think church attendance is dwindling because people see that. It's politically correct to be vague, not to come on too strong, not to talk about sin. But if you're a Christian, you have to address the nature of sin. Secondly, our churches always give children a low priority. They figure that having Sunday School is enough, but it's not. I often joke that we put our children in the corner of a dark basement with broken toys because we don't want to spend any money on them. But we need to understand that children are our primary seeds and what happens with those seeds is up to the family, the child, and the Holy Spirit. We [at Bishop Hamilton School] are on a mission to plant those seeds and nurture them well. The rest is up to them and God.

"Thirdly," she adds, "there's always been a close relationship between the Anglican Church and the State, to work with the State. I call it 'the faith commitment to public education' – the idea that everything will be better for our children and society down the road if everyone is educated together. And so Anglicans tend to support a multi-faith religions course within the public schools. While I think all children should be taught a multi-faith course, the Anglican support of it [instead of supporting independent Anglican schools] makes me question whether they belong to the multi-faith religion or the Christian religion. I think our limited resources should go to nurture children of the Christian faith. Maybe then they'll be able to create a more tolerant society."

The Ottawa Anglican School Society opened the Ottawa school in 1983, the Orleans school in 1992. The Ottawa school is housed in a former public school, taking up the whole of the first floor and filling three portables outside. In the fall of 1997, when Redeemer High School moves into its own building, it will spill over to the upstairs as well. Unlike Redeemer, the Anglican school doesn't require an acceptance of the infallibility of the Bible. But God clearly has primacy. Each classroom has Christian props – wooden toys depicting the parable of the Good Shepherd, maps of Israel in Jesus' time, children's Bibles, a long scroll called 'a time-line of life' that depicts the historic eras up to the birth of Jesus Christ, and the fact that human existence after Christ is, as Hopkins says, "just a small blip in history."

The children's uniforms – red tops and navy bottoms – lend an air of vitality to the classrooms. And it doesn't matter which classroom I visit, all of the children work with an intensity that's a joy to behold. When I arrive, they're well into their morning's activity, which means I've missed the morning worship. It takes place in the classroom and consists of a reading from the Bible, a discussion of what they've read, and the saying of prayers. Once a week, Hopkins leads a larger worship service. "We make it clear that God created the world and is in charge," she says. "As the children get older, we focus more on Jesus Christ and emphasize that he's the one they are to follow and to ask themselves, 'What would Jesus do in my situation?' Later, when they're studying world issues, we try to develop critical thinking from a Christian perspective. We don't have a school position on abortion, but if we do proper Christian teaching, then students have to ask, 'Is abortion something Jesus would condone?' We want their Christianity to have a practical application."

For small children, there's no talk of sin. There is, however, a great deal of attention paid to prayer. "That's one of the first things we try to establish with three-year-olds," says Hopkins. "And it's extemporaneous prayer – not the usual Anglican kind. We do this because we want to teach them about a God of love. And that God is with them all the time and is everywhere. Finally, we want them to establish a relationship with God through prayer. Children are natural believers and their prayers aren't the 'Gimme' kind of prayers that adults often pray, but are ones of thanksgiving. They *know* there's something, someone out there."

What about Catholic schools? Where do they fit in? Catholics, after all, have been operating schools longer than any other Christian group in the country. In fact, they're such an entrenched part of the education landscape that it's easy to slip into thinking of them in the same terms as their secular, public-school counterparts. In many provinces, for example, Catholic school boards are very powerful, their teachers' unions very strong. For the most part, parents don't play the same intimate role in these schools that they do in the Protestant ones I visited. And, of course, they don't have to be so actively involved – the survival of their schools is constitutionally assured, regardless of parental involvement. In fact, Catholic schools are rarely marginal to society, the way that most Protestant schools are. But what do they teach? What makes a Catholic school Catholic? Dennis Murphy, Catholic education director for the Ontario Separate School Trustees' Association, says they're directed at maintaining the heritage and traditions of the Roman Catholic faith. In other words, like their Protestant counterparts, these schools exist to teach children to be good adherents of their parents' religion. But Murphy, a realist, notes with sadness that Christian schools, including Catholic schools, are fighting an uphill battle.

"I'd say that education is a minor influence in children's lives today," says the priest. "It has less and less influence because of pop culture. Children have such access through the media to the information/technical culture. This has a huge homogenizing effect. Malls and McDonald's are a subculture in themselves, and that powerful culture is one of the most profoundly educational influences in their lives. That's why I think now, more than ever, we need an education system that stands over and against – at an oblique remove from – those pressures. Those outside influences are quite relativistic, quite individualistic. They don't give young people a direction in which to go. We need to be there to provide a moral compass, to ask, 'What is the nature of the human person? What is social justice?'"

Murphy's point about the need for schools to help provide students with a moral compass is an important one. That is an integral part of religious schools, and is found also, perhaps, in the best of the public schools. But religious content in a curriculum would strengthen all schools in this respect. In its best form, it would equip young people to make crucial, ethical judgments for themselves in the outside world. The treatment of religion as a subject deserving of a legitimate place in the curriculum would formally recognize this role on the part of schools.

In keeping with this philosophy, the motto of the St. Pius X Junior High School in St. John's is "To return all things in Christ." The school, which has 260 children in Grades 5 to 8, operates by a religious calendar, celebrating various seasons of the liturgy. Events in the school year are given a Christian emphasis. When school starts, for example, there's a religious celebration to inaugurate the year and to ask God's blessing on the new school year. Pat Hogan, the principal, says the pervading philosophy behind the school is "the recognition that there is a supernatural dimension to life. We start with that philosophy," he says, "and we try to maintain a kind of Christian community in the school. We would like to think that we have a very caring Christian atmosphere here. We would like to think that our teachers are, to a degree, role models in Christian living. We also try to think that in our school the gospel values prevail." These values, he says, when pressed, are "caring and compassion and forgiveness. Everything that Christ taught is lived out in everyday life, from the discipline policy of the school, to volunteer service in the school, to food drives. Even our school lunch program recognizes that there are poor families that can't afford to have quality lunches, so we take care of that. So, it's fine to talk about generalities and philosophy, but we'd like to think that we also try to carry it out in practical ways."

The Immaculata School in Ottawa also emphasizes community involvement and social-justice issues. Students work in a local soup kitchen, do volunteer work with seniors, and operate a clothing boutique for the needy. The school, with 1,200 students in Grades 7 to 13, recently moved into a building which used to house St. Patrick's College of Carleton University. A lot of money was spent renovating it and it shows; the result is a school that's airy, sunny, and spacious. I'd been hearing stories about Immaculata long before I embarked on this project. Two friends attended Immaculata in the fifties and often told stories about their experiences. Back then, it was an all-girls school run by nuns, with rules so strict, they said, that patent leather shoes weren't allowed "because they might reflect what was underneath your skirt."

There are few signs of such rigidity today. It is no longer run by a Catholic order, the lay staff dress casually, and the school is co-educational. Evelyn Kelly, the principal, says attendance at most Masses is not mandatory. "I believe students should be given the option to choose, but they can't make a good choice unless they know what they're missing." To Kelly, the most important feature of Catholic education is the fact that religion isn't compartmentalized, but is presented in such a way that it can permeate every facet of a student's life and studies. "We give them an environment to grow up in where they don't have to ignore or eliminate what is a given part of one's life," she says.

But what do Immaculata students think about their education? I was able to meet with twenty-five students from Grades 11 and 12. Interestingly, it was the only school I visited which allowed me to talk to students without a staff person present. These students were lively, thoughtful, and immensely critical of mixing Catholicism with their education. Many said they were Catholic because their parents were and that, if they'd been given a choice, they'd be attending public schools. But they weren't opposed to religion per se. In fact, Paul, who said Catholic schooling had turned him off religion, then went on to say: "But Grade 11 is the greatest because you get to learn about other people's religions." His major resentment was that Catholicism was mandatory. "The thing is a shaft," he says, "because you have to look at it in terms of applying to university. If you're in a public high, when you take eight courses, you get eight credits. But we only get to choose seven courses because we have to take religion, and universities don't recognize it. And if we don't take religion, we don't get to graduate on stage."

This lack of choice in the area of religious studies, particularly for students of high-school age, seems highly counter-productive. Repeatedly, students made the point that they've had Catholicism drilled into them for their past twelve years of learning, and they figure they know it inside out. Certainly, the Grade 12 religion class that I sat in on seemed to reinforce the assessment I heard repeatedly: "It's a bird course." Students looked at lists that compared true love with infatuation and were told why the Church disapproves of homosexual sex. From what I saw, there's no way the material could qualify for university entrance accreditation. It was designed, after all, not to meet educational needs but to teach Church doctrine. A truly educational approach would establish the importance of students reaching their own conclusions on vital human issues. This would mean that choice would be a crucial component in this area of study. Besides, in the absence of choice, how do young people begin to develop a sense of autonomy?

Many expressed resentment at the fact that they aren't free to express their own opinions. "Beliefs are forced on you," says a Grade 12 student named Andrea. "You can have an opinion [in religion class], but you're told not to put it on a test." A young male student disagrees. "You're talking about a battle between your views and the views of the Church," he says. "But religion class is about the views of the Church. It doesn't mean you have to follow them. It just means you have to know them. I mean, they teach you what they think in law or philosophy, so why not religion?" Chris, a Grade 12 student who'd recently moved from Alberta, says his experience at a Catholic school in that province was quite different. "Here, things are more forced," he says. "They're always telling you all you have to believe. There, religion was more unstructured. There was more discussion. It was good. They didn't say, 'This is the only way,' but would say, 'This is the way most people should behave.'"

A young girl, a non-Catholic, quickly jumps in to defend Immaculata. "I hear what's being said in religion class and I try to apply it to my life," she says. "It helps shape my identity, even if I don't believe what's being said. It makes me think about things I wouldn't normally have to address if they weren't being raised there." "Yes," adds a male student, who identifies himself as a Catholic. "Religion is important because, even if you don't believe it, it teaches you about Christianity and other religions. It enables you to better interact with others, because if you know nothing about religion you're at a disadvantage."

This student hit the nail on the head. How can we possibly expect young people to be prepared for a society such as the one Canada has become without recognizing that religion is a crucial element in the texture of our new society? Those who are most religiously literate have a distinct advantage in understanding the world-view of others. They're also in a better position to converse with them, provided part of their schooling has been to foster an attitude of tolerance. It goes without saying that this is best achieved if the school itself tolerates dissident opinion.

Visiting a range of religious schools from Christian to Jewish to Sikh to Muslim made one thing clear: the way in which a school teaches religion is crucial. Is it taught as doctrine, or as human impulse, as a quest that can lead to several answers? Unfortunately, few of the schools I visited meet what I think is a fundamental standard of good education. By that, I mean to foster in children the faculty of critical thinking, encouraging them to question and critically examine the subject they study. It's not as if religion is the only subject that should be judged on these grounds. Anything that's taught as received truth falls short of a proper educational standard. To me, the best schools are those that don't teach religion as doctrine, but instead treat it as a crucial human impulse, a passion, a personal quest. None of the religious schools I visited really met that ideal, but some of them at least observed elements of it. As one principal put it, "God doesn't have grandchildren." He said this by way of acknowledging that the children in his care have to come to their own conclusions about their spiritual life; they aren't simply passive vessels waiting to be filled with the beliefs of others.

Finally, in terms of what they deliver, it's hard to distinguish between the practices and products of the best Catholic and Protestant religiously based schools. This makes the inequitable treatment of the latter, in terms of public support in a province like Ontario, very hard to justify. There is no logical reason for denying the support given Immaculata to a school like Redeemer. It is merely legal and historical anachronism that permits such discrimination. Schools that produce young people who are capable of making astute observations about the value of religion within the changing situation around them are surely offering something of value to society. In fact, they're presumably offering something that's in our interests as a society to foster. These examples lend support for bringing this element of religious education within the public system.

6

TAXES AND TOLERANCE

If Allah so willed, He
Could make you all one People:
But he leaves straying
Whom He pleases, and He guides
Whom He pleases: but ye
Shall certainly be called to account
For all your actions.

The Koran

At an early age, I was indoctrinated in the compromises of casu-
istry and sophistry, to make a clear distinction between God and
Caesar and to render unto each his due; all the same it was most
disconcerting to find that Caesar always got the better of God.

Simone de Beauvoir, *Memoirs of a Dutiful Daughter*

Habiba and Mohammed Khalid's comfortable brick home in suburban Oakville is distinguished from its neighbours by a bed of roses lining the front walk and meticulously cared for vegetable plants nestled against the backyard fence. Although their garden plot is modest, a lot of rich produce is grown here – enough to give the family of six abundant meals of corn-on-the-cob in summer and nice, frozen tomatoes in winter. Everything is carefully tended, from the garden outside to the large, immaculate rooms inside. The interior is furnished with the basics: in the dining-room, for example, the only piece of furniture is Habiba's sewing machine, on which she makes clothes for herself and her two daughters. Even the living-room is bare. Communal time is spent around the kitchen table, which looks out onto the garden, or in the family room, which has a couch and chair. Everything is minimalist, in keeping with the family's priorities. There are no fancy gadgets in the kitchen, no catchy posters, only a lunar calendar indicating Muslim prayer times.

Habiba prepares the evening meal, working quickly and efficiently, shunning offers of help. And so I sit in the family room with Khalid, acutely aware of what I've chosen to wear that day, wondering if I'm dressed modestly enough. We talk about the Islamic school from which their two eldest children have graduated, and which their two youngest still attend. I meet the young people briefly when they come in to ask about dinner. They're nice-looking, polite, and obviously very intelligent. I try to imagine what their lives are like, straddling two drastically different worlds – the overwhelming pop culture of television and of most of North American society, and the Islam of their home, mosque, and school.

These four young people are the reason Habiba and Khalid have invested so much time, energy, and money in the ISNA–Islam School. Back in 1982, the school opened in the basement of a mosque, with seven parents, thirteen children and several teacher-volunteers. Its future seemed precarious. No one knew where the money would come from to pay the teachers, let alone to survive another season. But the following year, someone made a huge donation, which allowed them to buy a former public school in Mississauga (see Chapter 4).

The school has had an enormous impact on the family. Habiba, for example, spends a lot of time ferrying the children on the 401 expressway to and from school. She also helps out there as much as possible. Most parents do, as a way of keeping administrative costs down. But the school has had another, unforeseen, consequence. It's changed her wardrobe. Before their children started attending the Islamic school, Habiba never donned the *hijab*. But female students and staff must wear the head-covering in accordance with the school's interpretation of a verse in the Koran that says women should dress modestly. When she'd drop her children off at school amid a sea of *hijabs*, Habiba says she first began to feel uneasy, and then hypocritical. How could she herself not conform to the school's dress code? she wondered. She felt she was sending a mixed message to her daughters. And so she adopted the *hijab*. To some Canadians this gesture would be reason enough to refuse public funding of the school, smacking as it does, they allege, of oppressing women and resisting integration into mainstream society. Certainly, from where I sit, as a Western woman, it seems highly unfair that the female students are required to cover up. Some Western feminists regard it as puritanical, and argue that it reflects badly on both sexes: either women are genetically programmed to act in the sexually enticing and ultimately destructive way in which Eve behaved in the literal interpretation of Genesis, or men have such little willpower that they're totally incapable of controlling their sexual urges. Neither speaks well of human beings. The larger question – of whether the *hijab* is a symbol of resistance to integration (as is argued in France) – seems to me a red herring. If the *hijab*, for whatever reason, is a meaningful religious symbol to people, and doesn't infringe on the rights of others, then why should non-Muslims be offended?

Khalid, tall and bearded, has smile lines around his dark eyes. Soft-spoken and gentle, he works by day as an economist at Ontario Hydro. At night and on weekends, he does volunteer work for the school. For years, he's been its treasurer, and during the time I spend in their home the phone rings constantly with questions and requests about school-related issues. Khalid admits to putting in long hours on behalf of the school, but this is said without any sense of complaint. As the calls pour in, I can't help but think that their school is a community focus in a way that public schools would, ideally, like to be, but seldom are. Through the Islamic school, Khalid and his family are closely connected with others with whom they share basic values. I think how consoling that must be in a society such as ours, which is often so lonely, so alienating, and which offers so few points of meeting.

The cost of an independent education for four children seriously affects a one-income family, and the issue comes up early in our conversation. While the Islamic school is cheap education as far as most independent schools are concerned, it's still a hefty chunk of money for any family to bear, year after year after year. Tuition for one child is $240 a month, for example; for two children, $420 a month, $620 a month for four. But what are parents to do if they believe, as Khalid and Habiba do, that educating their children at the Islamic school is the *only* way to preserve their religion? Where the issue is put so starkly, they don't believe they have the luxury of choice.

Khalid describes how he came to Canada from Pakistan, knowing – and accepting – that he'd have to adapt and change in order to become Canadian. "I left basically everything behind," he says. "Every single thing. I hardly ever speak with my kids in my own language [Punjabi], hardly ever. Always English. But religion is a very precious thing to us. We want to preserve our religion. Culture, I don't care. I know you can only perpetuate it for a couple of generations at most. There's no way on earth that my kids could stay in Canada and I can keep my own language. As a matter of fact, people who've done a lot of research in this particular field will tell you that the maximum you can keep it is two generations. Like, I can teach Punjabi to my kids and they wouldn't have the same kind of commitment to pass it on to their kids. And then their own kids – forget it – it's a lost cause. But religion is a very, very universal thing. It is a very important thing. In our religion, you cannot even pray unless you know Arabic. You can't."

So the financial burden is something they bear, albeit reluctantly. But Khalid is working hard to get the Ontario government to change its policy and fund independent religious schools. He's joined the Ontario Multi-faith Coalition for Equity in Education, a group committed to changing the way government views religion and schools and composed of Christians, Sikhs, Muslims, and Hindus. Buddhists discussed joining the coalition, but ultimately decided against it. "We are the second-largest faith tradition in Canada," says Michael Kerr, co-ordinator of Karuna Community Services, a community-development and social-service agency funded by Buddhists. "We are on public record as not being in pursuit of our own independent schools because of a fear of division and fragmentation in society. The Buddhist Communities of Greater Toronto, which represents fifty temples, decided to put our efforts behind multi-faith religious education in all schools. We'd rather work to build shared understandings between people."

Yet shared understandings do result from the coalition – at least for the adults involved. In his quest to instil the Islamic faith in his children through keeping them separate from non-Muslims, Khalid has been forced to unite with them in political lobbying and legal action, although he doesn't seem bothered by the contradiction. He says that working with people from other religions sets a good example to his children. "Oh yes," he says, "I embrace them with open arms. As a matter of fact, any time Gerald [Vandezande, a Christian] phones me, he calls me 'Brother.' We are brothers in faith. We really are brothers in faith."

They also share a sense of discrimination. "If you are giving funding to Catholics, you are preserving their religion, not mine," says Khalid. "What's wrong with my religion? Don't I pay taxes? Don't I deserve to be treated equally with other faiths?" While many people might think that equality means treating everyone exactly the same, that's not what it means to Khalid. That's too narrow, too limited, a perspective and would only make sense to him if everyone were, in fact, exactly the same. But he, along with many Sikh, Jewish, and Christian parents, thinks that religion is so fundamental it should permeate their children's education. A school system that denies them the right to that kind of education, they believe, is denying them access to what everyone else gets – a tax-paid education. And so they feel double-taxed – forced to pay taxes for a public system they can't use, and after-tax dollars for an independent religious education. To them, that's inequitable.

Meanwhile, I'm trying to digest all of this. After all, I know all kinds of people who are also trying to preserve their religion through their children but who don't insist on educating them separately. Why is Islamic education so important to Khalid? In a nutshell, it represents how he can best fulfil his responsibility as a parent.

"We Muslim parents have to raise our kids in the Islamic way until they come of age, and then they are independently responsible," he says softly. "On the day of Judgment, we believe we'll be asked about these things. 'What did you do? The God Almighty gave you these children, what did you do with them? How have you raised them?' There are a few duties the Almighty has put on Muslim parents. One of them is to name them good names. Really good names, Islamic names that have meaning. Then you should teach them all the morals of Islam, which are basically the Christian morals, the Judaic morals. The Ten Commandments give them good morals, so they behave very nicely in this world. They don't steal. They don't do any bad things and, if they do, they ask God Almighty to forgive them. And to stay away from many of the vices – liquor, for example. Sexually, a person has to be very, very pure until he gets married. No dating business. There are examples in the Koran, even the prophets, where their sons, their daughters, went over to the other side, so it can happen.

But you absolve yourself from that if you give your children good morals and a good education. And if, in spite of all this, they go astray, this is not in your control. Then, on the day of Judgment, when you stand before the God Almighty, you tell him, 'I did what I was supposed to do.' When the kids come of age – puberty is the time in Islamic religion – they are responsible for their own behaviour. Whatever they do on this earth, they are to be accountable on the day of Judgment individually."

When he's speaking, I'm struck by the similarities more than the differences between people from various religions. In particular, by the overwhelming need to inculcate their specific religious dogma. When I travelled the country, visiting as wide a range of independent religious schools as possible, I tried to discover why members of each group required their children to be separated from non-believers. They'd always start talking in terms of values – about the need to impart their particular religious values. But when I'd press them to be more specific, they'd invariably cite values that seem to be considered universally desirable: kindness to others, fair play, honesty, generosity of spirit, and moral development. Upon further probing, it became clear, however, that the issue is not actually one of teaching a generalized set of values; it's one of dogma. Their particular religious dogma. To someone like Khalid, it obviously isn't good enough to raise his children to be good, moral people. Not when he believes he'll someday have to stand before God Almighty and answer for what he did as a parent. No, the people I spoke with firmly believe they must raise their children to be good Jews, or good Muslims, or good, born-again Christians, and so on. Much depends on it: their relationship with God, the preservation of their religion, or, in the case of many Jews and Muslims, the preservation of their culture.

Esther Enkin, for example, believes that the very survival of the Jewish people depends on Jewish children getting a Jewish education. She says this with some sense of amazement, as it wasn't a position she always held. Since becoming a parent, she's become increasingly aware of Jews as a minority group, and of the overwhelming nature of the larger society. She's invited me into her home in northwest Toronto, where we sit in a spotless room filled with the pungent aroma of cleaning solutions. Enkin, managing editor of CBC National Radio News in her professional life, has taken the day off to clean. She looks down at her hands, which are almost raw from scrubbing. Passover begins this evening, and she's cooking a huge kosher meal for an extended family gathering. First, everything had to be taken out of the kitchen cupboards and cleaned. It was no small job, and she's exhausted by the effort. But she's also exhilarated by the ritual. Enkin knows why she's doing this and who she is in the larger society. This Jewish identity is something she's determined to pass on to her daughter.

"I have to live a Jewish life in the home," she begins. "I don't depend on the school to do that for me. But the school is really important for a sense of continuity. It's so easy to teach the prevailing culture, because it's there, it's all around us. It's much harder to reinforce us, because we're a minority; we get completely lost. The public system has so many problems. It says it celebrates diversity, but it seems to deal with it by turning it into nothing. What message, then, are we sending our kids? At Hebrew Day School, my daughter is taught her self-identity, her community, culture, tradition, history, religion – although we teach Canadian citizenship, too," Enkin adds quickly. Then she pauses. A thoughtful person, she's prone to deliberate before speaking, although this is one issue she's grappled with for a long time.

"It plagues me that I'm turning my back on the multicultural, ethnic part that is Toronto," she says slowly. "If people like me abandon the public system and don't hold it accountable, then it's in danger. But I have to do right by my child. I see her education as essential to the survival of my people. I owe that to my history and to my people. At Hebrew Day School, I'm giving her a sense of herself and her people. Ultimately, you can't deny who you are." Another pause. "The world makes you 'other,' " she says. "There's no getting away from that. But this [sending her to a Jewish school] isn't about rejecting others. It's protecting a culture I see in jeopardy." Enkin says she knows how important it is to teach children about living together. "And here I am, educating my child separately. But there's a paradox," she says. "The more I teach her who she is, then the better she can live with others. She'll have a sense of herself, of her people, in the context of Canada and the world." Because the school she sends her daughter to serves this important social purpose, she believes it deserves public dollars.

Understanding why members of minority religions feel compelled to send their children to their own religious schools is one thing. Accepting the premise that the public should pay for them is quite another. In Canada today, all provinces require that children go to school, but there's considerable flexibility about what constitutes a school. In Ontario, for example, anyone with a minimum of five students can start a school. As long as the school is independent – outside the public system – it can basically do as it pleases. Certified teachers aren't required, the school can follow any curriculum it devises, and it can discriminate on the basis of sex and religion. Every province also recognizes the right of parents to choose where and how their children will be educated. But they draw the line at what kinds of schools receive public support. While Ontario fully funds one separate-school system based solely on religion – Roman Catholicism – it rejects extending that same support to other religious groups. British Columbia, Alberta, Saskatchewan, Manitoba, and Quebec each provide some funding to independent religious schools of various faiths.

Gary Duthler of the Federation of Independent Schools in Canada is appalled at the power exerted by the provinces over education, but especially that of Ontario. "It's pretty scary when the State has the power to be the antidote to the values of the home," says the affable executive director. "This is because education is never valueless. The only questions are: 'Whose values? What values?' The easiest way is for the State to determine which culture it will support to be dominant and then force the integration of everybody else into that culture, or to penalize people if they want to do something else. The more difficult route is to do what the democratic system always says it wants to do: to be a marketplace of ideas and see that those who want another option are free to have it."

The point that seems to be lost in so much of this debate is that the current public-education system in Canada – a secular system – is, in fact, a value system, and a value system that competes with those of the religious.

This is a perspective I have come to reluctantly. When a value system that one implicitly accepts is being debated, it's often difficult to see it for what it is. Certainly, the ruling by an Ontario court judge that Ontario's public-school system, while secular, is in fact neutral, seemed to underline the validity of my position. But after listening, discussing, and debating this issue with people from a wide variety of religions, I've been forced to rethink things. While the judge is correct that the intention of a secular school system is to remove the State from influencing people's choice of faith, it lends itself to secularism, which is an ideology intolerant of belief in God. My *Shorter Oxford English Dictionary*, for example, defines "secularism" as "The doctrine that morality should be based solely on regard to the well-being of mankind in the present life, to the exclusion of all considerations drawn from belief in God or in a future state."

It's true that there's no deity in secularism, but it is definitely based on a set of beliefs about the nature of life. That's why many of the religious scoff at the notion that a secular school system is "neutral." While there's no reason why a secular system can't treat the subject of religion in its curriculum, a secularist school system won't tolerate it. That's why many of the religious argue that a secular system determined not to have religion in the schools *is* a value system. So why should that belief system get public funding and not theirs?

Susie Adler decided to put Ontario's hard line on funding to the test. Supported by the Canadian Jewish Congress, this mother of two, along with a number of other Jewish parents, sued the Ontario government, charging that she was being discriminated against because Catholic parents' religious schools are publicly funded. Parents with children in schools belonging to the Ontario Alliance of Christian Schools joined them. This unusual alliance of Christians and Jews argued its case before the Supreme Court of Canada in January 1996. Khalid's group, the Ontario Multifaith Coalition for Equity in Education, had intervenor status.

It was quite an event. I'd never been to the Supreme Court before, let alone sat in on a hearing. There are two sets of security to pass through before entering the courtroom, and seeing it for the first time does take your breath away. Legally, this is the place of last resort, the repository of many heartbreaking stories. The visitors' gallery was packed with people who'd come in from various parts of the province. For ten years, Jews and Christians have fought Ontario on this issue in the lower courts; the fact that the Supreme Court would hear them out gave them hope. Interestingly, I wasn't prepared for all the pomp and ceremony: the deference of the lawyers to the nine judges as they repeatedly addressed them as "M'Lords and M'Ladies"; the sense of grandeur in that room; the beauty of the judges' red robes set against the dark, high walls; the sense of history in the making.

It was a day for lawyers, not parents. While many of the appellants were in court that day, the language was not theirs. It was the language of legalese, formal, stiff, and often very difficult to follow. The Jews and Christians argued that they are being discriminated against under the equality provisions of the Canadian Charter of Rights and Freedoms. This discrimination occurs, they claimed, because Catholic schools get full public funding, while they get none. They acknowledged that public funding for separate schools is guaranteed in the Constitution, and stated categorically that they weren't arguing for its elimination. But repeatedly, Ed Morgan, lawyer for the Jews, David Brown, lawyer for the Christians, and Peter Jervis, the coalition's lawyer, made the point that Ontario is very different today from what it was when it signed the British North America Act back in 1867. Then, the majority of people in Quebec and Ontario were either Protestant or Catholic. Guaranteeing publicly funded separate schools for Protestants in Montreal and Quebec City and for Catholics in Ontario was considered a way to protect minority rights. If that was the original intention, they argued, then in order to continue to be just and equitable, funding should be extended to the schools of the religious minorities that exist in Ontario today.

They lost. On November 21, 1996, the court ruled that refusing to fund independent religious schools is not an infringement on freedom of religion and that Ontario has no constitutional obligation to fund them. However, the majority decision, written by Mr. Justice Frank Iacobucci, held that, while the Ontario government has only a constitutional obligation to fund Catholics, as guaranteed in the 1867 BNA Act, it could legislate the public funding of private religious schools. In other words, such funding is constitutionally permissible, even though it's not constitutionally obligatory. These were comforting words to the Jews and Christians, but not what they wanted to hear; they've been waging this war for a long time, and had really hoped the Supreme Court judges might interpret the Charter the same way they did.

But they didn't think the ruling was a complete bust. The Ontario Alliance of Christian Schools, for example, maintains that protection of their right to religious independence was reaffirmed, "which means that neither the government nor a Charter challenge can threaten the autonomy of our Christian schools." It also took heart from the fact that provincial governments are free to fund the independent-school system if they choose to do so. And there was rejoicing from all religious camps when the Court reaffirmed entrenched government support for Catholic schools. They interpreted this to mean that religious schools are a legitimate part of Ontario's education system.

Susie Adler, however, said she was "somewhat stunned" by the judgment. She really believed the Charter would support her claim for equitable treatment. The $13,000 a year she and her husband pay to send their two children to Hebrew Day School in Toronto hurts. She was hoping for equity during her children's educational lifetime. "We try to teach our children . . . that equality is right," she says. "Sadly, they go to school in a province where the courts don't appear to be teaching equality." Moshe Ronen, chair of the Canadian Jewish Congress in Ontario, says, "The next step is to dance the political dance with the government."

That's how religious groups got partial public funding in British Columbia. There, the Independent Schools Association lobbied hard to get the Socred government under Bill Bennett to recognize independent schools with its pocketbook, not just its mouth. In 1977, it obliged, providing partial funding of a child's tuition at an independent school (*any* independent school, not just religious ones). J. Donald Wilson, an education historian and professor at the University of British Columbia, recalls what happened. He says he opposed Bill 33, the bill that brought in funding for independent schools, because he believed it would fragment the public system. However, he was in the minority. Dr. Pat McGeer, the education minister, was keen to fund the schools. Wilson claims this was, in part, because he sent his own children to élite private schools, and considered public schools mediocre.

"But there was also the political agenda," says Wilson. "The B.C. Teachers' Federation had come out strongly in support of the NDP in the '71 election when the NDP got elected, and so there was a punishment factor from the Socred Party when it came back in '75. Then, they made it clear that they would support the public funding of independent schools. This did get them a great deal of support, no doubt, because it ranged from people who were using these independent schools, from Roman Catholics on down, because there was no publicly funded separate-school system here."

The NDP, meanwhile, was split over Bill 33. Some of its members were Catholic and wanted the funding. Others argued that social justice demanded that equality of opportunity should be extended to religious minorities. Their opponents within wanted to save public education. In the end, the party chose not to address its internal split and chose not to oppose the legislation. In fact, NDP members simply didn't attend second reading. The only group standing up for the public system, says Wilson, was the teachers, and they were considered self-serving. "A fundamental change came into being which should have been debated in the House and it wasn't. I blame the NDP, because they were the official opposition," says Wilson. "One could understand that they were split, but they didn't perform the role of Her Majesty's Opposition at a crucial time when there was going to be a revolution, you might say. This reform was root and branch of the public-school system, because it had implications, clearly, for the public-school system to give money to these religiously based private schools for the first time in 110 years."

And the upshot of the legislation? Well, the number of children attending independent schools has increased in British Columbia from 4.3 per cent of the student population in 1977 to 8.2 per cent in 1994. (In fact, student enrolment in independent schools has been steadily rising in Canada, from 2.5 per cent in 1970 to 4.8 per cent in 1992. As mentioned, because Catholic schools are considered part of the public system in Alberta, Saskatchewan, Ontario, Quebec, and Newfoundland, these figures don't give a true indication of attendance at religious schools. On the other hand, if they weren't publicly funded in those provinces, perhaps more Catholic children would attend public schools. And if religious schools were fully funded in all provinces, perhaps the numbers of children at independent religious schools would be surprising. Who knows?)

Wilson is clearly upset about the fact that more kids are opting out of the public system. And he says there's been another disturbing effect. "Now you've got some Chinese parents in Richmond saying they want a Chinese public school in Chinese language with Chinese teachers and X number of subjects taught in Chinese and not open to non-Chinese," he says. "I mean, this has people really upset. . . . Now, there's been resistance to that – it's racist – but clearly it's much more than that. One could argue, without introducing the question of racism, whether it's a good idea or not to have a public school that's exclusive to one ethnic group. . . . Once you open the door, as the legislation here did, it's very hard to close it again. Once you say, 'Yes, you're entitled to this type of schooling because it's really important to you to have that knowledge base that comes from being a Dutch Reformed Christian,' or whatever, then where do you stop? It's very hard to close the door. I think that what's happening in Ontario among those people who are saying, 'No, we don't want to extend public support to independent religious schools,' is that they're anticipating the problems we're facing now."

In fact, British Columbia has strict guidelines for those seeking funding. And the degree of funding depends on adherence to the rules. Classification criteria include the quality of teachers and facilities and a curriculum that doesn't include programs that foster racial or ethnic superiority, religious intolerance, or social change through violence. Schools that charge a higher tuition than what it costs to send a child to public school get a lower percentage of public funding. This means that élite private schools don't get as much public assistance as struggling religious schools do. Ironically, when the province moved to change its funding categories to give a maximum of 50 per cent to those schools that meet its criteria, the Society of Christian Schools in British Columbia objected. It wanted 49 per cent of the cost of tuition, not 50 per cent, arguing that the more money the government gave, the more control it could demand. (The government won.)

Jean Barman, an education-studies professor at UBC, says that government funding has had a positive effect, insofar as it's subjected independent schools to intense scrutiny and public accountability. The result is that they've tended to become more like their public counterparts. B.C. legislation, she says, "puts children's rights to a basic education, whatever school they attend, above their parents' and the school's philosophical or religious predilections." Who can argue with that?

Still, I'm left very uneasy by this entire debate. What Khalid and Enkin say is very compelling. But publicly funding independent religious schools has enormous social implications. Inherent in it are such questions as "How do we best raise children to be contributing citizens in a pluralistic society, respectful of the rights and differences of others? Through religious apartheid, or forced integration, or other means?" Put another way: In Canada's increasingly diverse society, what education model best contributes to intercultural and inter-religious understanding? It's clear that there are two competing and wildly disparate perspectives here. First, there's the question of tolerance. Many members of religious minorities argue that a society best proves how tolerant it is through how it treats its minorities. They insist a tolerant society would recognize their right to teach their religious doctrines at public expense. Canada, after all, prides itself on its tolerance and appreciation of ethnic and religious diversity. Their detractors, however, maintain that to develop a truly tolerant society, people must learn to live together and to respect differences, and that this is best done at an early age through inter-mingling in the public-school system.

Second, both groups embody differing visions of Canada. For supporters of independent religious schools, the vision is one of "separate but equal." Advocates of secular, public education, on the other hand, envision a Canada in which people of wildly dis-parate belief systems can meet and mix in one of the few poten-tially unifying institutions remaining – the public-school system. Both claim their goal is mutual respect. These are not small dif-ferences. In fact, while doing this research, I often despaired. Sometimes the gulf just seemed too great to bridge. I approached Bernard Shapiro, hoping for some enlightenment.

Shapiro is an interesting person. He's very bright, very articu-late, and very experienced. A Harvard graduate, Shapiro was Ontario's deputy minister of Education and head of the Ontario Institute for Studies in Education during the eighties. In 1984, Shapiro was asked by Ontario Premier Bill Davis to lead a com-mission on the funding of independent religious schools. Davis had just extended public funding of Catholic schools to the end of Grade 13 and needed to deflect some of the political heat com-ing from the members of minority religions. Then, as now, they were demanding equity. In his final report, submitted to David Peterson's Liberal government, Shapiro wrote, "The constitution-al provisions usually advanced to justify the special status of such [religious] schools serve only to describe its history. They do noth-ing to inform us about what we ought to do." Shapiro concluded that, morally, Ontario was on very shaky ground by refusing to fund the schools of other groups.

He came up with a model that would include religious schools under the public system. He called them "Associated Schools." The idea was that they could operate under the public system with public accountability. While they might have been complex to administer, they also might have satisfied many advocates of religious schools, as their schools would have been eligible for public funding. However, Shapiro's 267-page report has been gathering dust since he submitted it to the legislature in 1985. Today, he's principal of McGill University, but continues to take an interest in this issue. When we meet, he seems discouraged about our ability as Canadians to get along with each other. He describes moderating a debate the previous evening on the then upcoming Quebec referendum. While everyone was civil, he says it was clear there could be no genuine exchange between the "Yeses" and the "Nos," because their presuppositions were so diametrically opposed. As he describes it, the issue of funding religious schools jumps to mind. These two things seem depressingly similar.

"I don't see 'separate but equal' as God's gift to the world," he says drily. "Given our history, however, that's exactly where we're going. The difficulty that Canadians are always having is they are a country that doesn't want to get along. This is a place where you don't have to get along. In some sort of funny way, it's not a radical not-getting-alongness, because you aren't usually trying to stand in the way of other people. You aren't usually trying to belittle them, or tell them they are trivial, or irrelevant. They just aren't what you are and therefore not as important. . . . Now we may become morally consistent [by funding other religions, as well as Catholicism], but then we'd be 'separate but equal,' and that's apartheid, isn't it? Why not separate hospitals? Why not separate labour unions? Why not separate everything? Why should we mix? We'll solve the problem of staying together by some kind of circulation of élites at the top. This is a model that could be used, but my point is it's the non-ideal road that we're marching down. And no one seems to care, because the separate faith communities are saying, 'It's irrelevant. We want ours.' I can understand that. But that's what everybody is saying."

Shapiro is speaking in the quiet of an early morning in his office in downtown Montreal. It's the city of his childhood. He attended Lower Canada College, a school that defined itself as Anglican. What that amounted to, he says with a smile, was everyone said the Lord's Prayer every morning and twice a year (Christmas and Easter) the entire school went to a local church. As a Jew, he says he didn't feel "put upon." On important holy days, he'd simply not go to school, and no one minded. Although we don't discuss it at any length, it must have given him great pleasure to return to this city as principal of McGill, a university that once had a quota on the number of Jews that could enrol. He does say that, when his appointment was announced, the first question he was asked by a CBC radio interviewer was "Can you believe it? McGill's appointed a Jewish principal. How do you explain this?" "I didn't know what to say, frankly," says Shapiro. "So I said, 'Well, it shows that people can get better than once they were.'

"You have to encourage people to believe they can't get an environment exactly to suit," he says. "You know, societies aren't custom-made. They're off the rack. That's because there are a lot of different people with lots of different needs. It's no wonder that people like custom-made better, because it fits better. But that doesn't mean you can have it. It just means it fits better. . . . In the end, the majority is in a different position than the minority, and there's no use pretending that isn't the case." Given all of this, I express surprise that he argues for the funding of religious schools if Catholic schools are publicly funded. "Isn't that inconsistent?"

"Well, it depends upon which way you start," he says. "As long as we're insisting on funding the Roman Catholic schools, I see no way other than giving other parents their opportunity as well. I will not take constitutional history as an excuse for a moral lapse. That's my point of view. So, from my point of view, there are only two ways to get out of the school question. One is to revise the Constitution so that we are no longer obligated to Roman Catholics, and that's about a zero. Or we redesign the school system so that, even though schools are in some sense separate – that is, there are different schools – they are also in some sense together [under the public system]." This is the Associated Schools model Shapiro first suggested in 1985 and which has, to date, been ignored.

There's a price to pay for ignoring sound advice. People get angry and frustrated when deeply held beliefs are played with – especially when the education of their children is at stake. Every government in Ontario since Bill Davis's Conservative government in 1984 has promised to examine the issue of school funding for members of religious minorities (the Liberals under David Peterson, the NDP under Bob Rae, and now the Conservatives again, under Mike Harris). And thus far every government has managed to sidestep it. It's true that people who choose to send their children to independent religious schools have opted to be outsiders. But government inflexibility on religion in the classroom merely pushes people into an increasingly untenable "we/they" situation. This breeds alienation and distrust. And it's bound to affect the children.

As long as religious schools operate outside the public system, they are responsible only to themselves. While most of these schools follow government curricula, because they want their children to have the option of post-secondary education, not all do. Their standards, admission criteria, and teachers' qualifications are set by them alone, based on their own perceived religious and educational needs. While I understand why many parents want their children educated in their specific religious schools, I don't think it's ultimately in anyone's interests to have these children outside the system. Providing public funding so they can stay separate and apart from the children of other faiths is surely not the only way to accommodate them. Nor does it provide a model for getting along in an increasingly multicultural, multifaith society.

But maintaining the status quo – telling people the only way the public will pay for their children's education is if they enrol them in a school system dominated by a value system diametrically opposed to their own – is obviously no solution. Yet that's what the Ontario government has been doing for more than a decade. The upshot is that more people have been pushed out of the system, and they're getting more and more frustrated and angry. While many religious parents would no doubt be vehemently opposed to the suggestion that their schools operate under a public system, it seems to me an eminently reasonable suggestion. History certainly isn't a help when it comes to this debate. Too much has changed since 1867. Canada is now home to increasing numbers of people from minority faiths and the growing complexity of Canadian society must be taken into account.

Successful public policy isn't designed to meet extreme positions, but to accommodate the moderate majority. If we were to adopt that approach on the part of educational policy, we'd be fostering practices that potentially could bring the largest numbers of children under the public tent. That would involve, of course, making a place for religion in the public curriculum – either through funding religious schools that meet government criteria, or through including religion in the public system. Either route would reduce the number of people who feel the only way their needs can be met is by going outside the public system. One thing is clear: new answers are required to meet the educational needs of diverse groups of people. Canada is at a point in its history when it simply can't afford to ignore the need to achieve peaceful integration of minority groups into a multi-religious, multicultural Canada.

While ours is a new dilemma, some other countries have been grappling with the issue for decades. In the next chapter, I take a look at the Netherlands and France and the two drastically different routes they've followed.

7

ASSIMILATION OR INTEGRATION? FRANCE AND THE NETHERLANDS

The Dutch spirit of freedom and tolerance has grown out of differ-ent factors at different times. What you might call a Dutch cocktail: a tradition of reasonably well distributed wealth and power, a cen-tral government that concerns itself with social questions but takes a detached position, and the pragmatic attitude of a trading nation that knows you can't make a profit by quibbling.

Bastiaan Bommelje, "Twists of Tolerance"
(in the magazine *Holland Horizon*)

The Enlightenment demonstrated that tyranny and religion went hand in hand: wherever the first oppresses, the other is at hand with the word of God to portray the ruler as a divinely designated authority and the wretchedness of the people as a divine test. They no longer had any respect for the Church, for in their eyes it had sanctioned the powerlessness of the common man.

Walter Grab, *The French Revolution*

M ost Canadians have heard the story of the little boy in the Netherlands who happened upon a hole in a dyke. Water had begun to leak through and, even though he was only a child, he recognized a problem in the making. Much of the Netherlands is actually below sea level, but over the centuries an ingenious system of dykes has been built to hold back the sea. So, should a dyke spring a leak and nothing be done, it would be a disaster. The boy instinctively knew this, so he stuck his finger in the hole. But keeping the water back meant he couldn't go for help, forcing him to spend the night, cold and alone. Growing up, I knew this story well and admired the boy for his quick-thinking heroism.

Ironically, it isn't a story that Dutch children know and love. People like Robert Tielman scoff at it, saying, "Only a foreigner could invent such a story, for to know Holland is to understand that this land below sea level has survived, not by simple solutions of one individual, but by centuries of human co-operation." Perhaps that's why, instead of learning that story, little Dutch children grow up with the saying "God created the world; the Dutch created the Netherlands." It's a perspective Tielman much prefers. A humanist, he accepts the premise that human beings have both the right and the responsibility to give meaning and shape to their lives – and to do so without relying on supernatural intervention. Tielman first caught my interest several years ago when he came to Toronto for a conference of international humanists. I covered the event for the *Toronto Star* and had a chance to talk to him. He seemed unusual in that, unlike many of the participants, he neither spoke disparagingly about people who believe in God and organized religion, nor was he defensive about his own belief system, humanism.

I knew he was very involved in the international organization, but I had no idea of the degree to which humanism infuses his life until I met with him in his office by a canal in Utrecht. Among other things, he's professor of humanist studies at the University of Utrecht, president of the International Humanist and Ethical Union, president of European Humanist Professionals, president of the Humanist Study Centre in the Netherlands, and director of the Teacher Training Institute of Humanist Ethics in the Netherlands. He explains that the Netherlands is the most secular country in the world, half of the Dutch being either atheists or agnostics, and that the humanist movement in the Netherlands is one of the strongest in the world (25 per cent of the population identify themselves as humanists). These are interesting statistics, given the state of Dutch education. I went there, after all, to find out about the long-term consequences of funding religious schools. The Dutch have not only decades of experience with publicly funded religious schools, but they also have an international reputation for being one of the most tolerant peoples in the world. Since many Canadians argue against publicly funding religious schools on the grounds that they breed intolerance towards others different from themselves, I was anxious to visit the country.

Since 1917, the Dutch have been funding religious schools, but it took sixty years of what they called "the school struggles" to arrive at that decision. The debate was long and divisive. Both Protestants and Catholics wanted their own schools fully funded by taxpayers. The socialists – or secularists, as we'd refer to them today – were vehemently opposed. They were committed to "the common school," or "the people's school for the entire people," in which religion would be completely banned. Their fear, as expressed by one opponent, was that the Netherlands would return to the conditions of the sixteenth century, when Holland was fractured along religious lines.

"At present, all children, 'Romish and un-Romish,' sit next to each other on the school benches, offer a single prayer to the same God," wrote Petrus Hofstede de Groot in the mid-1800s. "But if schools should come from the various communions – *Ach, mijn Vaderland!* – church quarrels would tear us apart again; fanaticism would be injected into the receptive hearts of children, and the gentle nation would become a prey to the most horrible of evils: religious hatred." Sounds familiar! It's a sentiment well known to anyone involved in the contemporary debate in Canada on the same subject.

Despite prophesies of doom and gloom, the Dutch experience has proved otherwise. In 1917, Dutch legislators decided that enough was enough. Everyone was fed up with fighting about schools. People wanted to get on with their lives. And so they took the route that was both most democratic and of least resistance. They decided to allow any group of parents – religious or non-religious – who wanted their own school to open it, and to operate it at taxpayers' expense. The upshot is that today 80.5 per cent of all schools are publicly funded religious schools. Almost 77 per cent of all students attend those schools.

But it isn't simply a matter of handing over money to any parents' group demanding it. Conditions for public funding are explicit. To receive public funding, schools must agree to hire only certified teachers, teach in the Dutch language, follow the government-prescribed curriculum (including mandatory teaching of evolution and sex education), and have at least 240 students to open an elementary school in the city, 200 in the country. Parents must also sign a declaration stating they agree with the mission statement of the school and are committed to sending their children there.

Tielman says the Netherlands has traditionally separated church and state, yet recognizes a State responsibility "to create the conditions under which the religious or humanist situation can take place." As a result, he has no problem with the State's funding religious schools. "Why would the State pay for all activities in institutions like schools, hospitals, prisons, and the army, but exclude those which are fundamental to giving meaning to life?" he asks. Nor does he find the rules and regulations that accompany that funding oppressive. In that regard, he finds the attitude of North Americans somewhat peculiar. "In North America, there's the assumption that, the more laws you have, the less freedom you have," he says. "We don't believe that. Because we live below sea level, we're aware of how much work it takes to survive. Our country exists because of incredible planning and regulation. This is the paradox of culture: you need a lot of legislation to guarantee freedom."

During his numerous travels, Tielman has discovered that North Americans in particular often assume that, because marijuana is legal and sex shops are available in the Netherlands, then he must make regular use of them. While Tielman isn't prone to visible displays of humour, this assumption makes him smile. "I don't smoke or drink, or use them [the sex shops]," he says. "And many people find that hard to believe. But that's the point. We have the freedom to use them, but are self-determining." This is where the Dutch Constitution enters the fray. "We feel that, if the State funds schools, then what goes on in them should not be against the Constitution," says Tielman. "And one of the leading concepts guiding our Constitution is the principle of self-determination. This means that people have the right to give meaning and shape to their lives as long as their actions don't prevent others from being self-determining. Perhaps because we Dutch come from various minorities, we recognize the need to defend minority rights."

Walk down any street in Amsterdam and the diversity of peoples in that country is overwhelming. A country with half the population of Canada is squeezed into an area four-fifths the size of Nova Scotia. People living together at such close quarters had to develop coping techniques. And so the Dutch chose tolerance. In reality, that wasn't as big a stretch as it might now appear. Although Dutch society was composed of diverse belief systems – Protestants, Catholics, Jews, and humanists – they shared many of the cultural values of Europe. But recently, a new wave of immigrants has brought with it not only new religions but radically different cultures. In the eighties, when there were large enough numbers of Hindus and Muslims to demand their own schools, the extent of Dutch tolerance was put to the test, sparking a brand-new debate. Some politicians argued that the old rules didn't apply to the newcomers. After a lot of heated discussion revolving around what is and isn't a religion, it was decided to stick to the original deal — to allow any group of parents who wanted a school to start one, as long as it had the numbers and would follow government rules.

Arie Oostlander was happy with the decision. A member of the Christian Democratic Party, he was recently elected for a seven-year term to the European Parliament. His party was actually founded over the issue of free Christian education, and so, despite all the other issues he has to contend with, he continues to support publicly funded religious schools. "Education isn't neutral," he says. "Back then [when the battle was under way], parents understood that religion is central to every activity in human life. They didn't want religion banned from public life. While Christian schools did exist, they were paid for by the parents. Protestants and Catholics considered this unfair and anti-social, because the poor couldn't afford the tuition. So they worked together to fight it. They never would have won if they hadn't joined forces." When the debate erupted over extending this right to new immigrants (non-Christians), Oostlander took the position that what's sauce for the goose should be sauce for the gander. "It's because we know how important religion is to us that we have a responsibility to create similar opportunities for others," he says.

It's hard to catch everything Oostlander says. He's at a constituency meeting in a village far off the beaten track, and the several hundred people in attendance are taking a meal break. The smell of baked ham and vintage wine hangs in the air. From the dining-room, we hear laughter, glasses tinkling, and the rise and fall of energetic conversations. Oostlander, however, is keen to discuss the issue. He says that, while he comes to it as a Christian, he's also a politician, and that side of him sees a political advantage in supporting religious schools. "Imams [Muslim leaders] come from Pakistan, Iran, and so on," he says, taking a quick gulp of coffee. "We don't like that because we don't understand the culture in which believers were living, so it creates a lot of problems. It's best for everyone if we insist on European Islam and not one created by people from Iran."

Oostlander sees publicly funded schools as playing a key role in developing that "European Islam." Refusing to fund religious schools probably won't stop people from having them; it simply means the State won't have any influence or control over what goes on inside them. However, when people take government money, they have to accept the strings attached to it. And those strings will have a socializing influence (insisting that they speak the Dutch language, have Dutch certified teachers, and so on). Oostlander's assumption is that it's better for society – and, by implication, for the children – if they are, indeed, educated in schools with some government control.

To date, religious groups want to take public money, knowing that they're free to teach what they want in terms of religion. Given the structure of the school day, though, they don't have a lot of time in which to do it. There are thirty-two hours in each school week, twenty-eight hours of which must be filled with the government's core curriculum. That leaves only four hours a week for the Arabic language (in Muslim schools), Hebrew (in Jewish schools), to say nothing of prayers, scripture reading, and religious history and tradition. The schools are allowed to discriminate in their hiring of teachers. A Christian school can insist on hiring Christian teachers, an Islamic school Muslim teachers, and so on. But given the requirement that teachers have to have a Dutch teaching certificate, they tend to be highly acculturated. And even though a school may discriminate in whom it hires, once they are hired, it can't fire them if they behave outside the parameters of the religion (become divorced or are gay, for example).

Peter Batelaan is at odds with these policies. He teaches would-be teachers and is very involved in intercultural education. He thinks it's a bad idea to fund religious schools. The fair-haired educator would like the Netherlands to adopt one public system that would, as he puts it, "give kids an idea of basic issues in life from a global perspective. The problem is, it'll never satisfy those for whom religion is the entire truth, people who say, 'There is only one God, and I'm glad it's my God.' Teaching basic issues from a global perspective could be done in a variety of subjects, and that's what I'd like to see," he says. "As a believer in human rights, I'd much prefer to see us move to religious and cultural diversity within schools. That's where people should become more interested in learning to live together. If education cannot con-tribute to society, then it is a missed opportunity."

Having said that, however, Batelaan admits that there's an upside to funding religious schools, and it's not insignificant. "Flexibility – a readiness to change the system to accommodate people – undermines fundamentalism," he says. "Our education is very de-centralized and that's a good thing. Authority goes more to local authorities and school boards. They choose and decide what they want within a framework of general goals for educa-tion. This discourages, I think, extremism or fundamentalism. If people feel rejected by a society, then religion becomes more of their identity, and that fosters fundamentalism. Here in the Netherlands, there's not much fundamentalism."

Batelaan's point feels more like a warning, indicating where State intransigence towards funding religious schools could lead. In fact, his words take on special significance when I later visit France and learn about some of the consequences of its hard line on religion in schools. Throughout my stay in Europe, I can't help but be struck by a paradox: by emphasizing religious differences we may actually minimize their social impact. Denying them, however, might well exaggerate them, forcing people to become more dependent on them.

I decide to visit an Islamic school to learn about its experience. And so I find myself travelling to the outskirts of Amsterdam to a multicultural housing development. I discover high-rise apartment buildings clustered together, balconies overflowing with furniture and other household paraphernalia. Footpaths link them, but people are scarce. It's past 9 a.m. and they're presumably either at work or in school. While I have no difficulty finding schools, they aren't the As Soeffah Islamic School I'm looking for. I'm confused. It should be in this field, on this site. Unfortunately, there are no Islamic symbols to guide me, no school signs. Finally, I meet someone who directs me a little farther and, there it is, looking just like all the other schools I've passed. In fact, I'm standing in a complex of schools – Protestant, Catholic, Hindu, Open (public, in our terms), and Islamic – which are housed side by side and which share a huge playground area.

Inside, I'm greeted by Rahmat Khan Abdur Rahman, the principal. He's dressed in a long, sparkling white tunic, worn over equally white long pants. On his head he wears a small, white, brimless hat called a *takia*. This, he says, is a way of treating both sexes alike. The girls, after all, have to wear the *hijab*. It's only fair, then, that the males also cover their heads.

He tells me how the school began in 1993. There were only 90 children that first year, but within two years there were 310, making them eligible for government funding. From the beginning, parents felt very strongly that their children should have an Islamic education. "They felt their children were losing their identity," he says. "Most know that, whatever their background, they'll have to adopt a new identity in this country. But they don't want their children to lose their religious identity. The one common goal here is religion, whether you're from Turkey, or Morocco, or Indonesia. If you're a Muslim, your religion forms your identity. If you are insecure, if you don't know who you are, then you have problems. It was the wish of the parents to bring up their children in the context of the home situation, to create an Islamic atmosphere in the home and in the school."

Rahman says the children get forty minutes of religion a day, and the Arabic language is embedded in it. There are prayers and readings from the Koran every morning. And, he says, the school has no problem giving sex-education classes. "We feel it's our responsibility to teach the children to have responsibility in life, and if you don't know about something you can't bear the responsibility. We feel it's also a religious aim."

I see the faces of children from fifteen different nationalities poring over their textbooks. Rahman explains that this school is their ticket to integrating into Dutch society. Somehow, I wasn't expecting to hear that word from him. In retrospect, I suppose it's because the general assumption in Canada is that, if people want to educate their children in religious ghettos, then they're actively resisting integration. Yet in the Netherlands, the word "integration" comes up all the time. "Our philosophy," adds the soft-spoken educator, "is, if we want to integrate into a multi-faith society, then children should know their own religion and culture. They should come from a position of strength in order to contribute to society. If they have nothing to contribute, then they will be assimilated."

Given Canada's quickly changing demographics, it's clear the Dutch have something to teach us. They obviously understand the difference between "integration" and "assimilation." They describe integration as an exchange between a minority community and the larger community. This means that newcomers don't have to sacrifice their identity in order to be accepted. In the process of living together, different groups adjust to each other, transform each other, and become something new. Tielman, for example, argues that separate schools actually stimulate integration. "There are three routes a society can take," he says. "Assimilation, integration, or segregation. 'Assimilation' means adaptation, and 'segregation' means making different rules for different groups. 'Integration' is a basic set of rules which is valid for everyone, and yet people have, in addition, certain freedom to develop their own identity."

Dutch Catholics argue that separate schools made their integration into Dutch society possible. At the turn of the century, Catholics were very much the underclass. Only 2 per cent of all university students were Catholic. This was disproportionately low, given that 35 per cent of the population was Catholic. But once they were allowed their own publicly funded schools, everything changed. Today, they're on a par with the rest of society. B. M. Janssen, the cigar-puffing director general of the Bureau of Catholic Education in The Hague, argues that Catholic schools spelled the beginning of Catholic emancipation. "And that led to integration into Dutch society," he says. "Because that's what it meant for us, we say, 'Give that right to Muslims and others.' If people can first establish their own school, then they'll be on a better basis to integrate into Dutch society."

Worldwide, Janssen is in great demand to speak about the lessons of the Netherlands. Articulate and aggressive, he makes his points succinctly. "Education always carries a value," he says. "I prefer to know what a school stands for, what view is being trans-ferred. I prefer that, rather than forcing people to go to a public school, where the view being transferred isn't made explicit. Then, you force people to live in an environment they don't trust. It's better to operate from a situation of safety in the world than to be forced to mingle with a society you don't trust. This leads to more seclusion and more insecurity. The main thing is that parents should have the freedom of choice."

I leave the Netherlands with much to ponder. It's clear that the Dutch decision to fund all religious schools is contributing to a stable society. While some Canadians later tell me it's a mistake to compare Canada with the Netherlands, because that country is historically and culturally so different from ours, I'm not convinced that this means we have nothing to learn from the Dutch. They have an eighty-year history of funding religious schools, and the result thus far seems to point to social integration, not social division. Their experience is especially interesting when compared to the way the French deal with religious minorities.

The French partially fund independent religious schools, but won't tolerate diversity within the public system. While the rigidity of France's approach is obviously not the only factor behind the continuing problems it's having with religious extremists, it could be a contributing factor. The French are extremely reluctant to compromise their culture. This prevents integration as defined by Tielman from taking place (in which concessions are made by both the majority and the minorities). The French, too, waged a battle over the relationship between church and state. The issue was solved by the French Revolution: complete separation. This meant that the Catholic Church lost control of education and paved the way for the creation of compulsory secular schools in 1905.

The rigidity of the French position is perhaps best revealed by the debate over religious symbols. In fact, religious symbols have been banned for more than a century; but with large numbers of Muslims immigrating to France, the issue resurfaced in the early 1990s with a vengeance. Muslim girls were being kicked out of school for wearing the *hijab*. Canadians sat up and took notice when a Montreal high school followed suit. When the Quebec Human Rights Commission censured the action, the school was forced to back down on the injunction (and the *hijab*-wearing Muslim retreated to another high school). But the issue suddenly had a relevancy in Canada. What are the social consequences of denying a group of people the right to their religious symbols in public schools?

Rémy Schwartz was willing to fill me in on the situation in France. He's an immensely busy person, wearing two professional hats. A professor in public law at the University of Versailles, he is also a member of the State Council, the body that goes through all legislation with a fine-tooth comb to make sure it's both constitutionally and legally sound.

When he wears that hat, his office is in the Palais Royale, next to the Louvre. Being the home of the august council, it's closed to the public, but Schwartz generously offers me a guided tour. I'm thrilled. This is where Molière's last play was performed, and where he later died. Napoleon was married here, in a tiny chapel. And Marie Antoinette sat imprisoned in these luxurious rooms before being sent to prison and her eventual beheading. There's no escaping a sense of French history, French culture, in this place. And it's the integrity of the French culture, explains Schwartz, that the French are trying to preserve when they take a hard line on mixing religion with education.

But isn't ordering females to remove something as religiously significant to many Muslims as the *hijab* demanding an enormous sacrifice? I ask. "Yes," Schwartz says. "It is. But when you move to this country, you agree to follow the rules of our country. Polygamy, female circumcision, violence against women – all these things you must abandon when you come to France. These are the rules of communal life." Schwartz tries to explain that the French don't accept the notion of special rights for different groups of people. "Everyone has the right to their own culture," he says, "but that doesn't give them, legally speaking, special rights. We believe that rights given to one must be given to another. That's why Jews, for example, have been so successful in France. Many have achieved high office and have done well culturally and socially, because they've accepted our way of doing things. If we gave special rights, where would it end? People would want more and more and more."

I was struck by the similarity between his argument and that of the Reform Party in Canada, which argues that the government's emphasis should be on extending civil rights to all members of society and not singling out any one group or groups. But the logic behind the French position is cultural homogeneity. It's the explicit denial of difference. It demands complete assimilation of minorities, a position that would not serve Canada's new, multi-cultural society very well. Obviously, tolerating "difference," if it contributes to the oppression and abuse of women (female circumcision) or is against the law (polygamy, violence against women) is totally unacceptable. But when the rights of others are not infringed upon – such as when females wear the *hijab* or when Sikhs wear turbans – what is the problem? Surely, accommodating "difference" in these situations is socially beneficial. After all, we don't get upset or cry foul when people wear crosses around their necks, or when nuns wear head coverings. What's the difference?

In France, public schools are secular; no religion is allowed. But on Wednesday afternoons, classes are cancelled to allow chaplains from various religions to come into the schools and meet with the students. Despite France's population of an estimated three to four million Muslims, there has been no request for a Muslim chaplain to date. Schwartz assumes this is because the Islamic community is very divided. The Paris mosque, for example, is controlled by Algerians, he says, other mosques, by Saudi Arabians and Moroccans. French Muslims, he explains, haven't been able to overcome their cultural differences to lobby together for something that might be in their children's common interest.

To make up for the time lost on Wednesday afternoons, classes are held on Saturday morning. Since Saturday is their Sabbath, this has created a conflict for Jews. So they asked for the right to keep their children at home. The State Council ruled that school attendance is compulsory, and that Jewish children must attend these Saturday-morning classes. It's another example of the French system's rigidity, its resistance to compromise. However, Schwartz says that, if in fact children don't show up, and their school progress isn't negatively affected, then their religiously based absences are tolerated. (As an aside, he smiles as he describes the "Great Rabbi" reminiscing to him about how "he went to school on Saturday, but couldn't lift up his pencil and write.")

Schwartz returns to the subject of the *hijab*. He says he thinks young Muslim women embraced it in such large numbers as a way of seeking identity in a time of crisis. The economy, he notes, is not good; there isn't enough work. Ethnic minorities, especially, suffer under such conditions. He also says the 2,000 to 2,500 *hijab* cases the State Council had to examine caused it to soften its stance somewhat. It ruled that girls should be allowed to wear the *hijab*, as long as they weren't wearing it to proselytize, and as long as they attended all classes. That meant they couldn't get out of gym because they were wearing them. They'd have to take the class and remove them. "But public opinion went against the council," he says. "Among the public, people felt all children must be the same – equality must be practised. And so school administrators told girls to remove the veil and expelled one to two hundred of them. This was eventually overturned by the court because they went against the decision of the State Council."

Jamel Oubechou, himself a Muslim, also doesn't think the *hijab* should be allowed in public schools. In fact, he even goes so far as to say women shouldn't be allowed to wear it to university classes. (One student was expelled for wearing the *hijab*, but a court ruled that, because she was an adult attending university, it was admissible.) Oubechou was born in France to Algerian immigrants. His father had fought for the French against Algerian nationalists. Later, those loyalists were abandoned by the French, and about a hundred thousand of them were killed by the Algerian army. Some sixty thousand were allowed to immigrate to France; among them was Oubechou's father. Oubechou grew up in the suburbs of Paris, in an ethnically mixed, working-class neighbourhood.

Education has been his route to success. He excelled at school, eventually being allowed to write entrance exams to the Grandes Écoles. Only the crème de la crème get into this school – people like Jean-Paul Sartre, for example. Out of the 1,500 who write the exams, only 120 succeed, and Oubechou was one of them. For four years, he specialized in modern English literature, eventually graduating at the top of his class. Today, he's a professor of English literature at the University of Lille, northeast of Paris. He says with a mischievous smile that he teaches the literary work of Salman Rushdie, anticipating protest from his Muslim students, but so far not getting any.

Like Schwartz, he accepts the adage "If you give people an inch, they'll take a mile." "If girls were allowed to wear the *hijab*," he says, "where will the claims stop? Soon, they'll be saying they don't want to take gym with the boys, or study biology, because they'll have to learn the theory of evolution, and on and on and on. The problem with accepting religiously inspired behaviour is you don't know how far it will go. It's true," he adds, "that you can go to a public school in France and ask for a meal without pork. But then people started saying, 'Why accept this and not that?' If people really want to have religion in school, then they can go to their own private ones."

This seems an extraordinary endorsement of assimilation by a member of a religious minority. But Oubechou is living proof of the success France has had with assimilation. Whether it's a model to be admired and emulated is another issue, but in his case it's certainly worked. Here's someone who might have been expected to defend the tailoring of public policy to meet the needs of religious minorities who turns out to be a critic – and a very articulate one at that. But in Canada, where we don't have a culture so identifiable or so entrenched as that of France, and where we say we seek to uphold the ideals of equality and tolerance, France appears to present an inappropriate model.

Ironically, despite France's insistence on secular education, it does fund independent religious schools. Two levels of funding are available, depending on the kind of partnership the school enters into with the government. Most agree to follow government curricula, hire certified teachers, and have open admissions. In that case, the State pays for everything except the initial capital investment and any renovations. To date, there have been no Muslim requests for separate schools – largely, as mentioned, because the Islamic community is divided on the matter.

So, what to make of this study in contrasts? A country that's adamantly against mixing religion and education – like many parts of Canada – but turns around and gives money to religious groups to run their own schools – unlike Ontario, Nova Scotia, New Brunswick, Prince Edward Island, and Newfoundland. And what of the Netherlands? A place that seems a model for the public funding of religious schools. Until, that is, one digs a bit deeper. Because for all the talk of separate schools leading to integration, there is an exception – the Jewish schools. Mind you, there's an historic reason for this, but the paradox exists nonetheless. I discovered it when I visited the Cheider School, a publicly funded Jewish Orthodox School in Amsterdam. It was a battle just getting inside the door. Coming from the freedom of Canada, I assumed I could just open the door to the tall, steel-reinforced fence and walk in. Not so. I was kept out until my name was phoned in and verified. Then I had to wait until a very large, very muscular man came out to escort me to my interview. The children are kept inside this fortress all day, the adults around them feeling continually under the threat of potential siege.

"We haven't suffered any attacks here in the Netherlands," says Dr. J. H. Sanders, school director. "But a bomb was set off in a Jewish schoolyard in Belgium, and we can't afford to take chances." Sanders describes how this school was built – partly with funds raised from Canadian Jews. He'd come to Canada several years ago to raise money, and people gave generously. He says he only agreed to meet with me as a way of letting Canadian Jews know how their money was spent. He's affable, while challenging some of my observations about Dutch education. "There is no issue of integration for us," he says firmly. "We aren't interested." In part, he's come to this conclusion because of his experience at a previous job. He worked on anti-racism issues for the government's social-services ministry. He says he came to the conclusion that, instead of fighting someone else's prejudices, he needed to work on strengthening the Jewish identity. "You have to look at why separate schools exist," he says. "If people go to them out of choice, it's a very different situation than if they go out of class or racial reasons. It makes all the difference in the world how they relate to the rest of society."

In fact, the Jews at this school break all the rules so carefully described to me by everyone else I visited. And they're proud of it. They adamantly refuse, for example, to have open admissions. They won't even allow a Reform Jew to attend, let alone a Gentile. They teach creationism as fact, only evolution as theory. And they teach Hinduism as the worship of idolatry. When I question him about what that is teaching children about tolerance for other religions, he says, "It doesn't lead to an appreciation of Hinduism, but we teach children to treat others decently without taking over their beliefs." And, despite the government's explicit requirement that religious schools teach sex education, the Cheider School doesn't. "Sex education is in the ministry textbooks, so we cut out the pages," says Sanders. "We don't teach sex education because Jewish law forbids it. It's early enough that they learn it when they get married. We have a committee to do that."

I ask why the school hasn't been closed down, given its in-your-face defiance of government rules. "Everyone knows we got a raw deal," says Sanders. "Today, out of a population of 15 million, there are around 30,000 to 40,000 Jews. Before World War II, we were a quarter of a million. Many people recognize that our survival now depends on Jewish education. Due to the war and assimilation, much of what people knew of Jewish life has disappeared. People want it back, but don't even know what they want back. So we're giving their children a depth of Jewish knowledge not available in the home." The war wasn't the only time Jewish knowledge was threatened, either. A Dutch education historian, N. L. Dodde, has documented that the Hebrew language and traditions of Jewish life were almost erased before the 1917 legislation. It was the guarantee of State funding of their schools that allowed that knowledge to survive.

Presumably, the fact that the Jews are defying government regulations could be used as a reason for refusing to fund religious schools (the "give them an inch, they'll take a mile" argument). But look at it from Sanders's perspective. The atrocities of Nazism almost eliminated the Jews. While more would have been killed had many Dutch not hid them, many more would have survived had more of the Dutch resisted the Nazis. According to Sanders, they know this and are now paying penance. Perhaps there's more, too. Perhaps the Dutch, like many members of minority religions in Canada, really do believe that the true test of a tolerant society is how it treats its minorities. And that one way is to recognize the rights of Jews (in this instance) and allow them to teach in their own way, even if it offends the majority.

Ultimately, it's impossible to predict the outcome of events. When the Dutch were fighting so vehemently over the school-funding issue more than one hundred years ago, who could have predicted that their society would become so secularist? The mystery to me is why religiously based schools are still so widespread, given increasing numbers of non-believers. The Catholic director general of education, Janssen, admits that the base of Catholics is shrinking, but refuses to admit that the need for Catholic educa-tion is disappearing. "We don't only provide education," he says stoutly. "We provide formation, character, morals. We want our pupils to think about the world they live in, the meaning of life. It's true that we're a very secular society, but recent research on education revealed that 70 per cent of students pray. So it's not clear what their specific views are about God, transcendentalism, and so on. But most are convinced that there's more to life than the material."

Janssen says every once in a while someone will argue that reli-gious schools have become secularist and that their funding should be eliminated. Instead of ignoring the debate, he welcomes it. "The debate is never-ending," he says. "But that's what education is all about. We should be discussing these issues. We realize it's important in a multicultural, multi-faith society to have a dialogue with others. But first you have to know where you stand before you can speak with others."

For those who believe the public funding of religiously based schools will lead to ghettoization, social division, and religious conflict, the Dutch experience suggests otherwise. People on all sides agree that differences have narrowed, not grown. This has undoubtedly been in part because a policy of equality and toler-ance has contributed to the integration and emancipation of religious minorities.

8

DOCTRINE AND DEBATE

Her loyalty to the Episcopal Church provoked a certain grimness, and I see her now of a Sunday morning . . . rounding up a cranky flock of children and grandchildren . . . for the 11 o'clock service. That was the trouble; the superego was always at hand telling her how to behave, telling her that she had to go to church every Sunday until she could no longer walk, telling her to badger her children and grandchildren and to be gravely offended if one of them refused her. . . . There was always in my mother a threshold where laughter stopped, where the rules were invoked and where discussion became impossible.

Mary Meigs, *Lily Briscoe: A Self-Portrait*

indoctrinate − *to teach (a person or group) systematically or for a long period to accept (esp. partisan or tendentious) ideas uncritically.*

The Concise Oxford Dictionary

Train up a child in the way he should go: and when he is old, he will not depart from it.

Proverbs 22:6

I t's one of those bleak and tediously cold Toronto mornings. So the prospect of sitting for hours sipping hot tea and piecing together the disjointed patterns of someone's recent past is a pleasing prospect. Christopher Hudspeth has agreed to tell me about his experiences in Christian schools. Even though he's just worked a night shift, he arrives full of energy and ravenously hungry. He's clean-cut, casually dressed, and sports an earring in one ear. There's little small talk. At the age of twenty-eight, he's still trying to understand what happened to him between Grades 6 and 10 – the years he attended Christian schools. In all, he went to three of them. The first one was affiliated with the Christian Reform Church, but he attended it for only one year, his parents objecting to its discipline policy. The others were Accelerated Christian Education (ACE) schools, affiliated with the Pentecostal Church. The ACE schools were very small; one was housed in two rooms in a church basement, the other one – with seventy-five children from kindergarten to Grade 13 – was in an old warehouse. They were also, in his words, "intolerant." He leans back, readying himself to begin the list.

"Gays, pop music, any other religion," he begins. "Until recently," he adds, "I felt other religions were a cult. I'd been taught that people from other religions weren't people. I had a huge distaste of Roman Catholics for years." He shakes his head. The list continues. "No movies, no dances. There was an intolerance of the media in general. I was taught to distrust anything that was outside the purview of the church. In fact, the last ACE school I went to even had its own co-op grocery store, because the larger co-op store had given money to Planned Parenthood. It was a very paranoid world. The minister was a god. What I did by questioning him was put my head on the line."

But Hudspeth says he couldn't sit back and let everything go by without challenging what was happening. "I questioned their approach, not what they believed," he says. "I felt like I got regular floggings, it was so oppressive, although it never got physical. Corporal punishment was practised, but every parent had to sign a release. My mum signed it, but my dad didn't, so I guess that's why I never got it." Dating was allowed, but everyone had to abide by the "twelve-inch" rule. This rule – which required that a distance of twelve inches be maintained between boys and girls at all times – was strictly enforced. So Hudspeth used to swagger around the school with a ruler hanging out of his back pocket.

"There was no sex education, of course," he says. "That was considered part of the parents' job." But there was a lot of sex talk. Talk about not having sex before marriage and talk about the sinfulness of homosexuality. "Anti-gay sermons happened regularly," says Hudspeth. "But I felt gay well before puberty. I felt attracted to men. I liked being around men. I liked their conversation. And I felt those sermons were directed at me, even though I'd never done anything. I felt guilty, so guilty, because I knew how I felt, but I had to stand with them saying things against people who were gay. I felt I had to. I didn't feel as if I had a choice." Pain and turmoil cloud his face.

How, I wonder aloud, is it possible to come out of such an experience without hating God? He looks at me, amazed that I might even consider such a possibility. "I didn't come out of that system hating God," he says. "I came out of it hating me, because I'd been told how wrong I was. It's true, there were lots of reasons for me to have hated God, but I never came to that point. I *definitely* hated the Church," he says. This statement is pronounced with such emphasis that several people at the next table glance over to see if anything exciting is about to happen. Disappointed when his voice returns to normal, they turn away. "But then," he adds, "I've always had more than that surface belief I was raised with. I truly knew God loved me. I've never been one to give up on people, so why would I give up on God? God loves me. I know that. My faith is very strong, very personal. I believe in the One who created me. As a gay man, I had to come to the place where I realized that nothing else matters but that God loves me and I love God."

When Hudspeth finished Grade 10, there weren't enough high-school students to keep the senior program going, so he switched to the local high school. "I was so fearful of going into the public system," he says, eyes rolling. "I thought I was going into Satan's den itself. Within two weeks, I realized I was a good student. I was a poor student in the Christian system, I guess, because I was completely unmotivated. Plus, there was no freedom. Someone was always watching you with a thumb over you. I mean, you aren't encouraged to think, let alone critique. You just sit there, filling in the blanks and answering multiple-choice questions. You don't write essays. You don't talk about a book and have various thoughts and views on it. When I went to public high school, I couldn't get over the fact that so many people had points of view. I thought there was only one answer, only one way to think, because in ACE, if you didn't hold their view, you were corrected and told to do it their way. But I found out that stories could be allegories and that what you think is the climax to a story won't necessarily be mine."

Although Hudspeth discovered he was actually a good student, he also discovered he was way behind his counterparts. He'd had no French, and had studied only American history, American geography, and American math measurements. ("I still can't convert to the metric system," he says with a sigh.) And so he had to repeat Grade 10. It might have hurt his pride a little, but that seemed a small price to pay for what he gained. "I felt set free," says Hudspeth. "I was a new person again. I didn't feel I was set free to become gay. But I felt set free as a person to think, to be, and to make my own decisions."

I'm amazed that he's neither bitter nor boiling over with rage. These would seem pretty legitimate and understandable reactions to five lost years. But Hudspeth is philosophical. He figures his mother, who was responsible for sending him to the Christian schools, was under a lot of peer pressure at the church and honestly believed she was doing the right thing. If there's a spark of anger, it's at the fact that he had no exposure to art, music, industrial studies, physical education, or French. And that there were no opportunities to travel or go on exchange programs with other students. Today, he figures he was lucky to find people who love and accept him for who he is – a gay man. His ongoing struggle is to do the same.

Religiously based schools unabashedly exist to indoctrinate children in the dogma of their particular faiths. Their motives might seem eminently reasonable: to maintain the continuity and survival of their religion, for example, or to give children a strong sense of group identity. But Hudspeth, for one, bears the scars of religious indoctrination – and they're deep. This doesn't surprise me; of all the religious schools I visited, the ACE philosophy seems the most oppressive. But no matter what type of religion is being conveyed to students, the fact that religion dominates the school's approach to education and its philosophy raises a number of fundamental questions.

What is education all about? Is it learning about the world in order to make independent, informed choices about how to live one's life? Or is it learning an inherited dogma as a prescription for living? Second, it raises questions about the relationship between indoctrination and education. Is all education ultimately a process of indoctrination? Is there such a thing as good indoctrination? If there is, how do you tell the difference between good indoctrination and bad indoctrination?

Needless to say, countless scholars have grappled with these questions for centuries. The irony is that scholars can't agree on what constitutes indoctrination. Some argue that it's the teaching of questionable content; others, that it's the way that things are taught. Some say it boils down to the intention, or the objective, of the teaching. Does it, or does it not, mean to produce an indoctrinated person?

Clive Beck is a professor in the Department of History and the Philosophy of Education at the Ontario Institute for Studies in Education. He thinks that content is the most important feature of indoctrination. In his book *Better Schools*, he writes, "One of the chief ways of indoctrinating is to teach beliefs and values which are objectionable in some respects . . . focusing particularly on the teaching of untruths as if they were truths and uncertainties as if they were certainties." He adds that the manner in which students are taught is also a key component of indoctrination. Everyone needs to be inculcated with moral ideas, he contends, but "these early beliefs should not be taught so forcefully that when children are ready to think for themselves they are psychologically incapable of questioning them."

In his book *The End of Education*, the American educator Neil Postman makes the point that, for schools to work, the students, parents, and teachers have to serve a god. Now, he doesn't mean "God," as in "Creator," in whom many religions believe. He means a god in the sense of a story, a narrative, that threads its way through the educational life of a child, providing a sense of meaning, continuity, and purpose. "To put it simply," he writes, "there is no surer way to bring an end to schooling than for it to have no end." In this context, he's using the word "end" to mean "purpose" or goal. For education to be meaningful, he says, it must have a narrative through which children are taught, not how to make a living, but how to make a life. With these thoughts in mind, I go in search of other recent graduates from religiously based schools.

Walied Soliman went to the ISNA–Islamic School in Mississauga for six years, graduating from Grade 8 in 1991. When I meet him, he's enrolled at the University of Toronto, and also working part-time for an Ontario Member of the Provincial Parliament. Despite his busy schedule – five university courses on top of a twenty-five-to-thirty-hour week at Queen's Park – Soliman takes time out to discuss his experience at the Islamic school.

Only the most glowing terms will suffice. "There's no question in my mind that what that system gave me were the three most important things you need to be a successful person in life," he says. "That's direction, belief, and discipline. From the very first time I went to the school, it was put in my head that there's a certain direction I have to go in. I have to be a successful student. . . . And I had belief in a religion that told me I had to lead a very structured life, and that whole ideology was implemented in my head. And then, things were very disciplined. You know, standing in an absolutely straight line. And there aren't any ifs, ands, or buts about whether I should finish my homework. You have to finish your homework. If you don't, you're a social loser among your friends. So this was the social atmosphere and I remember getting out of it and a lot of people saying, 'Oh, this whole system messed you guys up. You were in a cocoon for five or six years and now you're out of this cocoon, you're going to have so many problems.' But I didn't have a single problem when I got out of the school."

Soliman is wearing a double-breasted suit and carries a brief-case. He's lean, earnest, and very self-confident. He says public school wasn't the shock he'd been told it would be; that he ran for student council twice and won each time by an overwhelming majority. "And I was nominated for valedictorian and lost marginally. So it wasn't an obstacle going to a private school and then going to a public school afterwards." He admits that the Islamic school was very strict about male-female relationships, but says, "I talk to girls all the time now. I think it's just a very controlled environment is what it is. And frankly, when I look outside right now, I think the controlled environment that I was brought up in didn't affect me in a big way. *Fortune* magazine did an article about religion in the workplace and showed that when companies encourage it – have weekly gatherings where a priest, or someone, comes in and gives a lecture about the Bible – it gives people a reason to actually work, and so that's a very interesting and very important thing. I believe it is absolutely correct."

When pressed, Soliman says the ideal would be for children from all religions and ethnic groups to be educated together. "But the present system has a lot of biases, and we'll always have people who are going to give us a difficult time. So there will always be people who want to bring their children to schools like these, and I think it's wonderful. I think it's great. It hasn't affected me. I'm not any less Canadian right now. You know, I work for a political party. I work for a cabinet minister. I think I'm just as Canadian as anyone else."

Soliman may sound as if he protests too much but, as he rushes out the door to make another engagement, he really does present a picture of the well-rounded student, the committed worker, the politically interested and involved citizen – in short, a good Canadian. And he certainly shows no signs of being afraid to confront life in a secular society. This is something I'm on the alert for: the ability to embrace the world on an equal footing with people who come from very different backgrounds, with very different worldviews. Because, if schooling doesn't enable people to move confidently in a world larger than the one in which they were brought up, then to my mind it's failed the interests of both the student and the larger society.

I admit a bias: I don't expect graduates from Roman Catholic schools to have much of a problem in that regard. Catholic schools are not marginal to society. They are a firmly entrenched part of virtually every Canadian community. They follow government curricula, hire certified teachers. Being publicly supported in many provinces, the majority of them don't depend on families being able to scrape together private tuition. This allows them to attract large numbers of students. As well, many Catholic schools, in urban areas especially, are often very ethnically diverse. Size and ethnic diversity alone make them stand out from some of the religious schools I visited in which each class consisted of only a handful of white, middle-class students.

Allison Hanes attended Roman Catholic schools in Burlington, a community west of Toronto, from Grade 6 to high-school graduation in 1995. She's a bright, vibrant person with a sunny disposition and a positive attitude towards life. Now in her second year of university, she enjoys intellectual discussions, especially those that revolve around an issue she's thought about a lot. And this is one she's found particularly engrossing. "I was indoctrinated, yes," she says. "It was worse in elementary school than in high school, because you're more vulnerable, more credulous then, and they can put more fear in little kids than in rebellious teenagers. But the amount of indoctrination depended on the teacher. Some were worse than others. I mean, in our Grade 6 religion class, our teacher would just give us little prayers and we'd decorate them. Others really pushed conformity to Catholicism. Later, in high school, we were encouraged to think critically in some classes, like English and law and history. I mean, that's a key component of those subjects. But we were not allowed to think critically about religious issues. Oh, we could ask questions, but the basic premise was: 'We're right, and eventually you'll come back and God will forgive you for being so crazy.'"

And the morals? "They taught you to be universally tolerant of everyone," she says. "And forgiveness is a big thing in the Roman Catholic Church. And redemption, to have the choice to redeem yourself." These sound like pretty good morals to me. "But it was hypocritical," she hastens to say. "I mean, what really turned me off was when the same-sex law [a bill that would have extended benefits to same-sex couples] was being debated [at Queen's Park]. Archbishop [Aloysius] Ambrozic sent a letter to every church, and it was read out on Sunday, saying that the same-sex law was evil and should be lobbied against. It was so hypocritical, because we were taught that Jesus was so revolutionary and he cavorted with outcasts and morally questionable people, but he showed love and compassion. Yet the Church says, 'Love everybody, but not gays, because they're evil and bad.' That's what upset me."

I wonder if she's the exception – the thoughtful student who took to heart what she was told and then examined it deeply. "Mostly," she says, "people weren't even socially or politically aware about what they were being taught." But Hanes says that, for many of the eight hundred students at her high school, there was a community spirit. "It was a community spirit of cynicism. That was the unifying factor – to fight the system, to escape Mass. I remember the days we tried to escape. They'd have teachers manning every exit to try to stop us from getting out, and teachers posted in every washroom to give us detentions if we tried to hide there. Oh, they came up with different things, like making us take our classroom chair to Mass, so they could see who was skipping, or scheduling Mass in the middle of the day, or not letting us take our bags or books out of the classroom. We'd still find ways to escape. And when we did, it looked like a jailbreak. But they couldn't get us because we wore uniforms, and when we hit the sidewalks we all looked the same from behind."

Her description of the getaways is very funny and as she recounts it, she laughs at the absurdity of it all. But the laughter dies away as she plunges into recounting "the biggest shock of my life." In 1996, she entered Carleton University. Leaving home is always a big venture, but that wasn't what threw her for a loop. "I consider myself to be very open-minded," says Hanes. "I took a world religions course, and my family has some non-Roman

Catholic friends, but when I came to campus and saw Muslims observing Ramadan or Jews observing Yom Kippur, I realized how sheltered my world was. I felt as if I'd missed something. It's not intolerance, it's more an exposure thing. A Catholic school is such an insular world." She pauses to think about the implications. "In our school, we never had to worry about prayers or offending anyone, because we were all the same. When you only have to worry about the interests of one group, you start to think that you're all-important and you're right. You just don't think about how that affects others, how it affects your perspective on society." Today, she says she's anti-Catholic, but she makes a distinction between institutional religion and personal faith, having rejected the former, not the latter. But, almost as a postscript, she mentions how peculiar it seems that the Catholic students she meets who are the most devout didn't actually attend Catholic schools.

Michael Mainville's experience at Catholic schools was quite different from Hanes's. He grew up far from the urban sprawl of Toronto, in a small community north of Sudbury. The schools he attended were not only Roman Catholic but were also French. This meant that they tried to reinforce the values and morals of Catholicism, and they also attempted to cultivate student pride in their French identity. "There was a lot of English influence where I grew up," says Mainville. "We were barraged with English culture and English messages. School was the only place where we got information that wasn't from the English media or Hollywood. That was the only place where we learned about our own past and history. Not that anything was ever said negatively about Protestants," he says quickly. "I never felt animosity towards them. I only knew their church wasn't as pretty as ours." A fleeting smile. "That's about it. It was more the English–French thing. In history class we were taught to challenge authority. But it was more a question of challenging the traditional views of

Canadian history and replacing them with French–Canadian history. We were told that what people learned in English schools was incorrect."

Mainville says one of the strongest messages he got at high school came through the word "assimilation." It was repeatedly invoked as something immensely negative, to be on guard against, to be avoided at all costs, and to be actively resisted. "We were taught identity through religion and language," says Mainville, "and religion was about French culture. I remember that once a year the teachers would make taffy, and then they would serve it to us and we would eat it. It was to celebrate Sister Marguerite Bourgeoys. She opened the first school in Montreal in 1658 and she used to make taffy to entice the Indians to go to school. I look back on it now and think how awful that was. There we were celebrating the assimilation of another group."

Quiet and intense, Mainville is proud of his French heritage. He says he understands how important it is to get a sense of pride in your own identity. "The problem is they tried to instil pride through fear," he says. "We were terrified of being assimilated. Then again, I guess that, when you're a teenager, you're not interested in the beauty of your culture. So they took the easy way out and instilled fear in us."

When I ask him whether or not he was indoctrinated, his reaction is so abrupt, it's almost physical. I can feel him backing off. "That's a strong word," he says slowly. "I'd just say that we were given very strong moral messages about what's right and what's wrong, and not just in religion but in all classes. We were given a moral code. For example, in family studies, we looked at the roles of family in society. But we were given the Roman Catholic perspective. The family was always a heterosexual couple with children. And on divorce, we didn't look at the reasons behind it or the statistics, only that it is bad and why. Same with common-law relationships. And gays were not discussed. Not in any course.

I never heard the word homosexuality mentioned in school. A stand was taken on a lot of other moral issues. I mean, abortion was strongly opposed. But we had no sex-education classes. We weren't taught methods of birth control – just abstinence. The unfortunate thing is that students weren't getting the education they needed, because the teen-pregnancy rate in my home town was phenomenal." How phenomenal? "Well, there were about a hundred of us – boys and girls – who started in Grade 9, although only about thirty-five went on to Grade 13. During that time, fifteen girls had babies."

This is the area of his education of which Mainville is most critical. "We were so ignorant," he says. "We just weren't told anything that would have helped us cope with some of the things we were going through. I mean, students actually believed it wasn't possible to get pregnant the first time you had sex. Or they believed that a girl couldn't get pregnant if she washed afterwards. And religion class didn't have a lot of credibility. We had to take it every year. It was mandatory. The only religion class that wasn't mandatory was world religions. We spent half of a lunch hour every second day at religion class, so we got used to it. All of us had the values of the Church, because we weren't presented with any other options. But values can be easily put aside. I mean, Catholics rate their values. Being opposed to abortion is a very strong belief. But believing that you can only have sex for procreation is a good ten notches below abortion."

Perhaps this helps to explain the findings of Reginald Bibby, a University of Lethbridge sociologist, and Don Posterski, a social analyst. In their 1992 survey called *Project Teen Canada*, they compared teenage Catholics attending Catholic schools outside Quebec with non-Catholic public-school students across Canada (results accurate within 4 per cent, nineteen times out of twenty). They discovered that four out of five Catholic-school students approve of premarital sex and living together outside marriage, even though both contravene Vatican teachings. And 76 per cent of them approve of abortion for rape victims. In fact, Catholic high-school students are slightly more likely than public-school students to be sexually active – 51 per cent compared to 47 per cent. And more than two out of three Catholic-school students support homosexual rights. Only 37 per cent consider themselves committed Christians, compared with 29 per cent of their public-school counterparts.

Mainville also says he wasn't academically prepared for university. But he doesn't blame this on the fact that his education was religiously based. To him, it had more to do with coming from a small northern town with limited financial resources. "When I got to university in 1993, I was way behind other students," he says. "I knew Quebec history and a little bit of world history. But that was about it. I'd had no philosophy, read no books of thought, didn't know Canadian history. There was just no pressure to do well at school."

Nor was he equipped to mix with people from other religions, other ethnic groups. "I didn't know the difference between a Jew and a Jehovah's Witness," he says. Despite his experience, Mainville says he can't condemn religious schools. "People did a lot of good," he says. "We were taught to be proud of who we were and taught to be proud of the Catholic Church and the work it does. The largest club at our school was the missionary club, and every year fifteen or twenty students went to Haiti to help build homes and dig ditches. This isn't a simple black-and-white situation."

I know that, and it's precisely the complexity of this issue that makes it both so interesting and so difficult to come to terms with. Of course it's important for children to learn about their history, their culture, their religion, and to grow up with a sense of pride in who they are. Of course it's important that the values of the home aren't consistently undermined in the school.

But *how* children are taught and *what* they are taught are fundamental to how they cope in the wider society and how they relate
to people quite different from themselves. They are also a good
gauge of whether they are being educated to think independently, or whether they are being indoctrinated to accept what they've
been told.

There are other values that seem equally important; for example, surely it's in everyone's interests that young people learn about
sex and about ways to prevent bringing another human being into
the world until they're emotionally and financially equipped to do
so. Equally obvious, it seems to me, is that young people be taught
the value of autonomous thinking as they age and mature. When
young people are treated in the way Hanes describes – teachers
standing at doors to prevent them escaping from something that
the young people clearly believe is not in their self-interest – then
the message is that they aren't autonomous thinkers, that they exist
in a world without choice. (While I'm only examining the issue
of indoctrination in religious schools, similar practices no doubt
exist in secular schools. There's the same intolerance of dissent, of
autonomous thinking, and behaving. The question is whether one
system is more prone to it than another. It's quite possible that,
with the exception of religious teachings, there is little difference
between them.)

I also think that appreciating and celebrating diversity is an
important value. And this isn't one that comes automatically when
one enters adulthood or the paid workforce. It has to be taught
and then experienced through exposure to "the other." If children
grow up being taught that their way is the only way, or the best
way to be, then we might as well kiss the ideal of a pluralistic,
civilized society good-bye. All of this is easy for me to say, of course,
not being a member of a group that feels consistently threatened
and under siege.

★

Stephanie Levitz is Jewish and grew up totally immersed in the life of her synagogue, Jewish community, and Jewish school. Her parents sent her to Hillel, a conservative, Orthodox Jewish school in Ottawa for nursery school through Grade 8. Then, because there's no Jewish high school in the city, she was forced to attend a public high school. When we meet, she's finishing Grade 13. During the course of our time together, she gets news of yet another university acceptance. This is not a surprise. All of the universities to which she's applied have accepted her, and along with the letters of acceptance come offers of scholarships.

Levitz is clearly not going to have a problem coping with university. She's very articulate, very outspoken, and very impressive. Besides, she figures she's already been through the worst possible adjustment – going from a private Jewish school to public high school. "It was such a shock," she says, tossing back her shoulder-length hair. "It was the most traumatic experience of my life. I went from a small school where I'd known everyone since kindergarten to a huge school. I'd been really sheltered at Hillel. I don't mean that in a negative way," she hastens to add. "I saw it as negative then, but now I find it a good experience. Kids in public schools are exposed a lot earlier to things than we were at Hillel – smoking, drinking, drugs, dancing, sex. Being exposed to those things at eleven and twelve years of age is far too early. At Hillel, we didn't have dances and nobody smoked or drank or did drugs." Ironically, the real shock of public high school had nothing to do with those things. To her, it was the shock of being among people who were so radically different from herself.

"It was the first time I ever saw a Sikh," she says. "I'd never seen a Sikh before. I'd never talked to an Asian person. I'd never had non-Jewish friends before and, suddenly, there I was, having to explain myself – why I didn't go out on Friday night." Levitz says her preparation for public high school was totally inadequate.

"Public school was talked about a lot," she says. "We were told there would be a lot of anti-Semitism, and that we shouldn't be afraid to stand up for who we are, and that we should refuse to write exams on Yom Kippur. We were told we'd just be a number, and that we'd never know our teachers, and that they wouldn't care about us. And we were told that we should never date a non-Jewish boy, or else no Jewish boy would ever date us. I was terrified. I didn't make a new friend for my first year and a half in high school. Then I realized I was okay, that we were all going through the same things. It was weird being with Asian and Catholic kids, but we talked about our differences. And I made a point of not being a number. I got involved in things – students' council, the year-book committee – so no one forgot me in the shuffle. High school is big," she says, "but it's not bad. You get to be part of a small community and my teachers knew me well.

"There *was* an undertone of anti-Semitism. I'm a Zionist and I wear T-shirts with Israeli slogans. When I go outside, Lebanese students move away and give me looks. Some of our desks have swastikas carved on them. And remarks are made sometimes."

I ask how the school deals with these incidents. "When I pointed out the swastika, my teacher just said, 'If that bothers you, move to another desk.' And a comment was made in English class the other day. The quote was something like, 'He always wants more.' And a boy said, 'He's a Jew.' The teacher just said, 'Think before you open your mouth.' They aren't prepared to deal with it, yet the school I go to considers itself to be very politically correct. But then, I wasn't taught at Hillel how to deal with anti-Semitism. I really don't know how to respond when those things happen. But there really isn't much anti-Semitism at my high school. Most of the racism is directed at the visible minorities."

Levitz says she admires the values she was taught at Hillel. "Hard work is very important. And to be smart, to be a leader, to be a good friend. They stressed the importance of the family and

Judaism, the basic Jewish creed, the Ten Commandments, that it was important to keep the Sabbath. But it was very ethnocentric. I don't know anything about other people." This is obviously a sore point with her; it comes up repeatedly. "Why can't we learn Jewish history in relation to the rest of the world?" she asks. "Most of us were born and brought up in Canada. Why can't we be taught Canadian Jewish history?" But the word "indoctrination" doesn't scare her and she readily admits to being indoctrinated. "Hillel kids *are* different," she says. "I can't explain it, but all Hillel people are completely different from everyone else. Don't ask me how. It's an attitude, a persona. Hillel is just very different. It teaches you more maturity. Hillel guys at fourteen are leap years ahead of public-school guys at fourteen. We get a strong education. I think Hillel made me more intellectual as a person. . . . And we were encouraged to think critically." There's a quick intake of breath before she adds, "But not that critically. The joke was that if you wanted to stall a class, you'd raise your hand and ask a question about the Holocaust. The rest of the class would be spent with the teacher talking about the Holocaust. We were saturated with information about the Holocaust."

But sex education didn't exist. "It's taboo because it's never mentioned in the Torah," explains Levitz. "When anything goes against the Torah, then you have no need to know about it. We had no sex education, no information about AIDS prevention, or abortion, and no anti-drug campaigns. At Hillel, it's just assumed you don't do those things. But it's a problem, because students don't get sex education from the school and they don't get much from the home. That's not the best way to learn about these things. I have Catholic friends who are practising abstinence. They're doing that because they were taught that, but Jewish students aren't taught that. They aren't taught anything. It's a good thing there's so much information on television. Now I know about abortion and birth control because of television. I think Hillel's got to wake up. It's not good enough to say, 'Nice Jewish girls don't,' because they do. And they will, unless they're told why not."

While Levitz's comments may appear critical, they're all framed within a positive context. She believes that Jewish education is a force for good, an experience that she values. She'd simply like to see it get even better. And she figures being less ethnocentric would be a good place to begin. "We aren't prepared to function in a diverse society," she says. "You're made to think everyone out there is Jewish. No one ever tells you, unless your parents do, that schools don't close for Passover. That you must be prepared to explain what you're eating. That Sikhs wear turbans for a reason. I felt so stupid that I didn't know there were Sikhs. But then when I talked to a Sikh at school I found out he was just a normal, everyday teenager." Levitz is glad she had the opportunity to find out about such differences at high school, because she figures there'll be enough to cope with at university. "At least in high school, you're in your home and have a stable Jewish life," she says. "To adjust to these things in university when everything is new would be such a major change. It's like starting the rest of your life, so it's not a good time to learn." The prospect of going to university is obviously exciting to her, and she reels off a list of the universities she's considering. Queen's, she figures, is out. Not because of any academic failings, but because there's a scarcity of Jews.

"It means a lot to me to be a Jew," she says. "I know that the intermarriage rate for Jews is 50 per cent, and I find that terrifying. I'm not going to go to Queen's because I refuse to put myself in a situation where I'll fall madly in love with a non-Jew. Being Jewish is far more than a birthright. Oh, I dated a non-Jew once. It took me more than a year to tell my mother about it. It couldn't last. How could it? How could I not bring him home? I couldn't stand explaining myself all the time. There are expressions, ways of saying things, doing things, that are Jewish. And they're who I am. I don't want to have to explain myself."

It seems to me we've covered the field – the pros, the cons – and when we weigh them up, Levitz is adamant that Jewish education was good for her. "Religion and education are important," she says emphatically. "Very important. I don't understand how kids can grow up and not be anything. I have friends now who have relations in Scotland. But that's all they know. They don't go to church or synagogue. What do they believe in? Where do their values come from? I used to envy them because they didn't have any pressure. No pressure to be Jewish or Roman Catholic or anything. But while they might not have any pressure, at the same time they have nothing. No history, no culture, no background. It's a sad thing to have no history. At least Roman Catholics can trace their history back to Ireland [sic]. But I have friends who are Canadians now and who don't have a group history. They don't really know where they came from and why they do the things they do. They're nothing deeper than where they are at the moment. It's easy for me to become a more spiritual person because I have a basis for it. But they sit there and say, 'I'll be a Buddhist or a Protestant – it doesn't matter.' It's wishy-washy. They are the commercial people. They aren't into Christmas except as a commercial thing. They don't know who they are, and that's sad."

As I think about all the things young people told me, I can't help but admire the fact that they're so clear, so articulate, about their experiences. They know which "gods," to use Neil Postman's phrase, are being served at their schools. I think about the gods Postman describes as prevalent in the public system – Economic Utility, Consumerism, and Technology. (Many parents of children at religious schools would no doubt add to that list. Many say they won't send their children to public schools because they worship the gods of Individualism, Humanism, and Liberalism.)

But what are we to make of all these gods? More to the point, what kind of citizens, what kind of a society, are we creating if these gods don't foster the possibility of peaceful, respectful coexistence? Postman writes, "I wish to stress that all gods are imperfect, even dangerous. A belief too strongly held, one that excludes the possibility of a tolerance for other gods, may result in a psychopathic fanaticism." He quotes the Danish physicist Niels Bohr, who said, "The opposite of a correct statement is an incorrect statement, but the opposite of a profound truth is another profound truth." Postman states that this means that it's better to have access to more than one profound truth. "To be able to hold comfortably in one's mind the validity and usefulness of two contradictory truths is the source of tolerance, openness, and, most important, a sense of humor, which is the greatest enemy of fanaticism," he writes. "Nonetheless, it is undoubtedly better to have one profound truth, one god, one narrative, than to have none."

So what is one to conclude about the dangers of indoctrination in religious schools? There is obviously no doubt of its existence; the schools are often – too often – intolerant of disbelief, of alternative perspectives, of questioning, of autonomous thinking. These tendencies must be decried and rejected. But is indoctrination all bad? Ironically, while many of those I talked with were critical of their indoctrination, they displayed an admirable critical consciousness, in spite of their experience. While it's a tribute to them as individuals, it's also a sign of their contact and familiarity with religious ideas. This contact has helped them achieve a form of religious literacy, a capacity to navigate in areas far beyond specific doctrines of belief. Still, it's impossible to generalize. While many may grow up intellectually capable, the emotional damage from an experience such as the one Hudspeth described is incalculable.

Similar interviews with graduates of secular schools would no doubt turn up instances of intolerance of scepticism and dissenting viewpoints. Unfortunately, intolerance of autonomous thinking is a disease that's infiltrated many educational institutions. But when a school doesn't have qualified teachers and refuses to follow government curriculum and standards, it's not surprising if the quality of education suffers. Of course, this raises the question of whether the interests of children are given adequate weight when their parents decide on a religiously based school. While the rights of children are seldom mentioned within the context of a debate about religious schools, they're absolutely crucial to it.

9

RULES AND RIGHTS

Withhold not correction from the child: for if thou beatest him with the rod, he shall not die. Thou shalt beat him with the rod, and shalt deliver his soul from hell.

Proverbs 23:13–14

Your children are not your children.
They are the sons and daughters of Life's longing for itself.
They come through you but not from you,
And though they are with you yet they belong not to you.
You may give them your love but not your thoughts,
For they have their own thoughts.
. . . You may strive to be like them, but seek not to make them
*   like you.*
For life goes not backward nor tarries with yesterday.

Kahlil Gibran, The Prophet

The adult drags a whimpering first-grader across the room. She's been disruptive – talking – and must be punished. The little girl is flung into a chair. Immediately, the whimpers erupt into huge, volcanic sobs. "Do you want me to hurt you?" yells the woman towering above her. "No," cries the child, frantically attempting to avoid eye contact with her captor. "Well, I don't want to hurt you, either," booms the adult. "But I will if you don't obey." She then sits down beside the child and describes the pain she'll inflict if her orders aren't followed: three wallops. Unless, that is, there is no more talking. No more fidgeting. No more blatant disobedience. After the short sermon, the child's chest stops heaving and she murmurs assent to the rules. Today, for the moment, at least, she has avoided the strap. Now, only one more hurdle to jump. The adult closes her eyes and starts to pray – out loud – that God will forgive this little sinner.

This exchange might smack of a rigidity and authoritarianism associated with another, older era, but I witnessed it at an independent, partially publicly funded Christian school in Alberta in 1995. It was a devastating display of adult power; the child was humiliated, threatened, and emotionally blackmailed. In modern terms, her rights were flagrantly violated. But that's not the way her parents, church members, and schoolteachers see things. They believe that the threat of corporal punishment (a biblical injunction) and the power of prayer are fundamental tools of education. And they also believe, along with most of their counterparts in the public system, that parents have the right to educate their children according to a philosophy that reflects their values, their beliefs.

They're supported in this by the United Nations' Universal Declaration of Human Rights, to which Canada is a signatory. It states: "Parents have a prior right to choose the kind of education that shall be given to their children." And the International Covenant on Economic, Social and Cultural Rights, adopted by the UN in 1966 and signed by Canada in 1976, reads: "Parties to the present covenant undertake to have respect for the liberty of parents to choose for their children schools, other than those established by the public authorities, which conform to such minimum educational standards as may be laid down or approved by the State and to ensure the religious and moral education of their children in conformity with their own convictions." Not only has the Supreme Court of Canada repeatedly supported this position, but every government in Canada recognizes the right of parents to choose a system of education that teaches their specific religious values (within the limits of standards set by the State).

Yet provincial governments do restrict parental rights, largely through controlling the purse-strings. Parental choice is severely curtailed when parents have to pay their own, after-tax dollars to send their children to independent religious schools. And so the debate rages: Whose rights take precedence? The rights of the parents or the rights of the State? What seems to get lost in all of this are the children − faceless, nameless, and voiceless − totally devoid, it seems, of any rights whatsoever. The parents of children at independent religious schools maintain that they know what's best for their children, that their children need to be brought up in an environment in which they can become adherents of their faith. The State also says it knows what's best for its citizens, that children of all religious and cultural groups need to be educated together under the highest standards of government-approved education.

What I saw isn't against the law. Corporal punishment is legal in Alberta schools. While the school may have the right to administer discipline in this manner, the way in which that child was being treated went far beyond the bounds of physical intimidation. She was also psychologically manipulated and intimidated. This was so blatant, so outrageous, that I began to wonder what rights children actually have in our society. After all, we pride ourselves on being a society that upholds the right of children to food, clothing, and shelter. We also support through our taxes the right of children to free education and medical care. And we now, tentatively and slowly, are upholding their right not to be sexually abused or physically abused. Nevertheless, we remain equivocal about corporal punishment. Witness the debates that sporadically flare up around the issue, and the fact that it's still permissible in many public schools.

But do children have the right to be treated with respect, with dignity, as human beings with an evolving ability to think and reason for themselves? This is a question unheard of until fairly recently. After all, the right of adults to abuse children physically has only been challenged in our society in living memory. When adults take as their guide a holy book which actually advocates hitting children *for their own good*, then those people who defend the right of children not to be physically abused can be considered heretics. An increasingly secular society, however, has made it possible to question belief systems that support and condone corporal punishment and other forms of physical abuse – ritual genital mutilation, for example. And the growth of the field of psychology has fostered the documentation of the lives of people who commit violent offences. Invariably, it seems, they were abused as children themselves. It's hard to ignore the suggestion that people who were abused as children – physically and psychologically – grow up to be damaged adults who often re-enact their childhood abuse with others.

But questioning an adult's right to abuse children psychologically seems light years away. In fact, it may well be an impossibility. Unlike physical abuse, how should it be defined? Are there features to identify it or would ten or twenty years have to pass before its effects were expressed? How could psychological abuse possibly be monitored? And how could rules prohibiting it ever be enforced? Adrian Guldemond, executive director of the Ontario Alliance of Christian Schools, thinks we'd be creating a nightmare if we tried to eliminate the extremes. "You can't write laws to prevent things like the Alberta situation from occurring," he says. "It's just like you can't set road regulations in order to prevent accidents. You could, but basically you wouldn't be driving any more. I know there are extreme examples. You've described one. And I don't have an answer to the extreme cases. But my general rule of thumb is that extreme cases make bad law."

Guldemond's organization belongs to Christian Schools International, which has 30,000 students enrolled in 120 schools across Canada. The Ontario Alliance has 74 schools with 12,000 students. He fiercely defends the right of parents to decide what's best for their children. But he also accepts that children have rights. What he'd like is that those rights be defined. And that, of course, is the best way to limit, if not prevent, both the psychological and physical abuse of children.

The rights of children *have* been defined, although they aren't a tidy little set of rules easy to post on school bulletin boards. In 1989, the United Nations adopted the Convention on the Rights of the Child. Canada signed it in 1990, and ratified it two years later. In twenty-eight pages, it outlines fifty-three articles applicable to children under the age of eighteen. It upholds the child's right to freedom of expression, "to seek, receive and impart information and ideas of all kinds . . ." But it then says, "State parties shall respect the rights and duties of the parents . . . to provide direction to the child in the exercise of his or her right [to freedom of thought, conscience, and religion] in a manner consistent with the evolving capacities of the child." In other words, it recognizes parents' rights to nurture and direct children. But it doesn't give blanket approval to them to do with their children as they wish. In fact, it specifically refers to children's *evolving* capacities. I take that to mean there's a recognition that children should gradually be given the opportunities to think and reason and challenge and to use their critical faculties. Presumably, it also means it's possible, and desirable, to draw a line between a parent's right to act in the interests of a child as a guardian, and a parent's right to control the child. Creating an authoritarian environment, threatening punishment for not behaving and believing in a certain prescribed way goes far beyond the role of nurturing guardian. It also contravenes the spirit of the UN convention.

I should make it clear that it's a rare independent religious school that abuses children in the way I describe above. (And I hope the Alberta school doesn't subject children to this kind of treatment on a routine basis; I visited it on three other occasions and never saw anything similar.) Besides, it would be naïve to think that public schools don't also resort to psychologically manipulating and intimidating children. But religious schools pose a particular problem regarding the rights of children because of their insistence on prescribing a particular world-view. They argue, of course, that secular schools present a world-view as well (of individualism, humanism, materialism, and so on), but there is, nonetheless, an important difference. And that is that religious schools have only one perspective underlying all they teach; that's why they exist. Public schools, on the other hand, offer a mix of world-views, through ethnic, cultural, and religious diversity within both the student and teacher mix. This is not to deny that teachers within the public system often teach their "truth" as the only truth. Yet this is an individual failing and not one endemic to the system as a whole. The degree of diversity in the public system obviously varies according to the neighbourhood, but at least the openness to, the possibility of, a diversity of world-views exists. Religious schools, on the other hand, are religiously homogenous. If you go to a Christian school or a Jewish school or a Sikh school, you're going to find yourself surrounded by other Christians, Jews, or Sikhs – both as students and, depending on the school, largely as teachers.

Guldemond defends the need for homogeneity on the grounds that schools belonging to the alliance believe in "the cultural mandate." By that, he means they believe Christians have an obligation to improve the world in which they live. To do so, however, a training period is required. "And part of that training period," he says, "is to learn what you believe and the kind of world-view that you work with in culture. If a person isn't prepared properly through education, you don't get any significant cultural activity from them when they graduate." This view, he says, came out of the experience of members of the Christian Reform Church in the Second World War. "There was a big debate in Holland in the thirties," he says. "The pacifist group said, 'Hitler is just another fanatic; he'll go away.' And the other group said, 'No, we've got to arm the country because it [fascism] is coming.' When Christian Reformers immigrated to Canada, that debate was fresh in their minds. We're stuck with a dilemma," adds Guldemond. "If we want to do something distinctive, based on a certain number of scriptural principles, and if the general culture isn't doing that, what choice do we have? It's not a happy withdrawal. It's saying, 'We don't really have a choice here.' We know what the result is if we stick our children in public schools. The large majority leave the faith, judging from the statistics."

But if a "training period," as Guldemond puts it, is required, then presumably it's only meaningful if young people are encouraged to truly search to discover what they themselves believe. This can't happen unless choice, real choice – including the choice to disbelieve – exists. If it does, then what Guldemond is describing seems an admirable objective. But it's hard not to conclude that what he's really talking about is indoctrination. And, surely, holding the continuity of the faith as an education objective isn't a legitimate social goal worthy of public support.

Besides, Charles Ungerleider maintains that independent religious schools are no guarantee that young people will remain in the faith. He points to Catholic schools as a case in point. "The Catholic school system works as a school system," says the associate dean in the Faculty of Education at the University of British Columbia. "It doesn't work in terms of ensuring that the young grow up to be practising Catholics."

A firm believer in children's rights, Ungerleider argues that a basic right of children is the right to an education that expands their horizons. "If we have a system of schooling that simply replicates religious or family values, then that system of education has failed the young," he says. He believes that good education should encourage students to examine their experience and to make judgments about it based on logic and evidence. Because beliefs aren't subjected to that same standard of proof – and never can be – he argues against religious doctrine in education. He recalls a bumper sticker he once saw that summed up the opposite perspective: "God said it. I believe it. That settles it." "I think that's the view held by most strong adherents of including religious dogma in schools," he says. "But educating children in a manner compatible with family values is fundamentally miseducative, because what we're trying to do [in public education] is to get children to examine their values. Values are not simply a matter of beliefs – either you accept them, or you don't. Some are more defensible than others."

These are obviously highly contentious statements, but they'd probably be supported by Alice Miller. She's a Swiss therapist who's written extensively on child-rearing. In her book *For Your Own Good: Hidden Cruelty in Child-Rearing and the Roots of Violence*, she outlines what she calls "poisonous pedagogy." This is the method, she says, which is used to impart false information and beliefs to children from generation to generation. These beliefs, she maintains, are not only unproven but are demonstrably false. Although she cites seventeen aspects in all, here are the ten most applicable to this discussion. Poisonous pedagogy teaches that:

1. A feeling of duty produces love;
2. Hatred can be done away with by forbidding it;
3. Parents deserve respect simply because they're parents;
4. Children are undeserving of respect simply because they're children;

5. Obedience makes a child strong;
6. A high degree of self-esteem is harmful;
7. A low degree of self-esteem makes a person altruistic;
8. The way you behave is more important than the way you really are;
9. Neither parents nor God would survive being offended;
10. Parents are always right.

Miller isn't arguing that children be left to their own devices. In fact, she maintains that they need a lot of emotional and physical support from adults. But she doesn't think that that support should rely on manipulation and intimidation. Instead, she thinks it should revolve around respect for the child and tolerance of his or her feelings. "We need to hear what the child has to say in order to give our understanding, support, and love," she writes. "The child, on the other hand, needs free space if he or she is to find adequate self-expression. There is no discrepancy here between means and ends, but rather a dialectical process involving dialogue. Learning is a result of listening, which in turn leads to an even better listening and attentiveness to the other person. In other words, to learn from the child, we must have empathy, and empathy grows as we learn. It is a different matter for parents or educators who would like the child to be a certain way or think they must expect him to be that way. To reach their sacred ends, they try to mold the child in their image, suppressing self-expression in the child and at the same time missing out on an opportunity to learn something." Miller's views are implicitly critical of not only schools whose objective is the perpetuation of religious faith. Much of what takes place in public schools and in the home would also fail to meet her standard.

Detractors of Miller and Ungerleider could argue that what they're proposing is simply their value system and that they have no right to prescribe it to others. But there is a fundamental issue here, and it comes down, once again, to whether or not one accepts the premise that children have rights, and, if so, the extent of those rights. Do they have the right to be exposed, through education, to a world outside their own?

Manjit Singh not only believes they have that right, but he believes it's one that should be exercised. The Montreal activist speaks specifically in terms of the experience of the Sikh community, his community, many members of which are new to Canada. He points out that eventually their children will have to join the mainstream to survive economically. And like it or not, he says, the mainstream is dominated by what he calls "old-stock Canadians."

Singh tries to get his point across by appealing to the experience of his peers. He tries to get them to remember the kinds of barriers they experienced in dealing with these "old-stock Canadians" as adult immigrants. "The dominant factor that comes into play is the strangeness or unfamiliarity with each other's ways," he says. "Second- or third-generation children of immigrants don't have this particular experience of strangeness and unfamiliarity in their societal dealings. By sheltering our children in our own schools, we'll be ghettoizing them. So, when they come out of them, they'll be strangers to the mainstream children. Consequently, our children will have to relive the experiences of our lives as new immigrants. One generation later, we would be no further advanced in becoming better accepted and integrated into the Canadian mainstream society." He thinks children have the right to benefit from the experience of previous generations.

And what do young people have to say? It's their lives that are at stake, after all, but because parental rights predominate, few are asked what kind of education they want to receive. I'm not suggesting, of course, that six-year-old children be sat down and asked what kind of education they want. That would be patently absurd. But even a six-year-old can speak to her needs. What she has to say may be unsophisticated, but a parent attuned to listen can, and should, take such expression into account when deciding what's in the best interests of that child. This kind of interchange can start early and should develop throughout the life of a child. As children's capacities grow to express themselves, and to analyse their situations, they'll be in a better position to influence decisions being made about their lives. Parents obviously need to make decisions based on their knowledge of their child's needs and, of course, their education values will be a factor in the ultimate decision. But, as the United Nations convention states, children's capacities evolve; they not only grow up wanting to think things through for themselves, but they need to if they're to take their places as independent, contributing members of our society.

Both schools and parents have a tendency to misjudge the capacity of children to make decisions for themselves. In some cases, they do so wilfully. Take, for example, the following story a young Ontario Catholic told me. Her school, like most Catholic schools, requires students to wear a uniform, but on occasion they're allowed to wear "civvies." They pay a dollar for the privilege, and the money is then donated to a charity. The school's teachers made the decision that the money collected in a February 1997, dress-down day would go to an anti-abortion group. Although opposition to abortion is one of the primary things taught at the school, some of the students don't, in good conscience, hold that belief. So they found themselves caught between a rock and a hard place. If they paid their dollar to dress down, they were contributing to a cause they were philosophically opposed to. If they didn't pay – and this is what happened – they stuck out like sore thumbs and were harassed by teachers for taking an "immoral" stand. Clearly, the denial of rights and responsibility implicit in this case is wholly inappropriate to the highly evolved capacity of most teenagers to make such choices for themselves.

When I met with students at religious schools, all but one school had a teacher or principal sit in on the discussions. In some schools,

I wasn't allowed any access to students. If there were two themes that predominated in discussions that did take place, however, they were these: young people are genuinely interested in learning about people who hold beliefs very different from themselves, and they recognize when fear is being used as an educational tool. They also resent it. Oh, and they repeatedly mentioned how important friendship is to them. Many said that's why they didn't leave their religious school in their teen years and switch to a public school. While they couldn't accept all the things they were told to believe, they couldn't bear to leave their friends behind.

The concept of "rights" didn't seem to have occurred to them. Yet it seems to me they have a legitimate right to an education that exposes them to different viewpoints and religious perspectives and that doesn't rely on fear to meet the objectives of a religious or cultural group. They also, surely, have a right to that kind of education without having to sacrifice friendships to obtain it. The State, then, has an important role to play, by guaranteeing the kind of education environment that is both responsive to the needs of the community and meets high academic standards. And the State should certainly play a role in ensuring that the rights of students are acknowledged and protected. What this means is that parents don't have the ultimate authority over their children; there is a need for the State to act in the interests of children.

This position is shared by Will Kymlicka. The philosophy professor, who holds positions at both the University of Ottawa and Carleton University, is the author of several books about multiculturalism. He says he doesn't think parents have a right "to educate their children in such a way that they are unable to critically reflect on the value of the way of life that's been handed down to them." But he looks at the issue from the perspective of sustaining a liberal democracy. To him, the right that many religious parents claim they have — to educate their children in the insular world of their particular religious doctrine – is neither morally defensible nor should it be upheld by the State.

He's on very shaky ground. One of the things that's always bothered me in this issue is the question of "Who gets to decide?" Why do detractors of independent religious schools inevitably begin with the assumption that the State necessarily knows best? Kymlicka says it isn't a question of the State playing God. Instead, it's the survival of liberal democracy that's at stake. "A liberal democracy is grounded on notions of moral equality of persons," says Kymlicka. "And there are obvious cases of violations of that – slavery being one. We can work through a series of injustices that liberal democracy has to fight – racism and sexism and aristocratic privileges, for example. But the State has to decide. If we accept that the State ought to be premised on the assumption that all human beings matter equally, then it follows that we can't view children as the property of their parents. They have an independent, moral existence, and they matter, from the point of view of the State, equally with their parents. It follows from that that parental rights over their children must always be constrained by, and limited by, respect for the interests of the child as an independent moral being."

Kymlicka has no problem accepting that it's in the best interests of children to be raised in intimate family settings. But the State has a role to play, he says, in setting limits and constraints – a kind of "trust-responsibility" relationship, as he puts it. "The State recognizes the rights and powers of parents over children within these limits," he says. "And the State has the responsibility to monitor those boundaries and to step in when they're being transgressed. Whether it's through physical abuse or through failing to educate their children at all, or if they put them in some kind of separate schooling, to establish a common curriculum which insures that their children will be capable of making an informed judgment for themselves about whether the way of life they've inherited is worthy of their allegiance. Or, whether it's, instead, just false in terms of its underlying theology, or whether it's demeaning, or too confining, or too restrictive, or whatever. So it's not that the State knows best about what ways of life are good or bad. It's just that it has a responsibility to protect the interests of the children which, in turn, limits the rights of parents."

If we accept public funding of religiously defined schools, then the State must accept its responsibility to ensure that the rights of children are observed. This must extend to the toleration of dissent. Beyond that, even religiously based schools outside the public system should be required to meet this standard as a matter of public policy. These aren't arguments against religious schools, but they do suggest that, if we are to accept the principle of religiously defined schools, then they will have to comply with certain minimum standards as defined both by our Constitution and by our international obligations. All schools, religious or otherwise, should do no less.

Children aren't the only ones whose rights are thrown into question by religious schools. Some teachers at religious schools have been shocked to discover they don't have the same human-rights protection as their public-school counterparts. Unlike public-school teachers, they can be fired for falling in love with someone of a different religion, or because they discover they're gay, or because their marriages end in divorce, or because they change religious denomination. "The idea of dismissing teachers because they have made personal choices of a life partner or religion is offensive to many people," says John Staple, director of Teacher Welfare for the Newfoundland and Labrador Teachers' Association. "It's even more surprising to them that the Canadian legal system permits an employer to take such action."

It all stems from the constitutional deal that Canada made with the provinces when they agreed to enter into Confederation. Section 93

of the 1867 Constitution Act (BNA Act), as described earlier, pro-
tects the rights and privileges of denominations as they were at the
time of each province's union into the new entity called Canada.
"This constitutional provision recognizes the need to protect
religious minorities from the political strength of the majority,"
says Staple. "It also recognizes that the guarantee of religious freedom without some exercise of State support for religious education won't adequately protect these minority groups. Section 93,
therefore, constitutes a fundamental part of the Confederation
'bargain.' The architects of Confederation sought to avoid strife
between groups within the country by protecting rights to group
identity, even at the expense of individual rights."

So that's why Catholics in Ontario, Quebec, Saskatchewan,
Alberta, and Newfoundland get not only publicly funded schools,
but their group rights take precedence over the individual rights
of teachers. "Even though human-rights legislation can be powerful," says Jim Davies, counsel for the Edmonton Public School
Board, "it can't overrule federal constitutional legislation. This
means that, if certain rights of denominational schools were constitutionally preserved, then there is no infringement of human-
rights legislation."

In 1988, for example, a teacher named Richard Walsh was fired
by the Roman Catholic board in St. John's because he married
outside the Catholic faith and joined a Protestant denomination,
the Salvation Army. He grieved his dismissal, lost, and took his
case to court. His lawyer argued that Walsh had been denied the
fundamental freedoms of conscience and religion as guaranteed
under the Charter. The school board argued that it was simply
enforcing an employer's rule prohibiting its teachers from changing faith. The judge, however, accepted that the school board had
the right to require that its teachers remain Catholic. Walsh
appealed, but the Newfoundland Supreme Court of Appeal upheld
the earlier decision.

Staple says it's important to note that Walsh's teaching ability was never in question. At his arbitration hearing, school-board officials praised his abilities. In fact, he'd been teaching satisfactorily as a lapsed Catholic for some time before the board discovered his circumstances and dismissed him. "It would seem that the action was taken because Mr. Walsh's continued employment was perceived as a threat to the Church, since it was made clear in the evidence it was no threat to the school," says Staple. "Mr. Walsh was performing the requirements of his position more than adequately, and one has to question where the protection of his rights is centred, and whether the courts are placing too little emphasis on the rights of individuals in these matters."

One can see a parallel here to the issue of whether children in religious schools should have the right to question the sponsor's dogma. In denying that right, what defensible social interest is served? Or is that interest, as Staple suggests, only serving the maintenance of institutional power?

When Paul Dal Monte was fired from a Catholic school in 1995, he too discovered he had no individual rights protection. However, he never changed his Catholic faith. Nor did he lose his Catholic faith. But he did fall in love with a divorced woman. In 1986, the physical-education instructor started teaching at Vancouver College, a private Catholic high school. When he joined the school, he signed a contract agreeing to live in accordance with Catholic beliefs about moral behaviour. He didn't have a doubt in the world that he would be able to live up to them. So, in 1992, when he realized he'd fallen in love with a divorced woman, he did everything he could to meet the standards of the Catholic board. He went to school officials and told them about the relationship. He says he was told, "That's fine, but get the marriage annulled by Rome." The couple immediately started that process.

Two years later, there'd been no response from Rome, but by that time the couple was expecting a child. Again, he says, he went to school officials; the response was virtually the same. "We had a child together, but we weren't allowed to live together, because that's against Catholic rules and regulations," explains the former football coach. "But our son was approaching two years of age, and there I was, still living separately. In order for me to keep my job, that was part of the bargain. We finally just wanted to get on with normal life. June wasn't allowed to bring our son to any football games or any other school function, because it would give the perception that we were a family when, in the eyes of the Church, we weren't."

Dal Monte consulted two priests in the Vancouver archdiocese. They responded in writing, advising him to get married in a civil ceremony and then let the annulment process with Rome take its course. When he followed their advice, he was fired. "The school board said I violated the terms of the contract, and they were obligated to uphold the rules and regulations of the Catholic Church," Dal Monte explains. "I'm not arguing – I know what the rules are, even though I had been given different advice from priests. But if I was a non-Catholic in that school and got a divorce or married a divorced woman, I'd still be teaching there today."

And so, once again, the religious rights of the Catholic School Board took precedence over Dal Monte's human rights. But he taught in a province that isn't constitutionally bound to protect the religious rights of Catholics. So why was he fired? Well, in 1980, the Catholic Schools of Vancouver Archdiocese refused to continue to employ a teacher because, like Dal Monte, she married a divorcé in a civil ceremony. She sued and lost. So she turned to the Supreme Court of Canada. It found that the special nature of the Catholic school, and the unique role of its teachers, justify religious conformity as a "bona fide occupational qualification." Since then, various arbitration rulings under collective agreements have relied on the Supreme Court decision to rule in favour of religious school boards terminating teachers' contracts.

★

Still, it's understandable why religious schools want to have teachers who share their faith. They want them as role models for students, to set an example of someone living the faith. They argue that one of the salient features of religious schools is the "ambience," or tone, that permeates their schools. That what's important is that what they do (religiously) is done every day and in every way. In hearing about Dal Monte's situation, Bernard Shapiro, head of Ontario's 1984 Royal Commission into Private Schools, says, "Of course he has a right to marry a divorcée. That's not the issue. Instead, it's 'How does a teacher stand in relation to the young people that he or she is charged with?' He is some sort of leader. And once you are inside a religious school system, that really does limit the options you've got. So I see it as perfectly consistent: The guy was fired. I may not like the system but, if you're going to have the system, you have no right not to allow it to be its best self. If you don't like that consequence, it's the system that's going to have to change, not how it behaves towards a particular teacher."

Interestingly, not all religious schools make religious affiliation the primary qualification of the teachers they hire. Many Jewish, Sikh, and some Catholic schools hire people who don't share their religious faith. The schools maintain that they're looking for good teachers, period. They say that what's important is that the people who teach their religion, their culture, their history, and their language share their faith. For teachers of math, French, geography, and so on, they don't make religion a requirement. In fact, many Sikh schools in British Columbia make a point of hiring a Christian as a vice-principal. They argue that they live in a predominantly Christian country, and that this is one way for them to gain greater understanding of the beliefs and ways of Christians.

On the issue of competing rights, Alan Borovoy, general counsel for the Canadian Civil Liberties Association, says, "I can't argue with the proposition that an institution committed to a religious or cultural ideology has a right to promote its values and to prefer people of their own faith over others. Where the problem arises is if those institutions are receiving public subsidies and then want to engage in discriminatory practices, that's where the rub comes in."

Grant Tadman figures he's been particularly discriminated against under the Catholic school system. He's one of the approximately 250 public-school teachers who became "refugees" when Ontario extended public funding to Catholic high schools in 1985. They were mainly specialty teachers – home economics, physical education – who had to be let go, because the schools suddenly had fewer students attending them. Tadman, for example, had been teaching physical education for eleven years in the public system, but his school reduced the number of physical-education teachers from seven full-time to two. Under the provisions of Bill 30 – the legislation that extended full funding to the separate board – public-school teachers were supposed to be guaranteed comparable jobs in the Catholic system, or else be retrained. Tadman admits he could have refused to move to the separate system on the grounds of conscience, but he didn't. "How could I object to a system I had no knowledge of?" he asks. "I'm a member of the United Church and married a United Church minister's daughter. I was taught to be open to others. I had no reason to feel a sense of prejudice. I knew nothing about the separate board, although I did fall for the myth that uniforms made Catholic students better disciplined. I went into the system expecting equity, fairness, and the guarantee of my rights as a Bill 30 teacher."

When Tadman showed up at the separate-school board office on the first day of school in 1986, he says, "we were treated like cattle and told we'd get a paycheque, but they didn't know what to do with us. So we all went home to await instructions." When he finally got a placement the following year, it was as a teaching assistant. "I submitted my name for a short list of potential heads of physical-education departments, but was told my application was refused because I had no experience in their system," says Tadman. "I asked, 'How does it differ? I thought it was all education.'" Later assignments included supply teaching, assisting the attendance secretary, supervising lunch hours, filing, and acting as receptionist. He says he was subjected to slurs and harassment from students and staff because he doesn't share their faith. "I was denied teaching positions because I'm not a Catholic. I was flushed down the toilet," says Tadman. When he contacted his union, the Ontario English Catholic Teachers' Association, he was told nothing could be done because he was, after all, being paid. "But here I am eleven years later, still fighting because of the injustice of it all." Tadman has tried to get redress through the Human Rights Commission, the courts, and, most recently, arbitration. He says his experience points to the need for a unified, confederated school board – as called for by the Ontario Secondary School Teachers' Federation. He figures such a system would provide for the humane placement of teachers between the public and Catholic systems "so that people like me can avoid similar abusive treatment in the future."

Eli Maccabi is another Bill 30 "refugee." In 1986, he was transferred from the North York Board of Education to St. Michael's Choir School, sometimes called the "Bishop's school" because of its historical and geographical proximity to the local cathedral. According to Phillip Little, who investigated Maccabi's grievance, the beginning of an anti-Semitic campaign against him goes back to 1987, starting with an anonymous letter. It complained about a Jew teaching under a Catholic board, while it is a "historical fact that Our Lord was crucified by Jews." Maccabi was also threatened by the godfather of one of the students. Because he taught the ancient and contemporary sections of the history curriculum, concerns were raised about his teaching "faith history." The board also questioned his observance of Jewish holy days.

In 1993, Maccabi told the board he felt it should be protecting him from racial and religious harassment. When it didn't, he filed two separate grievances. On March 29, 1994, he got a response to his grievances, though not in a form he expected. A large swastika was painted on the school, with the words "No Jews." The board's response was to offer Maccabi a transfer. He refused on the grounds that action should be taken to stop the racism. In his forty-two-page report summarizing Maccabi's case, Little concludes that there were "strong anti-Semitic overtones coming from both the board and the union." His report is thoroughly documented and overwhelmingly sad. Little, himself a Catholic, paints a picture in which his Catholic teachers' union couldn't bring itself to defend a Jew. Maccabi has taken his case to the Ontario Human Rights Commission.

The above stories might make teachers at independent schools feel grateful that at least they don't operate under a pretence of having human rights. They know when they're hired that there's no union to protect them, no organization through which they can seek redress if they feel they've been unfairly dismissed. Independent religious schools can refuse to hire, or refuse to continue to have on staff, homosexuals or people who are divorced or people who switch religions, knowing that they are firmly within their rights to do so. But it's clear that government-supported religious schools can also violate what many Canadians consider fundamental human rights.

This raises a host of questions. If religious institutions are allowed to set their own rules, then where should the line be drawn in terms of what's permissible? Does it extend to the denial of the rights of women? To ritual suicide? And if not, then how do you draw the line between the right not to be discriminated against on the grounds of marital status from the right not to be administered a lethal dose of Kool-Aid by your parents?

The latter may sound absurd, but the point is that these differences are merely ones of degree. If an institution is allowed to discriminate against someone because of a religious belief, then in what other ways could it use "religious belief" to violate a person's rights? Surely rights are rights. Why should the law not apply equally to all institutions? As Bill McKim, psychology professor from Memorial University, notes, "It seems the ultimate irony that, in order to set a moral example to children, schools need to be excused from the constraint of basic human rights."

10

HOLIDAYS AND HOLY DAYS

Here where I am living in the western Pennsylvania hills, they want to hear nothing of Christmas. Their children grow up knowing nothing of brightly lit Christmas trees, nor Christmas presents. God have mercy on these Presbyterians, these pagans.

Rev. Henry Harbaugh, a Reformed Church pastor, 1867

As Philip Roth reminds us in "Operation Shylock," Irving Berlin revenged world Jewry upon Christendom by composing "Easter Parade" and "White Christmas," converting the two most sacred days on the Christian calendar into, respectively, a fashion show and a holiday about snow.

Tom Flynn, *The Trouble with Christmas*

A number of Christmases ago, we went to the "Festival of Lights" concert at our children's elementary school in Toronto. It was a wonderful display of the songs, dances, and stories of the various cultural and religious groups attending that public school. Hanukkah, the Jewish Feast of Lights, which symbolizes the victory of the spirit of Judaism, was celebrated. Tribute was also paid to the Hindu festival Diwali. We learned that this

Festival of Lights is a time to remember that evil must be overcome by goodness, just as darkness is overcome by light. The children also described and celebrated the traditions and religious beliefs of native Indians, Africans, and Sikhs.

But when it came time to pay tribute to people of the Christian faith, there was a purely perfunctory nod. It was the shortest item in the concert and consisted of a reading from Dylan Thomas's *A Child's Christmas in Wales*. That was all. I found myself overwhelmed by a mix of emotions. The multicultural, multi-faith nature of the event was thrilling, and the genuine exchange between the children was moving. But I was dismayed that the same standards weren't applied across the board, that there was no attempt made to describe through music, drama, or verse why Christians celebrate Christmas. It seemed that in this school's well-meaning effort not to offend non-Christians by referring to the birth of a child, let alone mentioning the name "Jesus Christ," a disservice was committed.

Through the years, I've discussed this event with a wide variety of people. Their responses have been revealing. Christians have often been reluctant to voice an opinion. Fighting to have their holy day acknowledged religiously in the public arena, they said, would probably be misinterpreted. They'd be labelled as promoting Christianity, even pushing Christianity onto non-believers. It was clear, however, they felt badly about both the omission of Jesus' birth at such events, and about their own seeming impotence to do anything about it. Many members of minority religions say they feel sorry for observant Christians in Canada. They say efforts on the part of politicians to ban Christmas in their legislatures and government offices, and on the part of school officials to ignore the religious reason for Christmas, debase the event. They say Canadians seem determined to deprive Christians of a public acknowledgement of their holy day and, as people of faith, they become concerned when any holy day is trivialized. Many secular friends, on the other hand, argue that the school did the right thing, that the Christian majority has no right to make everyone acknowledge the birth of a Messiah they don't accept. They also say that non-Christians are unfairly overexposed to Christmas, and the least we can do is keep it out of the school system. But we're all overexposed to Christmas – at least to a secular, commercialized Christmas. *That* Christmas is in our collective faces a good six weeks before the actual day. Little wonder that most of us are fed up with the very word by the time December twenty-fifth rolls around.

Bernard Shapiro, principal of McGill University and former head of Ontario's 1984 Royal Commission into Private Schools, simply shakes his head when I describe the school event to him. Then he calls it "criminal. You can't understand the history of this country or the culture of Western civilization if you don't understand Christianity. It's absolutely criminal to bring anyone up in this culture who doesn't understand what Christianity is and what it stood for. To not have people understand what Christmas is – which is not Santa Claus, it's Christ – is to be wilfully ignorant. And schools have no business being wilfully ignorant." He argues that, ultimately, "You can't pretend that 30 per cent of the people are the same as 2 per cent. Public policy isn't going to represent those people as if they were all the same. The notion of growing up in a Western country and not understanding something about Christianity is crazy. It just condemns you to not understanding the environment in which you live, and why it is the way it is, and what it might be in the future. You don't have to be a believing person to understand that. You just have to be a sensible person."

For a variety of reasons, Christmas presents a particular challenge for public schools. The Europeans who took over this country based its institutions on Judeo-Christian values. However, some lessons have ostensibly been learned from the attempt to assimilate native peoples, among others. Today Canada claims to uphold the objective of not imposing the majority's religious values on its minorities. This, combined with the overwhelming commercial nature of Christmas today, makes Christmas a problem for schools. Should it be observed as a holy day (referring to the birth of Jesus Christ) or merely as a secular day ("Santa Claus is coming to town")? How can schools claim to be inclusive if they ignore the religious aspect of Christmas? And how should they acknowledge the holy days of other religions: within classroom curricula and through school-wide festivals? Should they also close for the holy days of other major religions, the way that schools close for Christmas and Easter? These are controversial questions, but then Christmas has been controversial for a long time – and not least among Christians.

Christmas, as a religious event, has a rocky past. Early Christians didn't observe their Messiah's birth. But while it might not have seemed spiritually important to observe it, it did become politically important to do so. From the year 380, the Church of Rome was the only legal religion in the Roman Empire. Making a law was one thing; winning the hearts and minds of people was quite another. So the Church of Rome introduced Christmas in the fourth century as a way of coping with its religious competition. December twenty-fifth was a pagan feast to the Unconquered Sun God, and by creating a Christian event on that day the Church hoped to provide alternative rites for its followers. Besides, the birth of a Messiah at the time of the winter solstice was full of poetic symbolism. By 438, Christmas was declared a legal holiday throughout the Roman Empire. Eventually, an entire religious season, with liturgies and complex ceremonies, developed around Christmas. Even so, belief in the old religions remained, and so the Church became more innovative in its efforts to convert. Co-opting pagan rites – decorating homes and trees, adopting plants sacred to Druids (mistletoe), or associated with gods (Ivy, the Roman god of wine) and feasting – were by far the most effective.

Clement Miles, in his 1912 book *Christmas in Ritual and Tradition, Christian and Pagan*, wrote:

> The struggle between the ascetic principle of self-mortification, world-renunciation, absorption in a transcendent ideal, and the natural human striving towards earthly joy and well-being is, perhaps, the most interesting aspect of the history of Christianity; it is certainly shown in an absorbingly interesting way in the development of the Christian feast of the Nativity. The conflict is keen at first; the Church authorities fight tooth and nail against these relics of heathenism, these devilish rites; but mankind's instinctive paganism is insuppressible, the practices continue as ritual, though losing much of their meaning, and the Church, weary of denouncing, comes to wink at them, while the pagan joy in earthly life begins to colour her own festival.

The Reformation marked a major turning point in the history of Christianity. Those who protested against the power and authority of the Roman Catholic Church (*Protest*ants) questioned its interpretation of Christianity. A quest to return to a religious life based solely on New Testament documents put the observance of Christmas and other holy days in question. But Protestants weren't united in their condemnation of Christmas; Lutherans and members of the new Church of England appreciated its religious significance and continued to celebrate it as a major holy day. This led to a schism, with little tolerance on either side of the debate. In 1632, for example, a Puritan lawyer named William Prynne published *Histriomastix*, a condemnation of Christmas. He did not get off lightly. He was committed to the Tower of London, prosecuted in the infamous Star Chamber, fined five thousand pounds (payable directly to the King), and expelled from both Oxford University and the legal profession. If that weren't enough, he was forced to stand in the pillory, and his book was burned. When Oliver Cromwell and his Puritan Roundheads won the English Civil War, the balance of power shifted. They wanted to ban Christmas because of its "Popish" origins. (In fact, Scottish Presbyterians had suppressed Christmas long before – in 1583. In 1618, however, James I of England forced the Scots to retract.)

By 1647, the Puritans refused to allow the English to celebrate Christmas as either a religious or a secular holiday. This didn't go down well. There were protests and acts of violence which upset Parliament – but not enough that it modified the ban. In 1652, it ruled that "the 25th of December should not be solemnized in churches or observed in any other way, that town criers should each year remind the people that Christmas Day and other superstitious festivals should not be kept and the markets and shops should stay open." Anyone who tried to worship publicly on Christmas Day risked being imprisoned or exiled. Christmas was officially restored, however, with the monarchy under Charles II in 1660 (although Christmas wasn't largely observed in Presbyterian Scotland until after the Second World War).

The conflict over Christmas moved to North America. In many parts of the United States, celebrating Christmas wasn't socially acceptable until the late 1880s. Today, of the world's 200 countries, 151 observe December twenty-fifth as a legal holiday. They include Muslim countries like Bangladesh, Indonesia, Jordan, Pakistan, Sudan, and Syria, as well as religiously mixed countries like India, Brunei, Malaysia, and Sri Lanka. Countries that don't acknowledge December twenty-fifth as a legal holiday include communist China and Cuba, the Jewish state of Israel, and Japan, a country whose culture has been shaped largely by Buddhism and Shintoism.

What does all of this prove? That Christmas has pagan origins, so shouldn't we just turn it into the secular holiday that it is in many countries, thereby ensuring that it doesn't offend the sensibilities of a multicultural society? That's one interpretation, and it certainly seems to be winning the day. But it's a little simplistic. The point is, Christmas has always been controversial. The debate that's surfaced in schools is simply the latest chapter in the ongoing struggle between the pious and the profane. It is interesting that many public schools are now taking the side of the secular in this ancient battle, even though, as history suggests, the issue won't go away. In fact, the debate over Christmas is part of a wider debate over achieving equality in terms of the significance given to the holy days of a number of religions. The way that holy days are treated in the public-school system marvellously points up the inadequacies and absurdities that stem from its denial of the importance of human religious experience. It's also an area where opportunities to include, rather than exclude, growing numbers of Canadians from the ambit of the public system are being lost, where a chance to appeal to the moderate majority of the devout is being missed. I don't think we can afford to continue down this path to irrelevancy. This isn't simply an issue of holy days; it symbolizes a larger problem, and could be a very helpful tool in public policy.

But back to history. It teaches us that there's nothing particularly immutable about Christmas. Like many holy days, it wasn't ordained by God, but was constructed by human beings to meet a variety of needs. It would be naïve to ignore the fact that Christmas has significant religious meaning for millions of Christians around the world today. No real purpose is served by trying to deny the religious dimension of Christmas, whatever the arbitrary origins of the date observed. Besides, schools should be able to acknowledge a religious holy day without subscribing to it. It all depends on how it's handled by teachers within the classroom and within the school as a whole.

The Ryerson Public School in downtown Toronto, for example, has been commended in the press for setting a fine example through the way it deals with Christmas. Like the school my children attended, it tries to present the myriad ways that that particular season is celebrated around the world. Chris Bolton, the principal, says they simply call it the December holidays or winter solstice. There are "Merry Christmas" signs around the school and the "Christ" in the sign isn't replaced by an "X," he says. But then he adds that the school tries to keep it "non-specific . . . not strictly a religious kind of thing. It's the time of year, and the idea that everybody celebrates something in some kind of form. There's always something going on here. A couple of Indian festivals . . . the end of Ramadan . . . or Chinese New Year, or the lunar new year, or Black History Month . . . every group that is represented in the classroom should be honoured."

In December, however, Bolton says "carols" are sung in the morning throughout the school – everything from "Jingle Bells" to songs from *Joseph and the Amazing Technicolour Dreamcoat*. "It's pretty comprehensive," says Bolton. "But more 'White Christmas' than 'Hark the Herald Angels Sing.' Oh, and 'Frosty the Snowman.' They love that." Some songs refer to Christ's birth and, if a parent or child objects – as some Jehovah's Witnesses have – then the child doesn't have to participate. One teacher says she makes a point of teaching the children that presents aren't what Christmas is about – that it's about doing things for people. "You can take the religion out of it and still celebrate the occasion," she says.

Obviously, you can, as witnessed by the Ryerson school. And even though that teacher might tell the children Christmas isn't about presents, Santa does come into the school to give a present to every child under the age of six. And the children sing "Rudolph the Red-Nosed Reindeer" with the line about the other reindeer laughing and calling him names excised. They see a traditional

Chinese dragon-dance head hanging from a ceiling holding a Christmas wreath in its jaws. The Ryerson school seems to imply that the possibilities are endless. Virtually all is permissible – making it easy to see why it might be a tad confusing.

Mohammed Adam, a Muslim parent in Ottawa, says Christmas is always problematic for his family. In fact, he says his children are having a harder time of it than he did as a child. This is because, even though he too grew up in a predominantly Christian country, Ghana, Christmas was clearly identified as a religious celebration. He says the mixed messages his children get at public schools here confuse them. For example, he doesn't find it helpful when a teacher tells his child that everybody can celebrate Christmas. "The schools mean well by trying to make Christmas all-inclusive," he says. "They don't want to offend non-Christians and that's admirable. But I am not offended or threatened by the celebration of Christmas as a Christian festival that has spiritual meaning for millions. Trying to ignore that denies many children the right to the full teachings of their faith."

Sometimes the efforts of public schools to deny the religious significance of Christmas appear a trifle pathetic. Fear of religious expression has apparently ruled out a mature appraisal and appreciation of the meaning of this key date in the Christian calendar. It is truly absurd to censor the truth and deny the critical capacities of students in this crucial aspect of human experience, while expecting the same critical capacities to be active in other areas of study.

Religious schools, of course, breathe a sigh of relief whenever the issue of holy days comes up. They don't have to pretend to be all things to all people. They know when their holy days are, why they have them, and how they should observe them. Offending others is the least of their worries. Yet the Dashmesh Punjabi School in Abbotsford, British Columbia, an independent Sikh school, chooses to celebrate Christmas. Rajinder Dhaliwal says teachers prepare children for this holy day by talking to them about it and describing its religious meaning. "We explain it is Jesus' birth," she says. "Easter, too, we explain what it is. But the main focus is to help them understand the meaning. We have no Santa at Christmas, no party. We don't invite Santa in because our school is in a Sikh temple, and we celebrate religion the way it should be celebrated. And we explain Christmas to them as something positive, not negative."

Qasem Mahmud also believes it's possible to acknowledge Christmas without accepting it. But he understands why people of other religions often don't want their children exposed to tenets of the Christian faith. "They're afraid," says the Muslim. "But in that case, either they don't understand their own religion, or they aren't too sure of themselves. I don't know about Buddhism or Hinduism, but I know that the values and ethics, the beliefs and moral systems are the same in Christianity, Judaism, and Islam. So how can I be threatened? What I may not like in this society I am sure a Christian or a Jew doesn't like, either. I can convey that to my children. When it comes to the divinity of Jesus, I disagree with the Christians and agree with the Jews. It's not difficult to pass on this belief or this information to my child. But at the same time, we have certain values in common – telling the truth, being honest, being compassionate. It doesn't matter which religion they come from, because these values are shared. I cannot see where the threat is. No one is telling me, 'You have to believe in this or that.' It is up to me. I would say most mainstream Muslims think like me. They believe they can live in this society and they can keep their faith and their values and they aren't threatened."

Mahmud came to Canada in 1966, at a time when there were very few Muslims here. The former Palestinian had been looking for a country "to call my own," as he puts it, for some time. When

Jews claimed Israel after the Second World War, his family moved to Jordan. Later, Mahmud moved to Egypt to get his degree in engineering and worked in Kuwait for five years before finally immigrating to Canada. This is now home. This is where he and his wife have raised their six children. This is the country he's committed to, the country which he hopes will accept and accommodate people of all faiths, including Muslims. He also hopes that Muslims will be firmly grounded in their faith, to take their place as fully contributing members of Canadian society. One obstacle to achieving the latter, he says, is that two-thirds of young Canadian Muslims get no education in Islam outside the home.

"And most parents are poorly equipped to teach Islam. They pass on what they know, but they often mix up culture and religion, and the kids can't relate to it. They get confused, because what their parents present as Islam contradicts Canadian culture." So Mahmud has written an eight-part series for children entitled *My Book of Islam*, which covers the essentials of the Muslim faith, as well as its history and the demands it places on believers. It's sold about 50,000 copies since he first published the series for the Islamic School of Ottawa in 1984. Yet, Mahmud is a public-school supporter. "We live in a pluralistic society, a multi-faith society, and we have to learn from one another," he says. "And learning is a two-way street."

His goal is not separation from the public system, but equality within it. To him, acknowledging Islamic holy days shouldn't simply revolve around getting equal time in school programs or festivals, although observing them in these ways is, he thinks, necessary. Equality also means having the freedom to take part in holy days the way that Christian students are free to observe Christmas and Easter — by having their schools closed.

This is a goal of the Islamic Schools Federation of Ontario, although it didn't actively pursue it until 1994, when a number of

Ontario public-school boards adjusted their school year to accommodate the Jewish community. The Ottawa Board of Education was one of them. It delayed school openings by two days, because the dates coincided with Rosh Hashanah, the Jewish New Year. In making his presentation to the board, Ron Singer of the Jewish Community Council of Ottawa pointed out that "on Rosh Hashanah, Jews are religiously forbidden from doing work of any kind or attending school. Beginning school on Rosh Hashanah would create a difficult dilemma for Jewish students. The desire to be present on the first two days of school, when orientation, socialization, and administrative matters take place, would be pitted against their religious and moral teachings. We hope to be able to avoid a situation where one's school is in direct conflict with one's religious values."

Muslims were pleased that the board had responded so positively to the religious request and immediately decided to ask for a similar concession. Within two weeks of the board's announcement on Rosh Hashanah, the Islamic Schools Federation requested that it close schools in 1995 on the two most prominent Muslim holidays – Eid-ul-Fitr (March 3, 1995) and Eid-ul-Adha (May 11, 1995). Mahmud, who chairs the federation, and the president of the Ottawa Muslim Association appeared before the board to discuss the request. They were deeply disappointed with the response. Basically, they say, there was none. No questions were asked. No comment was made. Nor was permission granted to close the schools for those holy days. "The way they treated us was not equal to the way they treated the Jewish community," says Mahmud. "We said we'd like to sit down and discuss which schools would close depending on the population. We know that 8 per cent of students are Muslims and, in some schools, this percentage goes over 25. . . . So we said, 'Let's sit down and see what's feasible.' But the board's view wasn't even to think about it. This is unfortunate. We think that, if they can accommodate one holy day, then they can do it for other faith groups. And if it can be done in one year, it can be done all the time."

As initially reported in the press, the proposal sounded highly problematic. If public schools were to close for every religious group's holy days, there'd be little time left for learning. In fact, one educator estimated that schools would have to shut down for an additional nine weeks if every holy day were observed for every major religion. And that was only for the year 1994. Depending on the lunar calendar, school closings could be even longer.

Subverting education isn't what the Muslims were proposing, however. Instead, Emilio Binavince, lawyer for the federation, says they simply want religion recognized as a constitutional value. They also want the benefit of the equality rights guaranteed under the Charter. On July 11, 1994, he filed a lawsuit against the Ottawa Board of Education on behalf of the federation. Two Muslim students said their holy days put them in a situation similar to that of Jewish students. In the court document, applicant Abdul-Aziz said "attendance at school on these days results in a feeling of guilt" and he "consider[s] the treatment of [his] absence from school during these holidays as a serious disadvantage due to [his] religious belief."

The case was heard on November 20, 1996, with Binavince representing the federation in court. The Constitution was the basis of his argument. "The Constitution Act of 1982," he says, "reads as follows: 'Whereas Canada is founded upon the principles of the supremacy of God. . . .' Belief in God is religion. The question is 'Whose God?' The fact that it doesn't speak about whether it is an Anglican god or a Christian god or an Islamic god or a pantheistic god shows that there is sectarian neutrality. This constitution recognizes – Canada recognizes – that religion has a place in our state." Binavince says this means that Canada never intended that church and state be strictly separate, as is the case in the United States. "Constitutionally speaking, that's the wrong position to take," he says. "The only thing that will resolve this problem is not to separate God from the State, but to give equal opportunity to all religions. That is the middle ground — give equal opportunity. The only problem is people already entrenched in our institutions are greatly resistant to extending the same rights to others."

Resistance is a natural response to what might appear to be an unreasonable demand. But Mahmud stresses that accommodation is all that's being sought. "If a Muslim wants a holiday every Friday [to worship at a mosque], then the request is not realistic," he says. "We are only looking for reasonable accommodation for reasonable requests. We aren't in favour of taking Christmas away from the Christians," he says. "We don't want to take away a holy day."

So how could accommodation be realized without creating a nightmare? The Ontario Muslims suggest that each of the recognized world religions be allowed to have two holy days acknowledged by a school closing within the public system. Because each religion has many more holy days than that, it would be up to each religion to decide which two are the most significant. Then, the school would close if the number of students warranted it. Both Mahmud and Binavince are vague about how many students would be required before closing the school would be justified. They simply say a standard should be set and adhered to. "We want accommodation for those who can be accommodated equally with others," says Binavince. "If there are insignificant numbers, that's fine. Then you aren't discriminating if you don't accommodate. But you can enshrine it as a principle and make it permanent. When you become a significant number, then you are a factor in this society. The trick here is recognizing the threshold number. When people become significant in numbers, then what prevents you from giving them a holiday?"

Binavince says the answer is simple: administrative convenience. That's largely why boards don't want to consider the issue. "There is no law that requires all school boards to be open and closed at the same time," he says. "This is just a convenience issue, and a convenience is not a justification for violating the Constitution. Why is it that a school in North York with 80 per cent Jewish students should be closed for Christian holidays and open for Jewish holidays? Let's not have separate schools. Let's have flexibility within the system." Binavince also believes such a process would aid the cause of democratizing religion. "The kind of relationship we have now in my church, the Catholic Church, is where the authority flows from the Pope, going down," he says. "That's going to go away. There will be a disintegration of centralized power. It will be a democracy. The believers, the congregation, will govern the church. And this debate that you and I are talking about is precisely that.

"For instance, look at the Muslims. There are also certain sectarian divisions within the Muslim world. In one school, for instance, most of the people are Sunni. Why can they not vote for themselves in that school what day they should take? They'd do it at the local level. Why do we have to make everything conform? I think the administrative convenience is one of the biggest hindrances, the biggest argument of those who oppose those kinds of things. It's really the highest hurdle in achieving accommodation."

It is, however, obviously much more than an administrative issue. It's also the product of a system that has ruled out the acknowledgement of religious faith or the human religious impulse as worthy of study or observance.

(On April 22, 1997, the Ontario Divisional Court ruled that the Ottawa Board of Education had not discriminated against Muslim students by failing to recognize Islamic holy days. Canadian courts now recognize Christmas and Easter as secular pause days, said the court, not as religious holidays. The federation is appealing the decision.)

Gerald Vandezande of Ontario's Multi-faith Coalition for Equity in Education has no quibble with the Islamic model. He stresses that holy days could, and should, be used in classrooms as a way of raising issues. At Easter, for example, students could look at how the crucifixion of Jesus has been used historically to scapegoat Jews. "Otherwise, I think these religious holidays become an excuse to spend the day in the bloody malls, which are temples in themselves," says Vandezande. "I say use the schools in the most open-minded way to expose everybody to whatever others believe. That has made me stronger than anything else. We have nothing to fear from that. We [members of his church, Christian Reform in the Netherlands] learned everything we could about Hitler and the Nazis. In fact, that's how we learned to resist them. . . . I don't think schools need to have Easter Monday off, but they should use it. What if students spent the day looking at how Christians and Jews still fight over Jerusalem? I am very much for constant, ongoing, public examination of not only what happened in history, but what it teaches us for living today and how we develop new relationships in the future." Not a bad idea, but it would require a sea change in the present treatment of religion in most curricula.

Others would settle for less. McGill University's Shapiro says he'd be happy if schools simply showed "reasonable respect" to religious adherents. Allowing schools to close for every group's holy days goes way beyond that — to the point of coddling, he implies. Shapiro points out that schools are meant to be places in which people grow up, not in which they're treated like infants. "You just have to learn to cope," he says. "I don't think there's anything inherently bad about having the school calendar convenient to the stated religious commitments of the majority. So what? I mean, I can't get excited about it. It's not as if every day in school is precious. It's the combined days that are precious. And we have to understand that parents have obligations. If you're going to take your child out of school for reasons that are important to you, that's fine. You have to then prepare those kids so they don't suffer. The school has to be co-operative as well. They have to help you help them."

But Nathan Vardi says people should never underestimate the role that school holidays could play in the quest for social equality. The university student attended Hillel Academy in Ottawa for his elementary education, yet is now a proponent of one secular public system. To him, a truly secular system is one in which "everyone is equal and no one is made to feel an outsider, because the system would be set up in such a way that alienation would be impossible. But," he says, "we have a long way to go before this will become a reality. It will take a big commitment by society, and people probably aren't ready for it yet. But it does start with little things, like knowing – everyone knowing – that next Wednesday is Yom Kippur and you get a day off for it. Wow! You can't imagine what that's like for a kid. Nothing's bigger than a day off, and if everybody recognized it, knew what it was really there for, who knows?"

So where does all this lead? Obviously, pleasing everybody is impossible. But refusing to accommodate the holy days of Canada's increasingly numerous religious groups seems an extreme overreaction. It's not as if we're the first country in the modern world trying to cope with this issue. The Netherlands solved the problem by allowing individual schools to decide on school closings – as long as they also closed on civic statutory holidays, such as Christmas and Easter, and as long as they're open for the number of school days required by the Ministry of Education. There's even an example here in Canada of religious accommodation: the Edmonton Public School Board, for one, allows flexibility within its alternative school programs. Talmud Torah, the Hebrew-language school, opens a week earlier than public schools so it can close for Yom Kippur and the whole of Passover. During its nearly twenty-five years of operation under the public system, Talmud Torah's flexibility has enhanced its whole program.

As Vardi makes very clear, the issue of recognizing holy days is far more than a concession to a minority faith. It could be an essential ingredient in a broader strategy to make the public schools a more inclusive, effective tool in achieving an egalitarian, integrated, multi-faith society. Accommodating the holy days of Canada's recognized religious groups within public education – both through school closings where numbers warrant and by using them as points of discussion – could be a small, but necessary, step to increased understanding of our new religious diversity.

II

FROM LITERALISM TO LITERACY

Virtue and vice were warp and woof of our first consciousness, and they will be the fabric of our last. . . . We have only one story. All novels, all poetry, are built on the never-ending contest in ourselves of good and evil.

John Steinbeck, *East of Eden*

"Every effect has its cause," Leaphorn said to Chee. "Once in a while, maybe, a star just falls at random. But I don't believe in random."

Tony Hillerman, *Talking God*

. . . You know how it is. You ast yourself one question, it lead to fifteen. I start to wonder why us need love. Why us suffer. Why us black. Why us men and women. Where do children really come from. It didn't take long to realize I didn't hardly know nothing. And that if you ast yourself why you black or a man or a woman or a bush it don't mean nothing if you don't ast why you here, period.

Alice Walker, *The Color Purple*

In 1995 the small town of Abbotsford, British Columbia, found itself at the centre of a curriculum storm. Someone complained that the local school board was violating the province's school act, because it allowed the theory of creationism in science classes. This hit the news, big-time. The community was depicted as right-wing and out of touch with the modern world. Later that year, when I visited British Columbia, I found John Sutherland, chair of the board, totally exasperated. He was fed up with the way the issue had been depicted in the news and discouraged at the seeming inability of anyone to engage in meaningful debate. "All the media ever wanted to talk about was Adam and Eve," said the business professor at Trinity Western University in Langley, southeast of Vancouver. "I was just about driven to distraction. When CTV reported this, they started with Lloyd Robertson saying 'Adam and Eve in the classroom,' blah, blah, blah. Then CBC-TV phones me the next day, all hot and panting about it, and I said, 'Listen, I'll talk to you, but I want to tell you what we really do. I don't want to go on the air and do what CTV did and talk about Adam and Eve and Genesis One.' And the CBC reporter said, 'Well, that's CTV for you. We're not like them.' Well, the first three words the next night on CBC were 'Adam and Eve.' They're no different. I could never get them to talk in terms of underlying hypotheses or variety of opinions because all they wanted to talk about was a literal interpretation of Genesis One."

In the early 1980s, the Abbotsford school board, responding to the wishes of the largely Mennonite and Dutch Reform population, passed a policy that its science students be exposed to the theories of scientific evolution and "divine creation." The policy didn't say that "divine creation" meant that God created the Earth in six days and rested on the seventh, nor that it had to get equal time with the theory of evolution, only that students should be given the opportunity to be made aware of both theories. Teachers didn't object to the policy, probably because they weren't required to teach it. Sutherland says schools implemented the policy by sometimes inviting a guest speaker in to the class. Most often the initiative was left up to students; they could raise the issue for discussion or write a paper on it.

"Probably the people who framed the policy in 1983 believed in a literal interpretation," he says. "The community would have been about half the size it is now, and the strong Christian identification would have been very much more marked than it is now. But my understanding of creationism is a belief that a divine being created the world, created the universe, in whatever length of time. I believe in a Creator and I believe that creation reflects something about the Creator, and I believe that creation has a purpose – it's not random and meaningless. I accept that the evolutionary hypothesis is the better understanding of the scientific data, but it's an untestable hypothesis. And I accept it on faith, as it were. And the majority of the Abbotsford school board are the same way – they're all evolutionists. When today's board reaffirmed that they wanted creationism allowed in the classroom, everybody – despite every effort on my part to disabuse them of the notion – assumed we wanted a Bible study in biology class, which was baloney. In a typical year, Grades 11 and 12 biology students might have one period or less of exposure to creationism. And then, only on their initiative, because teachers weren't required to teach it, and I'm not aware that any of them ever did."

As Sutherland and a number of conservative Christians pointed out to me during the course of my research, the theory of evolution doesn't necessarily conflict with the idea of a Creator. Many scientists accept evolution, but they also believe in God. In fact, a survey of scientists released in London, England, in April 1997, showed that scientists are as likely to believe in God now as they were eighty years ago. The figure has remained constant at about 40 per cent (44.6 per cent for mathematicians). Only the most literal creationists, relying on the book of Genesis interpretation, resist the theory of evolution. Outside that literal interpretation of the Scriptures, it's entirely possible to reconcile the idea of a divine Creator with the notion of evolution.

Sutherland admits he knew the policy would probably land the board in trouble. "I had personal misgivings about it, because its reference to 'divine creation' seemed to suggest a particular brand of creationism, a certain conservative Protestant view, whereas many in the community – Sikhs, for example, and Roman Catholics – also accept creationism. I would have been happy if students would simply have taken a look in biology class at the scientific data and the underlying hypotheses, including alternative schemes, and how different groups interpret the scientific data. Nobody disputes the scientific data. It's the hypothesis that you use to explain the data that is under dispute, and the random, purposeless, evolutionary hypotheses are as untestable and as philosophic as any other. They're a belief system. So where else but in science class could you look at scientific belief systems? It would make no sense to me that you would do it somewhere else."

By the time I met with Sutherland, the issue was resolved. In June 1995, the board changed its policy. The process by which it was resolved was less than ideal. In talks with the NDP government, Sutherland says board members pointed out that they were simply following the Ministry of Education's own curriculum guide for teachers. This stated that the theory of evolution might conflict with the beliefs of some students and, if so, teachers should make sure to show respect for their opinions, perhaps by working conflicting beliefs into classroom discussion. The minister responded to the board's defence of its position by ordering a rewriting of the curriculum guide.

"This eliminated any possibility of discussion of anything except evolution," said Sutherland. "The B.C. Civil Liberties people even told us that we should be going into the classroom and monitoring teachers to make sure they never breathe a word about creation. They literally wanted us to send people in, spies, to make sure they were behaving themselves. I couldn't believe the B.C. Teachers' Federation was putting up with this – allowing their teachers to be muzzled, as if there was no respect for a teacher's professional judgment or open inquiry of students. They want to muzzle the students by saying you're not allowed to raise politically incorrect issues in class.

"I said, 'What possible harm can there be in allowing students, on their own initiative, to critique particular positions? Scientists critique themselves all the time. Why would we deny it to students?' The head of our local teachers' union said students aren't in school to critique, they're there to learn. That's the kind of empty-headed, politically correct blather that I got back from most of my discussions. So they rewrote the curriculum guide to disallow student-initiated discussion of anything outside the scope of the curriculum. And they gave us one week to conform to the new curriculum guide or be fired and be replaced by a trustee appointed by the minister. Well, our community wasn't anxious for that to happen."

So, what many automatically assumed was a story about religious fundamentalism invading the curriculum turns out to be, in truth, an example of overzealous *secular* fundamentalism. It underlines the fact that intolerance isn't the province of any particular school system. In the terms of American educator Neil Postman, British Columbia's Ministry of Education is serving the god of science, which has its own story. "It is a story that exalts human reason, places criticism over faith, disdains revelation as a source of knowledge and . . . postulates that our purpose on Earth is to discover reliable knowledge," he writes in *The End of Education*. He notes that there are good reasons for worshipping science; the science-god sends men to the moon, inoculates them against disease, and gives people a measure of control over their lives. "Nonetheless, like all gods," writes Postman, it is imperfect. Its story of our origins and of our end is, to say the least, unsatisfactory. To the question, How did it all begin?, Science answers, Probably by accident. To the question, How will it all end?, Science answers, Probably by accident. And to many people, the accidental life is not worth living. Moreover, regarding the question, What moral instruction do you give us?, the science-god maintains a tight-lipped silence. It places itself at the service of both the beneficent and the cruel, and its grand moral impartiality, if not indifference, has made it welcome the world over.

I think there's a moral in the Abbotsford story, and it has to do with the future of public education. Surely an important facet of education is acknowledging that there's an element of faith in every area of human study, be it economics, history, or psychology. Adopting any theory or explanation in any discipline inevitably involves a certain leap of faith, and the model Sutherland describes for discussing the faith basis of human knowledge sounds as reasonable as any. In a comparative-religion course in one of Abbotsford's senior high schools, for example, Sutherland says the class set up a forum on love. An evangelical Christian, a Hindu, a Sikh, and two women from Wicca (witches) described their concepts of love. "It was great," says Sutherland. "The students had a great discussion and they understood how each other viewed this significant topic. Why that couldn't be done in one session of biology is beyond my comprehension." Part of the problem with what happened in Abbotsford is that government officials now won't allow the presumptions of their own faith in the science-god to be put under scrutiny. They're demanding unquestioning adherence to one theory, a position that's not only a poor model for future citizens, but could have the effect of driving moderates out of the public system – neither of which bodes well for the future of public education. As Ottawa philosopher Will Kymlicka and B.C. educator Charles Ungerleider have pointed out in earlier chapters, good education requires an open, inquiring approach with an emphasis on questioning, challenging, and critical reflection.

Discussing the beliefs underlying various disciplines is one example of how to get at the idea of faith. There's also a need to recognize the role that faith has played in the development of knowledge. In fact, to go back to science for a moment, it developed historically within a tradition of belief in a God who was a scientist and a technician. Postman points out that such people as René Descartes, Francis Bacon, Galileo, Johannes Kepler, and Isaac Newton believed their work wasn't replacing Judeo-Christianity, but extending it. To ignore or deny the role of religious faith in that discipline is to provide a less-than-adequate (or honest) education.

This struck me most forcibly after looking over our son's course of study during his winter break. He's enrolled in a first-year university program called "The Foundations of Western Civilization," which covers the great thinkers from prehistoric to modern times. Extensive reading and essay-writing are required because of the breadth of material to be covered. As we discussed the program, he said something that surprised me: he said he felt he was at a disadvantage in the program because, unlike some of his peers, he didn't have a grounding in religion. "I didn't know that Western civilization was based on religion," he told us. Nothing in his previous thirteen years of study had given him an inkling of that. Not once had a link been made between the development of art, history, science, music, philosophy, and religion – not, that is, until he went to university. Accepting as we did the tenets of secularism, my husband and I never questioned that omission during his high school years. University now seems awfully late for him to be making those links.

★

The theories of evolution and creationism, sex education (including methods of birth control, AIDS prevention, and abortion), the selection of appropriate books for English-literature reading lists, and the teaching of religion are extremely sensitive issues. Like the holy days question, it's easy to understand why religious groups want their own schools; they can teach what they want in whatever way they want. And so, today in Canada, there are a variety of ways in which religious schools deal with these issues. Many of them do teach evolution, but along the lines that Sutherland suggests: that a divine Creator was behind it all – in however many days, years, or eons that it took. Most make sure that students get sex education, but present abstinence or chastity until marriage as the only acceptable moral option. Most refuse to acknowledge homosexuality, except as morally unacceptable. When abortion is mentioned, as it frequently is in Catholic schools, it's often presented with graphic images and moral injunctions against it. Some inject their beliefs much more blatantly than others. For example, all curricula used in schools belonging to the Society of Christian Schools in British Columbia are built around providing their answers to the following questions: Where does this world come from? What's gone wrong in this world? What can we do about the problems that exist? Where does our hope lie?

Public schools are in a completely different situation. They serve a diverse population from a wide variety of backgrounds with a wide variety of needs. They must be seen as fair and equitable and academically sound. As religiously neutral, publicly supported institutions, they cannot allow controversial morals to rule the classroom. For example, to present homosexuality as "immoral" is tantamount to teaching prejudice against a group that has human-rights protection. To avoid offending those who object to the sexual practices of gays by ignoring homosexuality as one expression of human sexuality would be to deny the humanity of those who are gay. It would also deprive students of learning about the myriad ways in which humans live and express themselves and would undermine the cause of equality. And so a conscious effort is made to be realistic, informative, and non-judgmental. But raise the issue of religion, and there almost seems to be a conspiracy against it. In the name of "neutrality," public schools seem to relegate religion either to a boring, unimportant area of study or to ignore it altogether. Sometimes, in the attempt to avoid bringing God into the classroom, history is actually distorted.

Harro Van Brummelen, assistant dean in the Faculty of Social Sciences and Education at Trinity Western University in Langley, B.C., has done extensive research on education curricula. A conservative Christian and a supporter of independent religious schools, he makes a point of examining the textbooks used in the public-school system, partly because religious schools are so often accused of being biased while public schools purport not to be. He also believes that school textbooks are a good indicator of what are considered legitimate views. Textbooks, says Van Brummelen, are the way society says to its future generations "This is how we would like you to be and how we would like you to believe." In examining history texts used in British Columbia in the 1980s, he discovered that religion was, for the most part, studiously avoided.

"Although both Protestant Christianity and Judaism have had significant impact on English-Canadian culture, neither is mentioned at all in the elementary-school textbooks used in British Columbia," writes Van Brummelen in a 1994 academic journal. "High school history books excluded mention of religion to the point of distorting history. One of the textbooks . . . ignored that the Roman Catholic Church, for all its faults, nevertheless was instrumental in building the most stable 18th century society in the New World. Another Grade 9 book . . . developed ancient and medieval history without one single mention of Christianity.

In short," writes Van Brummelen, "the authors of these textbooks, for one reason or another, deliberately withheld from students any knowledge of the religious ideals and values of Canadians and of their impact on Canadian culture." (In American textbooks, according to a U.S. National Institute of Education report, *Religion and Traditional Values in Public School Textbooks*, religion is the "great unmentionable." The lengths to which textbook writers went to avoid religion ranged, it said, from the merely deceptive to the downright ludicrous. In one textbook, Pilgrims were described as "people who travel a lot.")

In his research, Van Brummelen found that individualism was emphasized. The theme "Everything is possible when I am me" ruled the day. "Individuals were shown to band together in social institutions only when it was mutually advantageous; even families were portrayed as 'groups of people' living together for social and economic convenience." The books were not without values, however. Envy, hatred, killing, and theft were presented as unjustifiable, while helping the sick, the disadvantaged, and handicapped was considered worthwhile. But Van Brummelen undertook a similar investigation into the Grades 3 to 7 math textbooks used in British Columbia. "I was appalled at the kinds of problems in these books," he says. "The vast majority of them dealt with buying material goods like compact discs and movie tickets, and skis, and sports and entertainment events. I could find only one problem in all the books I went through that was non-materialistic. One student said, 'If I buy something a bit cheaper, then maybe I could send some money to the Third World.'"

No wonder religious schools get frustrated when public-school educators depict the education they offer as neutral. Ken Badley, author of *Worldviews: The Challenge of Choice*, a secondary-school text on comparative religion, and an education professor in Edmonton, says he'd like to believe neutrality is possible, but he doesn't actually think it is. "It's conceivable that I could go into a classroom and say that my job is not to promote my view," he says. "But I don't think any of us is in complete control over what flows out of our mouths or the tone of it. I think it's inevitable that my comments, even when I'm trying to be 'neutral' – although I prefer the word 'fair-minded' – will be flavoured by my perspective. We all have views about important questions, perennial questions about good and God and right and wrong. It's unavoidable that we could have such views and equally unavoidable to teach without having those views flavour a person's teaching. It's not that we go around all the time reflecting on what we do or don't believe. Most of us just try to get through the day. I'd say these things don't come out at an articulate level, but at a pre-articulate level."

Badley says that, while the public classroom isn't a place for teachers to advocate on behalf of a particular political party or a particular religious denomination, they don't seem to see anything wrong with advocating a certain perspective on the environment, or on nutrition, or on smoking. "My wife has a glass of wine," he says, "and the children attack her. It's not because of what they learned at church, it's what they learned in school. It's drinking, period. I used to get this at church. Isn't it funny that the school has taken over? But the school is unashamedly stating what's right and what's wrong. I might agree with what they teach about these things. But my bottom point on all this is that they are teaching a set of morals, and they shouldn't pretend that they aren't."

It's not just religious schools that get frustrated by the public system's projection of "neutrality." Many public-school supporters are also frustrated by the seeming inability of the public system to consider offering religious education in any meaningful or systematic way in its schools. In fact, as long ago as 1969, the Anglican, Baptist, Lutheran, Presbyterian, Roman Catholic, and United churches got together to form the Ecumenical Study Commission on Public Education. Initially, the group organized

to co-ordinate a response to an Ontario study on religious education in public schools. When that finished, it chose not to disband.
Instead, the group made a commitment to promote multi-faith
education about religion within schools.

Provincial governments have come and gone – and the ecumenical group has made an endless round of presentations and sub-
missions to virtually all of them. To date, no government has chosen
to act on them. The most recent submission was in 1993, when the
group made a presentation to Ontario's Royal Commission on
Learning. Members urged the Ministry of Education to prepare a
curriculum guideline for multi-faith education about religion. The
brief, written by Roger Hutchinson, now principal of Emmanuel
College within the University of Toronto, argued that: "Such a
guideline could help teachers and local school boards work out the
scope and sequence of religious studies without restricting the freedom of local schools to adapt the guideline to meet the needs of
their communities, and it would also preclude the necessity of each
school from duplicating each other's effort. There is a core of
knowledge and understandings that all students should become
aware of, no matter where they live in Ontario."

Despite the practicality and sophistication of this recommenda-
tion, it's gone unheeded. In fact, if the discussion even comes up
in the first place, it seems stuck at a basic level of terminology.
Should it be "religious education" or "education about religion"?
A document put out in 1994 by Ontario's Ministry of Education
and Training provides a guide to differentiating between religious
education (an indoctrinating approach) and education about religion (an instructional approach). The description comes from the
Elgin County ruling on the teaching of religion. They're good
guidelines and don't require a change in the law in order to be
implemented. What's required, instead, is a recognition of the
importance of education about religion, a change in public policy,
and a commitment to train teachers accordingly.

Suggested Guidelines for the
Teaching of Religious Education

This is the way the Ontario Court of Appeal has interpreted the difference between religious indoctrination and education about religion:

- The school may sponsor the study of religion, but not the practice of religion.
- The school may expose students to all religious views, but not impose a particular view.
- The school's approach to religion is one of instruction, not indoctrination.
- The function of the school is to provide education about all religions, not to convert to any one religion.
- The school's approach is academic, not devotional.
- The school should study what all people believe, but shouldn't teach what to believe.
- The school should strive for student awareness of all religions, but not press for student acceptance of any one religion.
- The school should seek to inform the student about various beliefs, but not seek to conform him or her to any one belief.

Source: *Education about Religion in Ontario Public Elementary Schools*, Ontario Ministry of Education and Training, 1994

Despite the explicitness of the guide, few school boards in Ontario have chosen to follow up on it. But it's not because no one has tried. In 1991, a small group in Ottawa called the Brotherhood of Anglican Churchmen was looking for a useful social project to support. Members tossed around a variety of ideas and, according to Rex Nickson, one of the members, a common theme emerged: all were concerned about what they perceived as increasing racism and violence in society. "We thought perhaps we might be able to offer something for use in schools to help stem the tide of racism and violence," he says.

They figured that one way for children to learn to appreciate their neighbours is to get a grounding in comparative religion. As they saw it, historical, religious, and racial prejudices could, in part, be overcome by such an approach, and could help bring a sense of cohesiveness to the new multicultural mix. Since the government had announced in 1990 that religious education may be provided in Grades 1 through 8 for up to sixty minutes a week – as long as no single religion is given primacy – they figured it was safe to proceed. So the group raised some money and hired Helen Prince, an elementary-school teacher with a master's degree in religion, to develop resource material on Buddhism, Christianity, Hinduism, Islam, Judaism, and native spirituality for Grades 5 and 6. Representatives from each religion formed a committee to work with her to make sure each faith was accurately represented.

Given the age group being targeted, Prince chose a storybook format. Called *Alexander's Journey*, it's the story of a little girl with a gender-bending name who wonders "Who am I? Who made our world?" "What might we learn from one another?" In an attempt to find meaning, she sets out on a journey, meeting people from the six religions along the way. As it turned out, it was much easier for Alexander to find answers to the questions that have plagued human beings since time immemorial than it was for the group that commissioned her search to get her quest into the classroom. When the interfaith group met with the Ottawa and Carleton boards of education, the initial response was positive. In fact, by 1993 some schools were willing to try *Alexander's Journey* on an experimental basis. In responding to the proposal, the superintendent of instructional support for the Carleton Board of Education wrote, "There is a need for a broad province-wide approach to the issue of education about religion. A provincial curriculum for the objective study of world religions, fostering tolerance, appreciation and understanding of the similarities and differences among the many peoples of our world, should be developed. Local boards choosing to introduce this curriculum in their schools could then adapt it to particular local circumstances if they wished."

But there were objections, particularly from the Humanist Association of Ottawa. In a five-page critique of the material to the board, the association's president Colin Downie told the board that *Alexander's Journey* is "biased in favour of religion and discriminates against the non-religious. It is propaganda for theism, and indoctrinates a liberal, syncretic, but basically Christian, set of beliefs. First of all, the study guide completely ignores the dark side of religious history. There is a bias in this one-sided favourable presentation of religion. Events such as the Inquisition, the religious wars of Europe, the Crusades, the witch mania, are never mentioned. The role of all the major religions in the oppression of women is never mentioned."

Downie's comments disturbed the program co-ordinator of the Carleton board to the extent that he asked Judith Robertson, assistant professor of teacher education at the University of Ottawa, whether *Alexander's Journey* discriminated against non-theistic children and whether it would be possible to include a humanistic and non-theistic perspective in the material. Robertson said, "While non-theists may hold that by virtue of teaching about God *Alexander's Journey* is discriminatory, in fact what they mean is that legislation which makes possible the teaching about God is discriminatory towards those persons whose lifestance discounts a conception of a supreme being." She said that a chapter on "non-theistic lifestances" could be included in the guide, but "would move the curriculum, in my opinion, outside the rubric of education about religion – a problem that may be more semantic than substantive. The social gains to be achieved potentially through such revision are worthwhile, in that the foundational text would include and work with expanded notions of human possibility."

In the end, *Alexander's Journey* wasn't pursued and children in the Ottawa–Carleton area continue to receive a "neutral" education. The multi-faith group, however, still meets to try and figure out ways to get education about religion into schools. Peter Evans, an Ottawa education consultant, isn't surprised at the school boards' reluctance to implement the resource material. "Religion is at the margin of Ontario's Common Curriculum," he says, "and merely to 'permit' its study, independent of the main curriculum – where it isn't given any practical support in curriculum design or teacher training – is tantamount to a dismissal of the religious dimension from serious attention altogether." Evans goes even further, saying that "the student's very right to learn is being undermined, and a distorted view of humanity and its traditions presented, instead. Those who criticize the public system as 'godless' have some legitimate grounds for their attack." The former high-school teacher of English, math, and world religions argues for a full program in religion. "The exploration of religion is essential because it's a very central component of human exploration," he says. "It encompasses a vast dimension of what humans are, what they've done. To omit it is to ignore a very important part of ourselves. Besides, it opens up young people's minds to other possibilities, if it's inquiring, and leaves many questions open-ended, rather than closed. I'd say that the systematic avoidance of religion is a different form of indoctrination. It's a deliberate avoidance of a whole area of human activity."

★

As I write this, thirty-nine bodies have just been found in a mass suicide in California. Stories in the *Globe and Mail* try to make sense of the deaths, describing the devotion of these followers to an authoritarian leader and their belief that they were going to shed what they called their physical containers (bodies) for spiritual ones on another planet. Still, it's difficult to understand how seemingly intelligent, capable people with much to offer life and much to get from life could possibly do such a thing. Difficult, that is, for people who do not appreciate the incredible power and attraction of faith. We live in an era so ignorant of religious conviction that it's understandable when the media have to scramble to make sense of it all. Yet deeply held religious convictions continue to lead people to war, just as they move people to work to improve the world. Some of the most divisive splits in our society today have religious dimensions – abortion, homosexuality, euthanasia, the rights of women. It's absurd to pretend that anyone can begin to understand human behaviour – both in the past and as it's unfolding before our eyes today – without understanding religion. Obviously, gaining insight into this is a process that should unfold in children growing through the developmental ages and stages. As the humanist Downie points out, there *is* a dark side to religion, but that's a poor reason to remove it from the classroom. That's all the more reason to explore it – gradually, as students build up their understanding of the complexities and varieties of human experience.

To suggest, as some opponents of religion in schools do, that this can be done solely in the home is patently absurd. Many parents today are themselves spiritually illiterate and have inadequate resources with which to impart such knowledge. Few have had a good model themselves of how this can be done. They were either totally immersed in the religion of their parents or have had no exposure to religion at all. Even strong adherents of a particular religion argue that parents are often in a poor position to teach children about their own faith, let alone someone else's.

Qasem Mahmud, for example, chair of the Islamic Schools Federation of Ontario, is a member of the multi-faith group backing *Alexander's Journey*. He says that, from his experience, Muslim children are often not taught the true Islamic faith, that cultural prejudices and misinformation are inadvertently passed on. Nor, he says, are they knowledgeable about other religions. And so he would like to see education play a role. "What is lacking in the public-school system is religion and nurturing the faith of the student," says Mahmud. "We aren't trying to pressure or convert children, just trying to provide information. Children have rights, too, and the public system is a safeguard for their protection."

In a magazine called *Teaching Tolerance*, Martin E. Marty, a professor of the history of religion at the University of Chicago, elaborates on an insight from Voltaire: "If England had one religion, that one would do what most monopolistic belief systems do – deny a voice to any other. If it had two, those would do what rival faiths often do – come to blows. But England had thirty religions, so they had to find ways of getting along." Perhaps it's not surprising, then, that England, in response to a new social reality, has made a concerted effort in the last decade to include religion in its school curriculum. It has done this by moving from an instructional approach (religious instruction) to an educational approach (religious education). John Hull, an education professor at the University of Birmingham, rejects the term "education about religion," because "it suggests a cognitive approach, and that isn't what we seek to do. Religious education, however, suggests a more open, critical educational description." To him, the school is the logical place for a child to develop both an awareness of the different forms of religious experience, and the capability to analyse and make sense out of the human religious quest.

The Anglican Diocese of Ottawa brought Hull to Canada recently to conduct seminars on "God Talk with Children." Co-founder of the International Seminar on Religious Education and Values, he's a passionate and articulate spokesperson for religious education in schools. Blind since the 1980s, Hull uses a cane to feel his way through a room. When he begins to speak, he abandons it and, drawing his audience along with him, loses himself in a world of age-old myths and ideas. He talks of the importance of giving children the language of symbolism, of the need to develop in them an awareness of evil, and describes scenarios in which God-talk with children requires cleverness, wit, and imagination. The father of six children, he's had a lot of experience doing just that, and he draws on it repeatedly. Perhaps whatever it is that's given this scholar the courage and ability to cope with being completely blind has also contributed to his love for the richness and power of religious belief. Later, when we meet for tea, he greets me by coming within centimetres of my body and then remains there, as if our physical proximity allows him to "see" me. Hull gives the impression that despite, or perhaps because of, his disability he's intent on being joyously and fully alive.

"We [in Britain] distinguish between learning religion, learning about religion, and learning from religion," says Hull. "Learning religion is learning to be religious and should be done in the home, church, synagogue, mosque, or temple. It doesn't have a place in schools. Learning about religion is the repetitive study of religions, a factual study. But learning from religion is encountering religious stories in such a way as to make a contribution to the spiritual, moral, cultural, and general educational way of students. We don't offer comparative religion. In fact, the last time that term was used was in the 1970s. It isn't used because there are many ways of studying religion, and the comparative is only one. It's a sophisticated activity and requires a high level of cognitive skills. You must understand the different religions first, so we don't do that. Also it's not helpful in the mind of the public, because it suggests superficial study without commitment. All of our syllabus [in the British education system] is a world-religion syllabus. At the same time it's controversial."

In 1986, Britain brought in the Education Reform Act, which applied to England and Wales only. It says that religious education is the responsibility of local education authorities. Their job is to produce a religious curriculum which will take up 5 per cent of a student's education time – about eighty minutes a week. For the younger grades, it's taught by the classroom teacher. At the secondary-school level, these teachers are specialists, in the same way that others are math and science specialists. Hull contends that such teachers require special pedagogical skills and personal attributes. "They should have a reasonable amount of subject knowledge," he says, "and be able to come to a mature relationship with the symbols of religion. Any well-trained person can teach it, regardless of faith. This is, after all, an educational activity, not a religious one. What matters is that teachers are mature in self-knowledge, must have come to terms with the great religious archetypes, and must be able to think and laugh about God, engage children in conversations about God. This doesn't mean they're believers. They must study from the inside and go outside. In fact," he adds, "people deeply embedded in their own particular faiths probably won't be good religious-education teachers. And people who pooh-pooh everything won't be good religious-education teachers, either. Some of the finest religious-education teachers we have are humanists." (Clearly, the humanist objections to including religion in some Ottawa schools are of a lower order of sophistication than the humanist sensibility implicit in Hull's description of religious education in Britain. It's very much the humanist vision of Robert Tielman in the Netherlands as well.)

Hull says that the debate in England was over the wording of a particular section of the Act. It read that any new agreed-upon syllabus "shall reflect the fact that the principal religious traditions in Great Britain are, in the main, Christian, whilst taking account of the teaching and practices of the other principal religions represented in Great Britain." Hull defends the way it's written, arguing that "the wording doesn't say there shall be predominantly Christian, but says 'reflects the fact.' This can be reflected in many ways," he says. "Conservatives insist on the importance of the first part of the sentence. They maintain that 50 per cent of the syllabus should be Christian and the rest shared. Liberals say the wording is vague and is flexible and that that's a good thing because it can reflect the make-up of local communities. There's also controversy over prayers, because the Act states that every child enrolled in a school shall take part in a daily act of collective worship. It doesn't say 'corporate,' which is an unanimous body of believers," says Hull. "It says 'collective,' which is collected individuals with different beliefs and points of view, but collected together. I believe in a collective act that highlights the spiritual element. I feel all spiritual traditions should contribute to it. It's okay for a rabbi to get up and read and say a prayer and say 'I hope you enjoy that.' That's sharing. You don't have to close your eyes. You don't have to say it. But I object to the assumption of unanimous religious belief, because the task of education is to examine."

The debates are frequent and often heated, according to Hull. He thinks that's good. "There are 175 armed conflicts in the world today, of which religion is a substantial issue in 125 of them," he says. "Religion is a major source of conflict, and people obviously won't be at peace with each other until religions are at peace with each other. It's part of citizenship education that people learn to be tolerant of other religions." And so the debate in England is widespread and, Hull says, led by the government. "Government is holding a national forum on values and education, which people from all walks of life will attend. We'll be talking about what core values should be communicated through the schools, because there's widespread concern about the deterioration of spiritual and moral values of society. There's also a recognition that religious education is the flagship of this enterprise." What Hull is describing is the antithesis of religious indoctrination, whose purpose is to convey a truth, or system of belief. Instead, he is describing the development of what I call throughout this book religious literacy. This amounts to not just a knowledge of one's own beliefs, but a capacity to encounter and analyse respectfully the religious views of others, and to see that enterprise as personally worth while.

All of this, of course, is a far cry from what we have here in Canada. Here, there is no teacher training in religion outside the Catholic system, no interest or commitment on the part of education authorities to examine religious issues – even to entertain the idea of a debate. And there's even less interest on the part of politicians. Quite the contrary. Still, there is a debate going on, however scattered and unfocused it may be. And while there may be some agreement from a variety of people that religion should be offered to children, there's certainly no consensus on how best to do it.

Gerald Vandezande, for example, of Ontario's Multi-faith Coalition for Equity in Education, says he'd be hesitant about making education-about-religion courses mandatory. He'd much prefer to see an education-about-world-views course offered. "Education about world-views would recognize the reality that so-called non-religious views are value-laden," he says. "They represent a view of life and of the world that lies behind it. You could get everything from Left to Right in it, but you should do justice to reality. Marxism, for example, is off the map these days, and it shouldn't be. And neo-conservatism, that should be examined at the high-school level. And I'd put feminism in there, too, and humanism. But let students examine these perspectives, so that they know what the current debates are all about. Such a course would also force the religious communities to articulate what they believe in educational lingo." In Vandezande's scenario, the multi-cultural, multi-religious mix in society would be represented at the policy-making level. "You'd have a plurality of participants making the decision as to what legitimately constitutes a world-view," he says. "Not everyone can be at the table. You'd have to show that your view has something to say about the environment, social issues, etcetera, in educational terms in order to be there."

Clive Beck, a professor in the philosophy of education at the Ontario Institute for Studies in Education (OISE), author of *Better Schools*, argues, on the other hand, that religion needs to be built into the teaching of history, English, social studies, and other courses. "And it has to be taught by an ordinary teacher, not specialized ones," he says. "Otherwise, it tends to become distorted. I've taught world religion for a number of years at OISE, and most ordinary teachers don't take it. And if ordinary teachers aren't willing to teach it, then maybe it shouldn't be taught. I feel values should be part of the ordinary curriculum. In this way, all teachers would need to become more literate in this area. And it'd be a good thing, too," he says.

Almost as an aside, he adds that he's noticed that even a little bit of religious education can change people. "I teach one course called 'Religious Pluralism and Education,'" he says. "We have six weeks of seminars on Hinduism, Buddhism, Judaism, Taoism, and so on. That's six three-hour seminars. Just learning a little bit about religion makes people more accepting of other religions and much more tolerant. This isn't something you can measure, obviously. But from what I've seen, what people say, the discussions they get involved in, it seems to make a difference. I do believe the study of other religions is the most effective way to reduce prejudice and inter-religious tension."

This certainly seems plausible. Yet I often get an interesting and very negative response when I raise it as a possibility. One principal, for example, when I asked to visit his public school and told him what I was researching, immediately scoffed at the very idea of religious education in public schools. Can't be done, he said. Mustn't be done. It's too divisive, too upsetting to people. Besides, no teacher in his or her right mind would want to teach it. Within minutes of saying this, however, he told me about a meeting of inner-city principals in which an Islamic imam came and spoke to them. "There was so much I didn't know about what Muslims believe," he said. "It was really helpful." I listened amazed. Here was someone who could wax enthusiastic about what he himself had learned as a result of his own brief exposure to the beliefs of someone quite different from himself. But he couldn't begin to consider that his students could benefit from the same opportunity.

Ken Badley, who wrote *Worldviews*, compares the situation to a current debate over the role of sports in children's lives. "There's this flare-up in Calgary about hockey," he says. "Is it about winning or is it about learning teamsmanship? And a breakaway team's been formed because of the difference. Now, I can't imagine a school saying, 'Oh-oh, here's a philosophical difference, so we're going to cancel the whole thing because we can't agree.' It's unimaginable. That's why it strikes me as odd that this is the one area of life in which we actually do that. There, on something that's so important to so many people, we cancel out. But on a less important thing we don't."

It's true, of course, that even if there were agreement on offering religion in schools, there would be tremendous controversy over who would teach it and how and when to offer it. But surely that debate would be an important part of the process, an important part of learning about others and of devising ways to talk not only about our differences, but to find ways to live with them.

Still, there are those for whom religious conviction is so fundamental to their identity that they simply wouldn't be satisfied with only a certain portion of each week devoted to a study of religion, particularly someone else's. Adrian Guldemond of the Ontario Alliance of Christian Schools is one of them. He maintains that religions like Christianity shouldn't be removed from the public square, but he isn't sure of the best way to fit them into a multicultural society. "The answer is not to authorize the government to teach religion in a public, compulsory setting by regulation," he says. "The answer is to provide equal opportunity for all legitimate philosophies of education through the parental right to choose the appropriate instruction." In other words, nothing short of public support for independent religious schools will do.

This is one solution, perhaps, and one with significant drawbacks, many of which I've identified in earlier chapters. But it's no solution for the majority of Canadian students who attend public schools and who, at the moment, are getting little, or no, exposure to one of the most influential forces in human development.

12

PUBLIC AND PLURAL

*. . . I must remind myself we are living creatures — we have
religious impulses — we must — and yet into what cracks do these
impulses flow in a world without religion? It is something I think
about every day. Sometimes I think it is the only thing I should be
thinking about.*

Douglas Coupland, *Life After God*

It is the not-me in thee that is to me most precious.

Quaker proverb

*You see, I keep thinking that we need a new language, a language
of the heart . . . some kind of language between people that is a
new kind of poetry, that is the poetry of the dancing bee, that tells
us where the honey is.*

Wallace Shawn and André Gregory, *My Dinner with André*

This winter a group from Vancouver called Asza performed in
the "Acoustic Waves" music series that we subscribe to at
home in Ottawa. From advance promotion about the quartet it
was difficult to get a handle on exactly what kind of evening to

expect. Blending "fibres from the world's music to form plush tapestries of sound and culture" was one description. An interesting image, certainly, but one that seemed more picturesque than informative. On stage, though, it soon became clear why the group is so difficult to describe. For one thing, they're a study in contrasts. Throughout the evening, diminutive Qui Xia, who sings beautifully and plays the pipa, an ancient Chinese stringed instrument, sat very still, very composed. Pony-tailed Joseph "Pepe" Danza, a tall, lanky Uruguayan guitarist and percussionist, was the exact opposite. His infectious smile enveloped his entire face and his body never stopped moving in time with the music. Then there was André Thibault, a French-Canadian flamenco guitarist, and Randy Raine-Reusch, a former Maritimer who plays a multitude of instruments. In sight and sound they represented the English–French sides of Canada. What everyone shared was a love of music. What they created was astounding.

Each one played music from his or her distinct cultural tradition. The others didn't fade into the background, however; they each picked up the theme in their own idioms and added interpretations that amplified the original theme. The result was an unbelievably exciting kind of music that did indeed weave a musical tapestry of "sound and culture." During the course of the evening, the musicians described the roots of the music they were playing, its cultural influences, and what they'd learned about their own traditions as a result of learning about those of their colleagues. Qui, Danza, Thibault, and Raine-Reusch are pioneers charting a new course in intercultural understanding through the universal language of music. I listened entranced, captivated, swept away by what they were doing. To me, Asza encapsulates the possibility that is Canada – the possibility we have in this country of coming together, distinct but equal, with something unique to offer that can be appreciated, respected, and acknowledged by others. And then, using diversity as a springboard, creating something new and strong and unique to this culture. Asza does this without diminishing or denying each member's cultural roots. In fact, not only is each person's tradition enhanced through merging and blending with those of the other musicians, but those who listen discover new insights and understanding themselves.

So what does this have to do with god in the classroom? Quite a bit, I think. It's easy to argue that music is in a completely different category from religion, that it's not a matter of faith. But the stories and traditions of a people often reside in their music, and music is a form of communication, a language that speaks to the soul. So the idea of sharing it with people foreign to that culture – to say nothing of its potential transformation in the process – can be extremely threatening. On stage, Qui, for example, described the reaction she often gets from members of the Chinese community when they hear about Asza. Their first reaction is disbelief. They simply refuse to accept that she, a pipa virtuoso, could possibly play with musicians who aren't Chinese. Worse, they cannot conceive of her playing non-Chinese music on the pipa. So then, she said, she goes to great lengths to explain what Asza is and what it does. Finally, she says, they nod their heads and say, "Oh, you play on the same stage with them. But you don't actually play with them – not at the same time as them." And so she begins again, patiently trying to explain that the music the group creates doesn't denigrate Chinese music, culture, traditions – or herself.

Inherent in what she described is fear. Fear of change. Fear of loss. Fear of the "other." It is a familiar theme. In the course of researching this book, I often got the feeling from religious-school advocates that fear was the major reason they'd rejected public education. Fear that public-school children, the teachers who teach them, and the curricula of studies would pollute their children. Fear that public schools subversively encourage children to question and challenge their faith, their traditions. Fear that public schools discourage children from expressing authentic identities, especially authentic religious identities. Fear that the forces of secularism, individualism, and materialism within public schools are simply too strong to resist. Fear that their children will end up rejecting the values, the faith, and the life that they themselves believe in. These concerns are genuine and should not be dismissed lightly.

But feeling afraid is by no means exclusive to them. I think fear is also a factor for those who want to keep God out of the classroom. Fear of indoctrination. Fear of offending. Fear of conflict. Fear of lawsuits. Fear of curriculum hassles, administrative hassles. Fear of dumping yet one more thing onto teachers who haven't been educated in this area themselves. Fear of the unknown. Of course, the religious quest covers rugged, unknown terrain, because we have, as a matter of public policy, largely denied its existence. To be open to the many ways in which this quest exists means to re-shape one's identity, and that's an extremely frightening prospect.

So, instead of concentrating on our fears, perhaps, like Asza, we could set our sights on what we can create by working together. Each of us shares the responsibility of building and sustaining a civilized, democratic society. Certain principles are involved in this task: justice, equality, mutual respect, and commitment to the dignity and worth of all peoples. Lofty-sounding words. Yet unless they are translated into how we actually behave towards one another, how we organize ourselves in relation to one another through our institutions, they'll remain nothing but lofty, meaningless words. Such an enterprise must be motivated by the goal of integration, not assimilation. It requires, then, accommodation by both minority and majority sides of the relationship. The result will be original, and authentically Canadian.

One of the most compelling arguments for public schools rests in the fact that they are our common meeting place, open and accessible to all. In this alienating and increasingly complex society, public schools remain one of the few institutions where people actually come together to meet, to mix, and, one hopes, to know one another more than superficially. Ideally, they are a social leveller of class, sex, ethnicity, and race. Ideally, they teach us not only how to live with people quite different from ourselves, but to respect those differences. But the ideal, unfortunately, can be elusive.

In 1984, Alberta's Committee on Tolerance and Understanding, headed by Ron Ghitter, released its report *Education for All*. The committee was formed in response to what's become known as "the Keegstra affair." Jim Keegstra, an Alberta high-school social-studies teacher, had been using his position to promote his anti-Semitic views. Eventually, he was stripped of his teaching licence, and convicted and fined for wilfully promoting hatred against Jews. In its report, the committee repeatedly cautioned against independent religious schools, because of their exclusionary, and therefore intolerant, nature. Public schools, however, were praised for providing "the best armour against unacceptable intolerance, lack of understanding, discrimination and stereotyping." What seemed to escape the committee members' attention was that the Keegstra affair took place in a public school, not in an independent religious school. Admittedly, the fact that it was a public school may have contributed to its coming to light, but, even then, not immediately.

Assuming the public schools are models of tolerance is an easy trap to fall into. Conventional wisdom holds that tolerance, understanding, and respect are automatic off-shoots of people sitting together in the same classroom. Bernard Shapiro, however, found that simply wasn't true. He says that, when he headed the commission into private schools in Ontario in the late 1980s, he was struck with how poorly the issue of tolerance was handled – in both public *and* private schools. "Separate schools – whether they were Catholic or Jewish or whatever – tended to believe that, because they create good Catholics, or Jews, or whatever, they will therefore be tolerant," he says. "And the public schools said, 'Because we accept everybody – all kinds of 'isms' – we will be tolerant adults.' Neither of those things is true. The point is, you don't get to be tolerant just because you are a practising whatever. And you don't get to be tolerant just because you happen to go to school with members of another race. No one knows the answer of how you get to be tolerant. But I think you have to be much, much more pro-active about it. If you want people to be tolerant, they have to not only see tolerance, but they have to understand it, they have to talk about it, they have to be pro-active. It takes will and it takes focus."

I believe it also takes a commitment to Canada as a pluralistic society. Today the word "pluralism" is bandied about with such regularity that it's not clear that anyone knows quite what it means, let alone what it looks like in practice. My dictionary defines it as "a form of society in which the members of minority groups maintain their independent cultural traditions." That's a good beginning, I suppose, but it raises more questions than it settles. I mean, how would such socially important institutions as our courts, schools, jails, and hospitals actually work if they conformed to that definition?

Perhaps the vagueness of the concept is why Peter Lauwers, the Toronto lawyer who often represents Catholic school boards, calls for "meaningful pluralism." He says meaningful pluralism is "diversity about things that matter to people." Diversity in dress and food, then, while welcome, wouldn't fall into that category. Instead, he's looking for a pluralism that comes about intentionally, by design, because it deals with important matters of public policy – with such things as religion and education. "Frankly," says Lauwers, "I have never understood why it is more consistent with the civil libertarian approach to exclude all religion from education rather than to create a system which makes religious instruction possible for all faiths. It seems to me that pluralism, properly understood, must be meaningful, demanding equal respect for each viewpoint. That respect is due each of us in our inherent dignity. It is not accorded where we are obliged to forsake our faith in exchange for a public benefit."

Gerald Vandezande of the Ontario Multi-faith Coalition finds it useful to talk about "inclusive pluralism" and "exclusive pluralism." Inclusive pluralism, he says, respects everyone, though it isn't what we have in this country today. Ontario's education system, for example, operates on the principle of exclusive pluralism, "which is either a secular system of education or a Catholic system of education," says Vandezande. "Any others don't count. I think, in light of a radically changed situation, Canada should have the courage of political, and other, convictions, to look at a new arrangement. How do we live together? How do we educate? How do we respect each other? That includes revisiting the peculiar place that has been given to the Catholic system. But it also means examining what makes our public schools public. A genuine public system is only public to the extent that it accommodates all members of the public. To exclude one or more segments of the public makes it exclusive and sectarian, because it fails to include minority groupings who are equally entitled to public protection." Accommodation of minorities is a good principle, but the challenge remains where to draw the line practically.

For the sake of argument, let's buy Lauwers's and Vandezande's arguments and accept the need for a society that embraces and exemplifies meaningful, inclusive pluralism. Where would that take us? What would our education system look like? First and foremost, I believe it would lead public schools to include religion in their curricula. It would do so, in more than a didactic sense, through an exploration of the idea and experience of faith, giving all students the tools to determine their own beliefs. In the process the students would come to acknowledge and respect the efforts and answers of others as well. I think this is absolutely essential. It's a way of telling students, concretely, that this is an important aspect of human existence and the source of considerable meaning for billions of people around the world. It's also a fundamental first step in getting to know our own neighbours. Respect and appreciation for others obviously doesn't come about through classroom lectures and books alone. But, as Shapiro points out, it also doesn't come about just because people share a classroom. If there is no teaching about the beliefs of different faith systems and how those beliefs are expressed in the daily lives of followers, how can children possibly begin to gain an appreciation for those who differ from them in their religious convictions? What's required is a commitment to developing in children "religious literacy." In our multicultural, multi-faith society, the classroom is a perfect place to begin educating children about religious differences.

It's also a way of incorporating children of diverse faiths into Canadian society. In her book *Democracy on Trial*, University of Chicago ethics professor Jean Bethke Elshtain writes, "Education always reflects a society's views of what is excellent, worthy, and necessary." When religion is denied and/or ignored in schools, a clear message is conveyed: Religious belief isn't significant enough to study, and the people who hold religious beliefs aren't worthy of our time and attention. If, instead, neighbourhood public schools honoured the diversity of religious belief in more than the superficial ways of dress, food, and festivals, I suspect that many religiously moderate parents would be much less motivated to put their children in independent religious schools. Why would they? They'd know that their local public school could be depended on for a sound academic education, including the serious exploration of the religious impulse as a reality and a motivating force in human history. They would know it was open to accommodating for students of different faiths – through setting aside a prayer room if requested, acknowledging their holy days through school closings, curriculum studies, or school-wide observances. They'd know that the languages essential to reading their holy scriptures would be offered if numbers warranted, and that public schools would actively foster tolerance among the wide variety of people who now make up Canada. They'd also be confident that the school wouldn't demand uniformity of them or seek to assimilate them in the greater interest of actively respecting the religious traditions and identities of its students.

Incorporating religious education into schools is also a way of saving public education. Opponents of independent religious schools argue that funding such schools would fragment public education. But public education is being eroded anyway, and it's not because independent religious schools exist. It's because public education isn't responding fully to the needs of a new Canada. While much of the demand for religious schools is coming from people of minority faiths, Gary Duthler of the Federation of Independent Schools says that, over the past ten years, more and more Christians from every part of the country have contacted him. They tell him that they're disenchanted with the way that public schools have been transformed from purveyors of Christian values to agents of secularism. They often say their first choice would be to send their children to the local public school. But they say the public schools are losing their support. And it's not just because they no longer inculcate "Christian" values, but because they see the public system as one without values based on any religion. I want to make it clear that I'm not advocating an educational system that promotes religious values. I am advocating one that supports a range of religious perspectives and that teaches respect for religious thought and religious diversity through the way in which children are taught and challenged to think about these matters.

★

Fortunately, not all school boards resist responding to the needs of members of religious communities. Edmonton, for example, points to one way of doing things. In September 1996, five Christian schools, known as the Logos Alternative Program, opened under the public system. The non-denominational programs operate out of existing public schools and must follow the Alberta curriculum. They must also hire teachers certified by the province and they must share the principal of the public school in which they're housed. Beyond that they can do as they please. And so, the 425 children in Logos's five programs (kindergarten to Grade 9) are being educated in a Christian environment in which there are morning prayers, Bible readings, and assemblies with a Christian perspective. The teachers are Christians. Parents have to sign a commitment to the school's mission statement, that "students, taught in a spiritually nurturing, intellectually challenging and dis-ciplined environment, [will] acquire the knowledge, attitudes, skills and training necessary to seek after 'whatsoever things are true.' That, sustained by Christ's teachings and God's love, students may develop binding commitments to their families, neighbours, coun-try, and the global community while leading moral, healthy and productive lives."

Religious alternative programs have been an option only since 1988, when Alberta translated an emphasis on individual rights into choice in education. It did this by changing provincial legislation to allow religious alternative schools within the pub-lic system. In Chapter 4, I described Talmud Torah, a Hebrew-language school with a religious component, that's operated under Edmonton's public system since 1975. The Edmonton board side-stepped the thorny legal problem presented by the religious aspect of the school by calling it a language school. The Calgary board did much the same thing with its school for native Canadians, the

Plains Indians Cultural Survival School. Although there's clearly a religious aspect to that school, the board emphasizes the cultural side only. Today, no such word games have to be played; any religious group willing to conform to the requirements of the public board can open a school in Alberta. It's not been a popular choice. In fact, until the Edmonton board acted, only one group took advantage of the offer. In 1993, a Christian school, called Drayton Christian School, opened in Drayton Valley, in the foothills of the Rockies.

(Ontario's Multi-faith Coalition wants the province to allow alternative religious programs under its public system. In May 1997, lawyer Peter Jervis argued the case – known as the Bal case – before the Ontario Court of Appeal. In June, the court ruled against the coalition, saying that no freedoms have been violated. The coalition will appeal the decision to the Supreme Court of Canada.)

Emery Dostall, superintendent of the Edmonton Public Board, welcomed the request for five alternative Christian programs from Logos. "We don't think that everybody has to have the same program that you're going to have in the local neighbourhood school," he says. "We can serve a diverse, pluralistic society with multiple different programs. So the menu should be as varied as we can make it. And it should be available within the public system, not outside the system." As a result of that philosophy, Edmonton probably offers the most varied education "menu" in the country. Since 1974, it's been committed to offering choices in education. In 1997, 8,000 students out of its total student population of approximately 77,000 were enrolled in alternative programs, ranging from bilingual programs in Arabic, Mandarin, German, and Ukrainian, to sports, ballet, all-girls, and native Indian.

That religion was the last to be offered is no accident. The Edmonton board actually had a thirty-one-year-old policy against developing alternative religious schools. It read, "Our system of universal public education can only be weakened by fragmentation on the basis of religious belief." And so, when trustees decided in January 1996 to break with that policy and open the door to Christian alternative programs, objections were raised. The most vociferous reaction came from the Alberta Teachers' Association. "The more we provide for break-off groups, the more we are encouraging people not to get along," says Bauni Mackay, president of the ATA.

That was exactly what I said when I first began researching this issue. But now I don't see things in such an absolute way. To use the example of Asza again, the diversity of the musical group was impressive, as was their sharing of culturally based musical roots and the way they created something new and collectively distinctive from them. Yet the reality is that they could neither have respected and appreciated each other in this way, nor created so imaginatively, if they hadn't been so firmly grounded in their own individual traditions. And so, when Jewish, Sikh, Muslim, or Christian parents argue that their children can best become fully participating members of society when they are firmly grounded in their own religious traditions, I understand what they're saying. They're talking about identity and empowerment. When you know who you are, you can confront the larger society from a position of strength.

And so the question becomes "How is this best done without undermining social relations, social values?" Well, Edmonton is doing it by trying to keep children within the system rather than forcing parents to go outside the system for an education that conforms with their religious values.

Being housed in a public school means the Logos children have a chance to play and interact with children in the regular public program. It also means they can participate in all the events and activities available through the public board. And the rights of teachers are protected so that they work for the public board and are members of the ATA. The board monitors the program and, according to Faye Parker, who supervises the monitoring, the Logos program works well. Parents, teachers, and principals seem to be happy with it, she says. And the children will be tested on the core curriculum to make sure they're getting what they need academically. "Part of measuring success is looking at how the program lives and breathes," says Parker. "One thing that's been very important to its success is the program is non-denominational and the children aren't isolated by themselves within a school building, but are part of the larger society."

Dostall adds, "We want a Canada that recognizes cultural diversity. We want a Canada that is going to say that you can do that within the public system and that your tax-dollars will support that. And that while you're doing it we can find ways of integrating you and teaching you tolerance. I think this is best done within the umbrella of public education. That's where we build a positive Canada."

The Edmonton model is one step towards a more just and equitable system of education. It means that children are guaranteed access to the resources of the State, including teaching of an accredited curriculum by certified teachers. The students can have that access without being completely isolated from their peers who don't share their parents' beliefs. A diversified model also increases support for public education – financially and at the community level – as parents see their tax-dollars supporting a system of education that reinforces their values. It also reduces the likelihood of paranoia. If people feel excluded from the wider society, they might assume they're being religiously persecuted and pass that fear on to their children. This can feed extremism.

The problem with the Edmonton model is that it continues to promote a limited kind of one-sided learning. While children in the secular system might get to know the children from the religious program if they happen to share the same school, they are not formally exposed to their beliefs – or to anyone else's, for that matter. And the children in the alternative religious program only develop awareness and grounding in their own particular religion. Right now, there is no province in this country committed to developing the kind of religious literacy I think is essential in our new Canada.

Without a doubt, some religious groups would be threatened by such literacy. Religious literacy can't possibly develop in a vacuum. If such learning is to be meaningful, it will have to impart more than simply facts. It will have to challenge students to grapple with the meaning and implications of different religious beliefs, while developing their own perspectives. In other words, they'll be challenged to consider their own views in the context of knowledge about the beliefs and views of others.

Amy Gutmann thinks that learning about the ways of others is essential to the perpetuation of a democratic society. She calls this kind of learning "citizenship education." The professor of politics at Princeton University, and director of the University Center for Human Values, elaborates on this idea in her book, *Democratic Education*. She says that citizenship education includes "equipping children with the intellectual skills necessary to evaluate ways of life different from that of their parents," because "many, if not all, of the capacities necessary for choice among good lives are also necessary for choice among good societies." This means that young people learn "not just to behave in accordance with authority, but to think critically about authority if they are to live up to the democratic ideal of sharing political sovereignty as citizens." She maintains that people who "are ruled only by habit and authority . . . are incapable of constituting a society of sovereign citizens."

This is a theme also developed by the Ottawa philosopher, Will Kymlicka. He argues that the ability and willingness to engage in public-policy debates – and to question authority – are what distinguishes citizens in a democracy from subjects of authoritarian regimes. "Hence," he says, "it's not enough to invoke scripture or tradition. Liberal citizens must justify their political demands in terms that fellow citizens can understand and accept as consistent with their status as free and equal citizens. It requires a conscientious effort to distinguish those beliefs which are matters of private faith from those which are capable of public defence, and to see how issues look from the point of view of those with differing religious commitments and cultural backgrounds."

Kymlicka says that, if schools both taught and practised civility, then cultural barriers would likely break down. And this is precisely why religious literacy and citizenship education might threaten some groups. Not only do they fear that knowledge about others' beliefs might pollute their children, but they're unwilling to see their own views challenged – especially by their own children. While it's true that this kind of education carries a risk – independent thinking is always risky – it doesn't follow that thinking for oneself would automatically lead to rejecting the faith of one's parents or group. "The virtue of public reasonableness does not require that children come to admire or cherish other ways of life," says Kymlicka. "But it does require that children be exposed to competing ways of life, and be encouraged to view them as the expressions of coherent conceptions of value which have been sincerely affirmed by other reasonable people." Kymlicka maintains that exposing children to alternative ways of life and equipping them with the intellectual skills necessary to understand and appreciate them promotes their autonomy. And that's citizenship education, he says, because it's how people develop a sense of "us."

Today, it's not at all clear that this development is happening in any school. But Kymlicka argues that the very separateness of religious schools makes it difficult for them to provide appropriate citizenship education. "It is not enough to simply tell students that the majority of the people in the world do not share their religion," he say. "So long as one is surrounded by people who share one's faith, one may still succumb to the temptation to think that everyone who rejects one's religion is somehow illogical or depraved. To learn public reasonableness, students must come to know and understand people who are reasonable and decent and humane, but who do not share their religion. Only in this way can students learn how personal faith differs from public reasonableness, and where to draw that line."

Duthler of the Federation of Independent Schools doesn't buy that argument. Why shouldn't all schools, as part of their mandate, be required to educate children so that they'll become positive, contributing members of society, with the skills necessary to function in a democracy? he asks. "If children are being educated in this country, they must be educated to meet those standards," he says. "And it is very possible that you can do that more effectively if you are a francophone student within the francophone education system, in which a student is recognized for what he or she is, helped to be that, and then given the vision of being a contributing francophone within this culture. Same with natives. We know from bitter experience that trying to make little white kids out of native kids simply alienates them and makes it impossible for them to really feel as if they've got something to give. I would say that applies to a whole range of things. I think it's partly the excitement of being in Canada to say that it's very possible for a Chinese community to set up a program of studies that studies Canadian history, all the skills they need to function in Canadian society, and at the same time does that within traditional Chinese values. The students will integrate quickly enough – there'll be cross-fertilization that will happen automatically. If they can do that, and at the same time develop a sense of excitement about being Chinese in this Canadian culture, more power to them. But they must meet the standards set by the province. And the standards include those of socialization, integration, and contributing to society."

★

There are also other principles schools should be teaching, principles such as democracy and equality and justice. Supporters of independent religious schools say that children best learn these principles if the society to which they belong treats its minorities democratically, with equality and justice.

Duthler, for example, likes to quote Edmund Burke, a favourite statesman of his. He says that, during a heated debate in the British House of Commons about the American Revolution, the Irish-born Burke stood up and said that, in his opinion, Methodists, Baptists, Catholics, and other religious minorities should have the freedom to have their own chapels outside the Church of England. As long as, he added, they continued to pay their tithes (10 per cent of their incomes) to the Church of England. "Now, that was the height of tolerance in his day," says Duthler. "We live in a society where we don't have established churches any more. But we do have another social integration unit, and we call it the public school. And so we say, you're free, you can have any school you wish as long as your tithes – your taxes – go to the public system. That's not freedom."

Well, it's certainly not equal treatment. Every day, people from a variety of religious groups experience inequity when they see one religious group – Catholics – receiving full funding in many provinces, while in others they receive none. It seems blatantly unfair.

What's the difference, after all, between Catholic education and the kind of education they want their children to have? Catholics say they need their own system because it's essential for their religion to permeate the entire environment – from the teachers they hire, to their dress codes, to mandatory classes in the Catholic faith, the freedom to pray with students and refer to their faith in subjects not conventionally considered religious (such as history or English or science), and the way holy days are observed. These characteristics are shared by the people of many other faiths. But

Catholics have a constitutional guarantee to their own publicly funded education. Do they need an entire bureaucracy to support this? Why couldn't Catholic education be offered as an alternative program under the public system?

These aren't welcome questions. Initially, most Catholics simply fall back on the Constitution as reason enough for maintaining the status quo. In this day and age, that isn't good enough. Too much has changed since 1867. The Constitution derived from a simpler era as a compact between French and English, Catholics and Protestants. Today, such divisions no longer reflect our country's population. The constitutional obligation to fund Catholic schools could be changed. We need look no further than Newfoundland and, earlier, Manitoba, to see that constitutions aren't "carved in stone," as constitutional legal scholars will affirm. Instead, they argue that constitutions are meant to evolve. Dennis Murphy, education director for the Ontario Separate School Trustees' Association, says that, theoretically, he could buy into one public system. Realistically, though, he doesn't think it would work. "It's because of what I see in the public system," he says. "It's run by people with a profoundly secular agenda who want to have a profoundly secular education system. It simply wouldn't work at all, because part of the secular agenda that they've bought into is that religion is a private thing. We need an education system that stands over and against that."

While I understand what Murphy is saying, the Alberta model suggests that accommodation for religious belief and religious values is indeed possible under a public system. What is required is the will to make this happen, and Alberta is one of the few places that's entertained such a possibility. Murphy is absolutely right about the dominance of today's secularist education agenda. But today's reality doesn't necessarily have to be tomorrow's reality. What we require is a new openness in discussing these issues. It will be a slow process; if people continue to dig in their heels and refuse to accommodate any perspective outside their own, then it probably won't happen at all.

It will be interesting to see whether the World Interfaith Education Association of Ontario (WIFEA) has any success in this regard. This organization, run on a shoestring by a volunteer staff, is trying to promote a citizenship model as a way of introducing religion into public schools. Sue Tennant, executive director of the organization, argues that a civic framework is non-threatening and allows people to focus on what they share in a community. "I believe we are all children of God," she says. "And I believe the message we've been given is to 'Love one another.' How do you love one another in a pluralist society? Well, first you must get to know them. The 'how' comes back to the issue of their beliefs, their values. I've discovered that the same fruits of faith that were in other people's lives were also in mine. The fruits of the spirit are faith and trust and loyalty and forgiveness and charity. These are common to all religious backgrounds. Theologically speaking, what is meant by the commandment to love my neighbour on a day-to-day basis in this age means to know my neighbour."

Tennant's organization is trying to raise the profile of religion in education. It's a hard sell, as members of the Ecumenical Study Commission on Public Education know only too well. But Tennant is singlemindedly trying to get educators and members of various faiths to work together. She had a taste of what would be involved in 1994. With the Royal Ontario Museum, WIFEA organized a multicultural, inter-faith celebration of family life in Canada. Looking at how every religion supports the family seemed such a straightforward thing to do. It wasn't. Museum officials were afraid of a public protest, because they might be seen as celebrating the traditional family. There was some dissension between the Greek Orthodox and the Roman Catholic churches. And then the gay and lesbian church of Toronto, the Metropolitan Church, asked to be part of it.

"It was a stretch for people," says Tennant. "My interest was education, and part of that is learning about our differences. We don't do well to hide our differences. When you know about them, the challenge of staying in a loving relationship is a triumph. We found that, as long as people were willing to stay in community, we had a tremendous resource for solving problems. It's when people quit that everything weakens." But no one dropped out and the event was a huge success.

Now, Tennant is concentrating on raising awareness of the importance of religion with the view to having it included in school curricula. This is a quest supported by the Buddhist Communities of Greater Toronto, which represents fifty temples. Michael Kerr works for a social-service agency supported by the inter-denominational group, and he says the umbrella organization joined WIFEA "as a way of putting our efforts behind multi-faith religious education in all schools. We want all children to have a chance to see each of the windows on truth."

Tennant also underlines the visual image. "To deny how we develop the spiritual potential is like looking out of one eye, not both," she says. "But people seem to feel there's so much to fear by exploring this and they don't know how to deal with conflict. Using a civic framework gives you the confidence to deal with difference because you know differences can be resolved without war. Civic framework is what we hold in common. It's the values that we agree on, as a people, and it transcends the issues. If people come together in a broader framework, it facilitates dialogue."

Dialogue *is* essential if we are to create an education system capable of fostering religious literacy among our children. Unfortunately, there is tremendous resistance to discussing the value of this kind of education. Interestingly, the resistance doesn't come from the young. When I travelled the country, I'd invariably wind up talking to people about this topic. Resistance to non-indoctrinating

religious education in public schools came, I found, from adults –
no doubt the unfortunate legacy of a history of sectarian rivalries
and oppression.

I believe we're capable of overcoming the past. In fact, I'm
convinced that a public debate could open the door to a reconsideration of an education system that excludes religious education from its schools. It should also lead to a reconsideration of the
justice, or equity, of our current attitude to public funding for
independent schools. As we enter the twenty-first century, a
fundamental part of this debate must examine whether we can
afford to perpetuate a preference for one branch of the Christian
faith, Roman Catholicism, on the basis of a constitution devised
in another era. I think not.

If, however, public opinion favours the continuation of this
historical anomaly, then those provinces that refuse to fund independent religious schools should make amends. Consciously
perpetuating an inequity sets a terrible example to our young.

Who knows where a passionate, informed public debate on this
issue could lead? I would hope it would spark a commitment to
offering education about religion in public schools. While I
believe this would be for the social good, I also think it might satisfy those members of the religious moderate majority who are
increasingly alienated from the public system. For those who
demand more – such as teachers who share their faith, and frequent references to their religion throughout the curriculum –
then Edmonton's model of allowing alternative religious schools
within the public system has much to recommend it. To my mind,
it's much, much better to keep people within a public system than
to force them outside it, beyond the reach of State standards. It's
also a way of upholding the rights of children.

When all is said and done, however, I hold to one hope: That it
will be possible for all of our children – Buddhists, Muslims, Sikhs,

Hindus, Christians, Jews, secular humanists, and so on – to play together in the school yard and to study together in the classroom, without fear of either religious compromise or religious harassment. Accommodating religious difference within a public system through teaching about it, acknowledging and honouring holy days, and respecting religious symbols are important steps towards mutual understanding, healthy equality, and integration. The new fabric we weave as a result could well produce a Canada in which tolerance will be a matter of practice, not mere rhetoric, a country that could truly be a living example of what's possible when a liberal democracy takes the pluralist ideal seriously.

Bibliography

Papers, Theses, and Journal Articles

Bourgeault, Guy, France Gagnon, Marie McAndrew, and Michel Pagé. "Taking Cultural and Religious Diversity into Account in the School Setting: Some Fundamental Principles and Guidelines Derived from Ethics and Political Philosophy." Submitted to the *Revue européenne des migrations internationales*. Oct. 1994.

Burgess, Donald A. "Denominational and Linguistic Guarantees in the Canadian Constitution: Implications for Quebec Education." *McGill Journal of Education*. Vol. 26, no. 2 (spring 1991).

Callon, Eamonn. "Common Schools for Common Education." *Canadian Journal of Education*. Vol. 20, no. 3 (1995).

Calvert, Gordon C. "Growth of Non-FISA Christian Schools in British Columbia 1975–1985." Thesis submitted in partial fulfillment of the requirements for MA in the Faculty of Graduate Studies, Department of Social and Educational Studies, University of British Columbia. Dec. 1987.

Cochrane, Donald B. "The Stances of Provincial Ministries of Education Towards Values/Moral Education in Canadian Public Schools in 1990." *Journal of Moral Education*. Vol. 21, no. 2 (1992).

Cornell, M. Louise. "Education for Eternity: Evangelical Responses to the Secularization of Quebec Education." Paper presented to the Comparative and International Education Society of Canada. June 1992.

De Morr, Ary. "Tolerance in Religious Education: Three Dissenting Worldviews in Canadian Education." MA thesis in Philosophy of Education, Department of Educational Foundations, University of Alberta (fall 1994).

Duthler, Gary. "A New Look at the Origins of the Common School in Upper Canada." Paper completed for history course at University of Waterloo, 1983, and given to author.

Evans, Peter J. A. " 'Education about Religion' in the Public System: Policies, Practices and Possibilities." Paper presented to the World Inter-Faith Education Association (Ontario), Toronto. Dec. 5, 1995.

————. "Religion and the Common Curriculum – Ontario." Paper submitted to the World Inter-Faith Education Association (Ontario), Toronto. Jan. 1996.

Hiemstra, John L. "Religious Schooling and Prejudice in Canada: Implications for Public Funding of Christian Schools." *Journal of Research on Christian Education*. Vol. 3, no. 2 (autumn 1994).

Kymlicka, Will. "Education for Citizenship." Draft paper written for *Foundations for Moral Education*, Feb. 1995, and given to author.

Lauwers, Peter D. "Meaningful Pluralism and the Law." Presented to forum sponsored by the Centre for Renewal in Public Policy, Toronto. Nov. 18, 1995.

————. "Legal Images of Our Schools in the 21st Century: Religious Education in the Public Schools of Ontario." Presented to the Canadian Bar Association – Ontario, Toronto. Jan. 25, 1996.

————. "Religious Voices in Public Discourse." Presented to a symposium of the Centre for Renewal in Public Policy, Toronto. Feb. 1997.

Makhado, Samson B. "A Comparison Between ACE Schools and Traditional Calvinist Schools." Paper submitted to the Master's program in Philosophy of Education, Institute for Christian Studies, Toronto. Nov. 1993.

Martin, Yvonne M. "A Comparative Legislative Analysis of Parental Participation Policy in British Columbia, Alberta and Quebec." *Education and Law Journal*. Vol. 4, no. 1 (1992).

Staple, John. "The Liability of Teachers for Off-Duty Conduct and the 'Just Cause' Standard in Denominational Schools: The Case for Individual Rights." Paper submitted at conference of the Canadian Association for the Practical Study of Law and Education, 1993.

Thiessen, Elmer John. "Educational Pluralism and Tolerance." Paper presented to a meeting of the Philosophy of Education Society of Great Britain. Feb. 19, 1986.

Tielman, R. A. P. "Humanist Education in the Netherlands." *Rekenschap: Humanistisch Tijdschrift Voor Wetenschap en Cultuur*. July 1992.

Valk, John. "Religion and the Schools: The Case of Utrecht." *History of Education Quarterly*. Vol. 35, no. 2 (summer 1995).

Van Brummelen, Harro. "Faith on the Wane: A Documentary Analysis of Shifting Worldviews in Canadian Textbooks." *Journal of Research on Christian Education.* Vol. 3, no. 1 (spring 1994).

Vriend, John. "Eden Despoiled: A Questionable Experiment in School Choice." *Journal of Research on Christian Education.* Vol. 3, no. 2 (autumn 1994).

Wilson, J. Donald. "Multiculturalism and Immigration Policy in Canada: The Last Twenty-Five Years." Paper given at conference on "Migration and Global Change," Lohusalu, Estonia. Aug. 19–22, 1993.

Books

Beck, Clive. *Better Schools: A Values Perspective.* Falmer Press, 1990.

Bibby, Reginald. *Unknown Gods: The Ongoing Story of Religion in Canada.* Toronto: Stoddart, 1993.

Bissoondath, Neil. *Selling Illusions: The Cult of Multiculturalism in Canada.* Toronto: Penguin, 1994.

Carter, Stephen L. *The Culture of Disbelief: How American Law and Politics Trivialize Religious Devotion.* N.Y.: Basic Books, 1993.

Elshtain, Jean Bethke. *Democracy on Trial.* N.Y.: Basic Books, 1995.

Emberley, Peter C., and Waller R. Newell. *Bankrupt Education: The Decline of Liberal Education in Canada.* Toronto: University of Toronto Press, 1994.

Flynn, Tom. *The Trouble With Christmas.* Buffalo: Prometheus Books, 1993.

Glenn, Charles Leslie, Jr. *The Myth of the Common School.* Amherst: University of Massachusetts Press, 1987.

Guldemond, Adrian, ed. *Religion in the Public Schools of Ontario: Progress in the Courts.* Ancaster, ON: Guardian Press, 1990.

Hammann, Louis J., and Harry M. Buck. *Religious Traditions and the Limits of Tolerance.* Chambersburg, PA: Anima Books, 1988.

Kymlicka, Will. *Multicultural Citizenship.* Oxford: Oxford University Press, 1995.

————, ed. *The Rights of Minority Cultures.* Oxford: Oxford University Press, 1995.

LaPierre, Laurier L. *Sir Wilfrid Laurier and the Romance of Canada.* Toronto: Stoddart, 1996.

McKim, William A., ed. *The Vexed Question: Denominational Education in a Secular Age.* St. John's, NF: Breakwater, 1988.

Menendez, Albert J. *The December Wars.* Buffalo, N.Y.: Prometheus Books, 1993.

Miller, Alice. *For Your Own Good.* 3rd ed. N.Y.: Noonday Press, 1990.

Must, Art, Jr., ed. *Why We Still Need Public Schools.* Buffalo, N.Y.: Prometheus Books, 1992.

Postman, Neil. *The End of Education.* N.Y.: Vintage, 1996.

Taylor, Charles. *Multiculturalism: Examining the Politics of Recognition.* Ed. and introduced by Amy Gutmann. Princeton, NJ: Princeton University Press, 1994.

———. *Multiculturalism and "The Politics of Recognition": An essay by Charles Taylor.* Ed., Amy Gutmann. Princeton, NJ: Princeton University Press, 1992.

Van Brummelen, Harro W. *Telling the Next Generation: Educational Development in North American Calvinist Christian Schools.* Lanham, MD: University Press of America, 1986.

Wilkinson, Bruce W. *Educational Choice: Necessary but Not Sufficient.* Montreal: Institute for Research on Public Policy, 1994.

Wilson, J. Donald, ed. "Religion and Education: The Other Side of Pluralism," *Canadian Education in the 1980's.* Calgary: Detselig Enterprises, 1981.

Wilson, J. Donald, Robert M. Stamp, Louis-Philippe Audet, eds. *Canadian Education: A History.* Scarborough, 1970.

Young-Bruehl, Elisabeth. *The Anatomy of Prejudices.* Cambridge, MA: Harvard University Press, 1996.

Reports

The Ecumenical Study Commission on Public Education. Untitled submission to the Ontario Royal Commission on Learning. Toronto, Dec. 13, 1993.

Department of Education. Government of Ontario. *Religious Information and Moral Development: The Report of the Committee on Religious Education in the Public Schools of the Province of Ontario.* Toronto, 1969.

Ontario Ministry of Education. Government of Ontario. *The Report of The Commission on Private Schools in Ontario.* Bernard J. Shapiro, Commissioner. Toronto, Oct. 1985.

Ontario Ministry of Education and Training. Government of Ontario. *Education About Religion in Ontario Public Elementary Schools.* Toronto, 1994.

Ontario Multi-faith Coalition for Equity in Education. *Ensuring Choice and Equity for All Students (An Alternative Governance Model for Ontario Education).* Submission to the Ontario Royal Commission on Learning. Toronto, Mar. 1994.

Other Publications

Canadian Jewish Congress Ontario Region. *Government Funding for Independent Religious Schools Briefing Book.* Prepared by Manuel Prutschi and Bernie M. Farber. Toronto, 1996.

Commission des droits de la personne du Québec. *Religious Pluralism in Quebec: A Social and Ethical Challenge.* Québec, 1995.

Federation of Independent Schools in Canada. *An Overview of Independent Education in Canada.* Edmonton, 1996.

Macmillan Education. *Celebrating Meaning: Religious Education in Primary Schools.* London, 1979.

Macmillan Education. *Conveying Meaning: Religious Education in Primary Schools.* London, 1979.

Macmillan Education. *Seeking Meaning: Religious Education in Primary Schools.* London, 1979.

Ontario Alliance of Christian Schools. *Short Answers to 25 Common Objections to Independent School Funding.* Ancaster, 1995.

Ontario Department of Education. *World Religions.* Toronto, 1971.

Ontario Ministry of Education and Training. *Education about Religion in Ontario Public Elementary Schools.* Toronto, 1994.

Ontario Public School Boards' Association. *Does Legislation Permit Credit Courses in Catholicism to be Offered by a Public School Board?* Toronto, 1994.

Patterson, Renton H. *Not Carved in Stone: Public Funding of Separate Schools in Ontario.* Burnstown: General Store Publishing House, 1992.

"Private School Monitor," *Canadian Education.* Publication of Associates for Research on Private Education. Vol. 17, no. 2 (winter 1996).

The Evangelical Fellowship of Canada Task Force on Education. *Why Do We Educate Our Children?: Some Biblical Reflections.* Markham, 1997.

————. *Diversity and Faithfulness: Reflections for Christian Teachers on Plurality and Pluralism in Canadian Public Schools.* Markham, 1997.

The Ontario Institute for Studies in Education. *Three Approaches to Religious Education.* Ed., Hugh Oliver. Toronto, 1972.

Van Brummelen, Harro. *The New Christian Right and North American Education.* Institute for Reformational Studies. Potchefstroom, South Africa, June 1989.

Index